Tourism, Land, and Landscape in Ireland

This study, exploring a broad range of evocative Irish travel writing from 1850 to 1914, much of it highly entertaining and heavily laced with irony and humour, draws out interplays between tourism, travel literature, and commodifications of culture. It focuses on the importance of informal tourist economies, illicit dimensions of tourism, national landscapes, 'legend', and invented tradition in modern tourism.

Kevin J. James is Associate Professor of History at the University of Guelph, Canada, where he also is a core faculty member in the Centre for Scottish Studies. His research explores tourism, literature, and identity in the Victorian era, including comparative Irish and Scottish economic, social, and cultural history.

Routledge Research in Travel Writing

EDITED BY PETER HULME, *University of Essex*
TIM YOUNGS, *Nottingham Trent University*

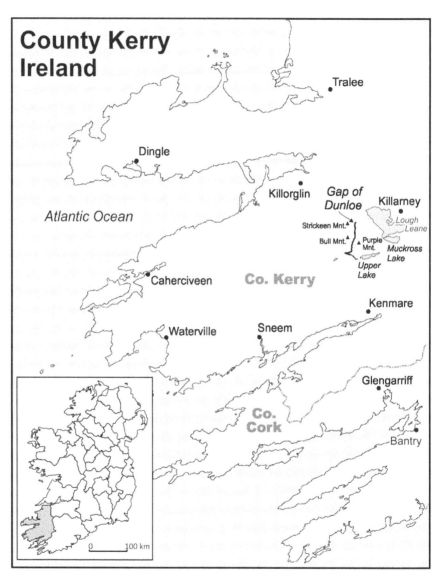

Map of Killarney, with County Map of Ireland inset

Tourism, Land, and Landscape in Ireland

The Commodification of Culture

Kevin J. James

Routledge
Taylor & Francis Group

LONDON AND NEW YORK

First published 2014 by Routledge

2 Park Square, Milton Park, Abingdon, Oxfordshire OX14 4RN
52 Vanderbilt Avenue, New York, NY 10017

Routledge is an imprint of the Taylor & Francis Group, an informa business

First issued in paperback 2019

Library of Congress Cataloging-in-Publication Data
James, Kevin J.
   Tourism, land, and landscape in Ireland : the commodification of culture
/ Kevin J. James. — First edition.
      pages cm — (Routledge research in travel writing ; 9)
   1. Travelers' writings, English—Ireland—History and
criticism.   2. Travel writing—Great Britain—History.   3. Travel
writing—Ireland—History.   4. Tourism—Ireland—History.   5. Culture
in literature.   6. Ireland—In literature.   7. Ireland—Social life and
customs.   8. Ireland—Description and travel.   I. Title.
   PR756.T72J36 2014
   820.9'32—dc23
   2014000076

ISBN13: 978-0-415-71355-9 (hbk)
ISBN13: 978-0-367-86876-5 (pbk)

Typeset in Sabon
by IBT Global.

To Monica, Charles, and Helen

Contents

Plates

Acknowledgements

I wish to thank many scholars who have shared their keen insights with me in the evolution of this study: Dr Alastair J. Durie, Dara Folan (who provided crucial insights and sources on tourism in the context of the Gaelic Revival), Prof. Margaret Kelleher, Prof. Maria Luddy, Dr James McConnel, Dr Éamonn Ó Ciardha, Prof. John K. Walton, Prof. William H.A. Williams (who read an early draft of the manuscript, and commented extensively on it), Dr Eric G.E. Zuelow, and two anonymous referees whose suggestions led to development, and recasting, of core elements of this study. The series editors, Prof. Peter Hulme and Prof. Tim Youngs, have provided unstinting support for its realisation in book form. I also wish to thank Nancy Chen, Elizabeth Levine, Emily Ross, and Josh Wells at Routledge for editorial advice and assistance, and Michael Watters, for help in the stages of page composition.

Through the years, and especially in my early forays into Canadian, British, and Irish history at McGill University, Prof. Catherine Desbarats, Prof. Elizabeth Elbourne, Prof. Suzanne Morton, Prof. Brian Young, and Prof. John Zucchi were especially influential in my formation—Prof. Zucchi as my MA advisor. So too were Prof. Graeme Morton, now at the University of Dundee, and Prof. R.J. Morris at Edinburgh University, when I was a PhD student there. At the earliest stage in my scholarly pursuits in History, Dr W.T. Matthews provided an invaluable introduction to social and economic history, in the context of expert and humane pedagogy.

I am grateful for the support of colleagues at the University of Guelph, notably Prof. William S. Cormack, Prof. Jamie Snell, and Prof. Linda Mahood, who read a copy of the manuscript and offered valuable advice on it. Prof. David A. Wilson of the University of Toronto has been generous in sharing his wide understanding of the field of Irish history. During a sojourn to London to undertake research towards this book, Dr Even Smith Wergeland hosted me in Hackney, and provided great companionship as we both worked to see our projects through to completion.

Graduate student members of the Tourism History Working Group have created a tremendously collegial and vibrant atmosphere for intellectual exchange at the University of Guelph: Alex Clay, Wade Cormack, Monica Finlay, Erica German, Shannon O'Connor (who contributed greatly to early research on this book), Chris Quinn, and Evan Tigchelaar. Patrick Segsworth, in the hours after completing his BA, carefully edited a final copy of the manuscript before my submission to the press. These students, and many more who participated in my undergraduate and graduate classes on tourism history, provided inspiration, intellectual immersion in the field of tourism studies, and practical help with sources and editing.

Parts of chapters one and three appeared in my chapter "Meeting Kate Kearney at Killarney: Performances of the Touring Subject, 1850–1914", in Benjamin Colbert, ed., *Travel Writing and Tourism in Britain and Ireland* (Houndmills: Palgrave Macmillan, 2011), pp. 181–200. Dr Glenn Hooper organised the workshop from which that collection emerged; its participants provided valuable feedback at an early stage in this project's development. I am grateful to them for their encouragement, and to Palgrave Macmillan for permission to reproduce elements of that chapter here. Dr Josh MacFadyen produced a map of Killarney, for which I am thankful. Marie Puddister adapted it to the requirements of this text.

Research support, in the form of a Standard Research Grant, was generously provided by the Social Sciences and Humanities Research Council of Canada, which also funded a Research Time Stipend matched by the College of Arts at the University of Guelph.

My mother, Jane Marie James, my father, Joseph C.M. James, and my brother, Mike and his family deserve my sincere thanks for their interest and support. My late grandmother, Helen M.N. McNab, inspired an early interest in Irish history that she encouraged through many years. Finally, I reserve my deepest thanks, and my dedication, to my wife Monica Rieck, my son Charles Ansley Theodor, and my daughter Helen Emma Gretchen, for faith, fortitude, and forbearance. They have provided encouragement and many happy hours of family time throughout the long gestation of this book. Indeed, as I was putting the finishing touches on the typescript, I intercepted my five-year old daughter, who had surreptitiously donned a costume of winter clothes and slipped out the door of our house one stormy afternoon in mid-December, with the wind howling and temperatures plunging below -20°. It turns out she planned to hawk small trinkets that she and her older brother had made; she was carrying them in a knit snow-cap. Her brother had counselled her that scrawling an endearing "for sale" sign would telegraph youthful innocence and attract more custom. This study had come full circle. I was reminded with equal measures of poignancy and force of the powers of imagination and enterprise.

Introduction

When the celebrated East Coast American architects Thomas W. Silloway and Lee L. Powers toured "somewhat leisurely over important parts of Ireland and Scotland, and in a yet more deliberate and critical manner over the principal parts of England", a visit to the Killarney Lakes in southwest Ireland was *de rigueur*.[1] In their account of these travels, published in 1883, they offered a synopsis of what "their New England eyes, ears, and minds saw, heard, and discovered". Perhaps the most entertaining passage recounted their visit to the ancestral home of the legendary "Kate Kearney", whose fame they (mistakenly) attributed to the poems of Thomas Moore. The encounter, slyly indexed in the book as "KEARNEY, Kate, her cottage and eye to business", took place at a site which they described with the precision of their trade: a one-storied thatched cottage made of stone, plastered and white-washed, surrounded by high hills on the left side of the road, 40 feet long and 20 feet wide.[2] It was not the edifice that intrigued them so much as its far-famed inhabitant, who claimed to be the "granddaughter" of the late Kate, a seductress whose exploits were famous the world over. Silloway and Powers described a relatively unremarkable woman who came to her door to greet them. Small and around 60 years old, "[s]he wore a short dress, heavy shoes, the inevitable kerchief, or miniature shawl, folded diamond-ways over her shoulders, and a frilled white muslin cap on her head."[3] In one hand she held a mug, and in the other a wine bottle of goat's-milk and a glass tumbler. Pouring the milk, she asked "naïvely, with an almost young-maidenly tone of voice . . . 'And will ye not have put into it a drop of the mountain dew?'".[4] Though professing to be "abstinence men", Silloway and Powers recounted that they must "run a bit of risk now, to do all that curious tourists do, so we said Yes". They described how she then proceeded to concoct the admixture, while the realisation came to the two visitors that "at home the dew would have been so like whiskey that we couldn't convince ourselves it was not, and so we cried 'Hold! Enough!' She held, and it *was* enough." To thousands of excursionists and many more who read narratives of travel in Killarney—Ireland's tourist Mecca—this was a familiar transaction, during which the woman turned increasingly forceful. On presentation of a shilling for her hospitality, Silloway and Powers wrote that "she had done business too long, and her distinguished grandmother before her, to be out-generalled by the Yankees, and so came a demand for more, which was refused." They then remarked on a sudden change in the old woman's countenance, as "[h]er maiden-like demure condition changed, and we left, thinking discretion and valor were synonymous terms; and she, probably of the same opinion, retired to try her luck with the next comer that way," while Silloway and Powers proceeded through the Gap of Dunloe—"one of the notable places of Ireland . . . a narrow, wild, and romantic mountain pass".[5]

Silloway and Powers's evocative narrative of an encounter with this colourful local character echoed in many accounts of Killarney tours, raising questions about the relationships between landscape, tourism, performance, and "hospitality" at a time when Killarney was becoming as famous for its tourist kitsch as for its varied scenery. These appear weighty questions to attach to such a brief meeting, but they are deeply revealing about the nature of tourism—not just as a business, but as myriad sets of performances inflected by class, gender, and culture. The exploration of tourism along these lines seemed, for many years, to be incompatible with the largely applied focus of "tourism studies" scholarship—to say nothing of the textual source base of critical tourism scholarship on Ireland, which attached great merit to serious-minded "surveys" of the island's condition in the nineteenth century. Amongst many scholars, tourism as a topic for "serious" scholarly inquiry was bedevilled by its association with "recreation", "frivolity", the supposed research theatre of the beach—and consequently with an implied binary opposition to work and the workplace: the farm, the factory floor, or other sites where the "meaningful" actions of individual and collective identity formation were situated. Scholars now recognise that theatres of "play" are important places of social, economic, and cultural production and reproduction.[6] Tourism is important not only to our contemporary economy, but also to earlier eras, when it gave birth to tourist "spaces"—towns, spas, and touring districts—as well as distinctive commercial, social, and cultural practices, from the Grand Tour to Cook's holidays.[7] Scholars debate the distinctions between travel and tourism;[8] they have variously focussed on topics as diverse as adventure tourism and the environmental impacts of "going away". But their interests converge on people's historical engagement with, and their renderings of, cultures and places that they encounter on tour. They had myriad motivations for travel (indeed, Silloway and Powers described degrees of critical "deliberateness" and leisure in their tour of the nations of the United Kingdom), and scholars have proposed equally varied definitions of the term: here I borrow an especially expansive formulation which broadly defines travel as "human movement through culturally conceived space, normally undertaken with at least some expectation of an eventual return to the place of origin".[9] This study explores local tourism's relationship to wider programmes of economic development, cultural preservation, and landscape production, and how it related to depictions of, and forms of self-presentation in, rural Ireland. It asks how Killarney, as its premier tourist site over many decades, was situated within broader discourses of nature and nationhood, in an era before the state played an especially prominent role in actively stewarding it.

PLACE, PILGRIMAGE, AND PLEASURE

In exploring the production and reproduction of landscapes and the place of the tourist in wider "national landscapes", we need to account for the variety of activities that took place in tourist space—from pleasure to pilgrimage—and understand the politicised character of even the most prosaic recreational tour. Sites such as Blackpool and Brighton have long been fertile ground for British historians interested in the intersections of leisure, place, and identity formation.[10] The act of seaside holidaying, for instance, did not involve a mere reproduction of workplace identities: solidarities and divisions could be negotiated differently in these theatres. Indeed, scholars contend that travel offers a liminoid space where systems of authority are contested, and where alternative identities and practices than those associated with the "everyday" realm are produced (recall how Silloway and Powers, professed "abstinence men", nonetheless submitted to the "granddaughter's" hospitality).[11] Within geography, sociology, and other social sciences, scholars taking the "cultural turn" have examined processes of ideological production through tourism in which landscapes are constructed and contested, and have also explored how they relate to national identity and the symbolic repertoire of the nation.[12] Tourism occupies a central place in studies of how national geographies are imagined and reimagined. The scale of the modern tourism sector, and forms of commercial leisure, are widely regarded as inextricably bound to the project of European nation-state-building.[13] And through the promotion, production, and reproduction of spaces imbued with specific political and cultural values—"The West" and "The North", for instance—regions and localities are constructed and freighted with ideological power. In Ireland, national spaces and precepts of nationhood were highly contested as the tourism sector matured. If the chronology during which nationalism and unionism crystallised is still a matter of debate, historians have underscored the ways in which strains of political opinion mutated, and stressed how they were largely contained within the political structure of the Union through the nineteenth century (consider, for instance, on the nationalist spectrum, the nuanced positions on Irish political autonomy associated with Daniel O'Connell's Repeal movement, and Issac Butt's Home Government Association and Home Rule League in the 1870s). Irish tourism history offers as a prism through which we can explore many ambiguous dimensions of Irish cultural politics in the years before partition in 1922 and the creation of the 26-county Irish Free State and six-county province of Northern Ireland, both of which subsequently engaged in vigorous tourism promotion campaigns.

THE LANDSCAPE OF THE GAP

The Gap of Dunloe, which lured Thomas W. Silloway and Lee L. Powers beyond Kate Kearney's Cottage, was a deep recess hemmed in by the Tomies and Purple Mountains on one side and a range known as Macgillycuddy's Reeks on the other. Its bridle-path, which followed a narrow seven-and-a-half-mile route through the pass and the Black Valley beyond it [Plate 1], was generally navigated by pony or foot, and was a famous tourist site within Killarney—a region in Co. Kerry, in Ireland's south-west, centred on its eponymous town. Nineteenth-century travel writers praised the diversity of scenery that could be viewed within a short tour, from rustic cottages to wild mountain passes, to beautiful lake-islands, even if specific places, such as the Gap, some eight-and-a-half miles distant from the town, did not always meet expectations. Writing in 1897, for instance, the Gaelic Leaguer Thomas O'Neill Russell, having returned only two years before from a lengthy, self-imposed exile in the USA,[14] praised Killarney's attractions, claiming that "[m]uch has been written about this 'Eden of the West,' but most of those who have attempted to describe it have omitted to mention its chief charm—namely, diversity of scenic attractions within a small compass. Almost everything that Nature could do has been done within a tract of country hardly ten miles square."[15] Indeed, Killarney offered the tourist something resembling a microcosm to which humans and nature had skilfully contributed, even if in total it would not surpass the monumental national landscapes of other countries:

> Those who expect to find in Killarney the grandeur of the Alps, the Rocky Mountains, or even of the Scottish Highlands, will be disappointed. It is too small to be sublime, for it could be ridden round in a day. The most wonderful of its many wonders is variety of scenery in a small compass. In this respect few parts of the known world can compare with it. Almost every possible phase of Nature, almost everything she could do with land and water, can be found in Killarney, and found on a little spot of earth hardly larger than the space covered by London. Mountains, lakes, rivers, rocks, woods, waterfalls, flowery islands, green meadows and glistening strands, almost exhaust Nature's materials for forming the beautiful. But all are found at Killarney. Man, who mars Nature so often, has helped her here, for the castles and abbeys he raised of yore still stand, and their ivy and flower-decked ruins, tenanted only by the bat and the bee, put the finishing touch on this earthly Eden, and make it one of the scenic wonders of

the world. If Killarney had glaciers and eternally snow-clad peaks, it would have everything that Switzerland has.[16]

Still, Russell contended that an essential feature of Killarney's beauty was "the admirable proportion its scenic features bear to one another";[17] its mountains, rivers, and waterfalls, being complementary in size, rendered Killarney "the most perfect effort of Nature to bring together without disproportion all her choicest charms". Besides the awe-inspiring Gap, through which the narrow stream the Loe passed, variously opening into five small lakes, there were neighbouring sites which offered prospects from commanding heights, including Macgillycuddy's Reeks, Purple Mountain, and Mangerton, where the intrepid tourist who ventured beyond the "Devil's Punch Bowl" would be rewarded, another writer promised, with a view of the district which took in a "magnificent panorama", including the "broad Atlantic", mountains, and the three Killarney Lakes.[18] By Russell's time, "doing" Killarney denoted a visit to these natural landscapes, typically as part of a day excursion that encompassed the Gap of Dunloe and perhaps ruins at Aghadoe and Ross Castle, along with the Dunloe Cave discovered in 1838 (near Dunloe Castle, the seat of Mahony family), the Upper Lake, a magnificent precipice called "the Eagle's Nest" situated within the Long Range, the Old Weir Bridge near the "Meeting of the Waters", where the Lakes intermingled, Dinish Island, and Muckross (or the "Middle Lake").[19] These places, many of long-standing interest to the traveller, also became staples of the Victorian Killarney tour in which tourist kitsch and hints of the (lost) romantic intermingled. In guide-books, travelogues, and other texts, tourists were given explicit directions on how to proceed to, progress through, and then depart from them, and how to knit several such visits into a day's excursion. Legions of excursionists to the Gap of Dunloe arrived, as Thomas W. Silloway and Lee L. Powers had, at "Kate Kearney's Cottage"—the "entrance" to the Gap—and proceeded through the deep recess, fully expecting to meet cloying peasant girls, buglers, artful guides, and, of course, the indomitable "granddaughter" of a fictional beauty, who exacted a toll for the privilege to enter this world of ruse and disguise. They then paid another—more formal—toll at Lord Brandon's Gate, where the Gap tour ended, and proceeded on a boat excursion through the Lakes. This themed route was the focal point for dynamic tourist encounters, complex performances of mobility and stasis, and engrossing sensory immersion.

TOURING IRELAND: HISTORIOGRAPHICAL CONTEXTS

While scholars of Irish travel writing have mined a corpus of texts to excavate travellers' views of Ireland's prospects under the new political Union of Great Britain and Ireland in 1801, as well as its experience of Famine and the cultural landscape of the post-Famine era, practices of recreational travel have received comparatively scant attention in explorations of land-scapes, travel writing, and tourism.[20] This is in part due to the compara-tively weighty motivations proclaimed by writers who toured Ireland to "investigate", "delineate", and "explore" the contours of its economy and culture, as opposed to the putatively frivolous purposes of leisure that intensified after the Famine. The two decades following the Union have been seen as the critical years in which the epistemological exercise of "mapping" Ireland through statistical and other means was undertaken—with shifts in the 1830s to more pessimistic appraisals of the condition of the country (one often witnessed at first hand in Britain, where a flood of Irish men and women were now migrating, including many families whose livelihoods had been shattered through technological transformations in textile production). During that decade, writers grappled with questions of poverty and how to alleviate it, and debated whether England supplied an appropriate model of relief for the poorer, more rural western island. In the 1840s, the Famine years witnessed the arrival of a steady stream of investigators alarmed by, and offering often conflicting appraisals of, Irish poverty and its causes. Those years have also been seen as a turning point in scholarly surveys of travel narratives. Tracing modes of travel writing from the Union to 1860, Glenn Hooper has detected the emergence of a new master-narrative of post-Famine travel—one imbued with optimism for the prospects of emptied space.[21] At the same time, a more durable and critical, if overlooked, development was taking shape in the textual field of travel: what Éadaoin Agnew has identified as the expanding number of materials related to the Irish holiday.[22] These accounts of leisure travel, when explored alongside other narratives, reveal the complex positioning of tourism within debates over Irish politics and culture—especially in the post-Famine era, when it figured subtly within debates over the status of Ireland under the Union. As Susan Kroeg asserts in a deeply illuminating study of the Irish guide, tourism is an epistemological project informed by a specific set of motivations, inquiries, and actions,[23] with great value in exploring the Irish tourist "product" and the exchanges through which it was created. Only recently have Irish historians begun to explore tourism as a subject of scholarly inquiry. Many draw on the insights of the social sciences,[24] where the study of contemporary tourism in Ireland has been a long-standing interest, particularly in relation to tourism and economic "peripheries".[25] With Ireland often studied as a successful global "brand", the purported inauthenticity of Irish cultural commodifications has been scrutinised by scholars who question the rhetorical and substantive fea-tures of authenticity itself.

In the context of these wider social scientific inquiries into tourism and commodification, Ireland has supplied verdant terrain for tourism histo-ries. In a society in which fierce political debate historically centred on land, the ideological "landscapes" that underpinned the politicisation of territory are often made explicit through tourism. Eric G.E. Zuelow's ground-breaking examination of tourism policy and its links to nationalism and national identity is a seminal analysis of Ireland's tourism sector in the post-partition era.[26] Zuelow maps a network of national and transnational policy actors, exploring relations between the Free State/Republic on one hand, and Northern Ireland on the other, elucidating inter-relationships between Ireland, the United Kingdom, Europe, and America (whose influence extended through Marshall Plan aid after the Second World War). This sophisticated exploration of the political economy of tourism in post-partition Ireland, interwoven with sociological analysis of nationalism and national identity, parses specific enactments "on the ground", as in the An Tóstal initiative of the 1950s, which was deeply informed by ideological notions of culture and national landscape.

In contrast, Irene Furlong's work on tourism history is grounded in a framework that highlights the roles of political and bureaucratic actors. Framed by the century stretching from 1880, it encompasses the first decades of "tourist development" in late-Victorian Ireland, spanning the three Home Rule Bill debates, the Great War, and the Emergency (as the Second World War was known in the 26-county state). If her chronology implies a degree of continuity in the sector's development, Furlong underlines the impact of the Great War, the Anglo-Irish and Civil Wars, and the Emergency on the volume of traffic in Ireland and on policy directions related to the tourism sector in Ireland, North and South.[27] Furlong, like Zuelow, explores tourism as a policy domain, though she does not apply the lens, or techniques, of social scientific analysis, or propose that landscape is a discursive production. She instead supplies an expansive and empirically rich political and administrative history. It lays the foundations for new scholarship that marries political and cultural narratives for an era in which, as both Furlong and Zuelow note, the state played a key role in fashioning and promulgating ideas of Irishness through tourist promotion—a role adopted in the twentieth century by regimes of various dispensations, democratic and authoritarian, in all corners of the world, from Nazi Germany to post-War America, to communist Mongolia and myriad postcolonial states.

In a markedly different approach to the analysis of eighteenth- and nineteenth-century Irish tourism which draws not on archival but on literary sources, and explicitly and principally engages with landscape as a cultural product, William H.A. Williams explores tourism as a set of cultural practices. His studies marry eighteenth-century aesthetic theory, travel literature, and semiotics and span the century before 1850.[28] Drawing on the elegant and jargon-free semiotics of Jonathan Culler,[29] Williams dissects skillfully the variety of meanings of Irish culture in tourist narratives, and the totems of Irishness that they constructed. In so doing, he contributes to a body of scholarship that dates back to L.P. Curtis's seminal, and controversial, work on images of the Irish, references studies of the Irish on stage and in literature, and incorporates an interest in material culture and cultural practices.[30]

Seeing tourism as involving dynamic intercultural encounters, and landscape as an imaginative and deeply value-laden construct, Williams shows the extent to which iconic images of Irishness (the pig in the cottar's cabin, for instance) were products of specific (mis)readings of Irish culture—and uses case studies to illustrate how, through the lens of the British travel writer, rural cultural practices were construed. He meticulously reconstructs the sensibility of travellers to Ireland, drawing on a wealth of published narratives which can be "read against the grain". If Williams elides, to some extent, the inflection of gender and (sub)nationality in the performance of tourism (though his work on the Scots in Ulster is an exemplar of the subtle and skilful analysis of identification between "guest" and "host"), his approach offers a remarkably imaginative theoretical tool-kit to examine travel as a gendered and intercultural practice—and landscape as a contested product of these practices. This study elaborates on his insights, extending its lens to the period between the end of the Famine and the beginning of the Great War—an era of intensifying development in the Irish tourism sector, and of a growth in writing about leisure travel to Killarney—and also an era in which the calls for more direct state sponsorship of tourism agendas, from infrastructural development to landscape conservation, became louder, and generated, as we shall see, markedly ambivalent responses.

The growth of tourism in Ireland and Killarney occurred against a backdrop of important changes in codes and conventions of travel—particularly with the fading dominance of Romantic landscape aesthetics, the evolution of new languages and forms of scenic and cultural evaluation, and a broader merchandising of the tourist experience. These trends were informed by economic developments (the growth of tourist traffic and the changing socio-economic profile of the tourist), social developments (such as the evolution of transport networks associated with the commercial leisure sector), and wider politico-cultural environments (the Land War, the Home Rule debates, and the "Celtic Twilight", which nourished, and sometimes recast, imageries of the Irish people and Irish landscapes). Killarney—promoted as "Beauty's Home" and "Heaven's Reflex"—was ambiguously placed within debates over tourism, symbolic and legal proprietorship over land, pollution, purity, cultural preservation, and paths towards economic and social modernisation. And as it evolved into an almost surreal realm of peasant kitsch, some tourist narratives were suffused with irony, heightening their comedic effect, while others interlaced earnest professions of patriotism and philanthropy, "reading" the site as a place of privation and degradation, demanding its preservation or its restoration.

THE PEOPLE IN THE LANDSCAPE: TOURISM AND PERFORMANCE

The episode that introduced this chapter recounted the intricate choreography of two American tourists meeting an artful old woman at an advantageously

situated cottage in the Gap of Dunloe. The tone of these self-described leisure travellers, mixing curiosity with a drop of incredulity as generous as the
"granddaughter's" mountain dew, was common to recreational travel narratives, suggesting how the meeting was at least partially pre-scripted and also
more than subtly ironic. Recently, the question of how identities are inscribed
in space through leisure tourism has been fruitfully engaged from the perspective of performance. Dramaturgy and social performance can explain
tourist behaviour as a dynamic process of enactment and narration;[31] it also
illuminates how performance is implicated in tourist "place-making", involving diverse mobilities and networks.[32] Performance need not merely denote
a scripted "entertainment" (the stage-play, for instance); rather it can denote
wider ways of "creating" and "being" in the world through embodied acts.[33]
Through iteration and reiteration, it constitutes the often unconscious performance of self. Social performance is thus an art implicated in the very
invention and stabilisation of identity—and the invention of space, too.[34]
Landscapes are not merely blank canvases on which specific narratives are
inscribed or which offer backgrounds to tourist enactments: landscapes are
produced by performance.[35] Moreover, performance is not prescriptive, and
the dramaturgical lens must not treat the "script" as inflexible, or preclude
the "exploration and experiment" afforded by dynamic embodied practices
which are outside parameters of the established choreographies.[36] In the Killarney tour, irony played a central role in narrating people and place—and in
many episodes it turned on locals' self-presentations as authentic carriers and
custodians of rural tradition, and tourists' professed surprise as they (often
playfully) denounced the patent inauthenticity of it all, professing to resist its
sensually engrossing, carnivalesque elements.

The formidable hostess at Kate Kearney's Cottage whom Silloway and
Powers encountered claimed stewardship not only over her "ancestor's"
abode-cum-shop, but also over the wider landscape to which the white-
washed building served as a symbolic entry-point. As the century progressed, her proprietorship was challenged both by those who demanded
the right to preserve Killarney on behalf of the Irish nation, and by a mot-
ley crew of rogues, hucksters, and hawkers who determinedly chased the
tourist pound, proffering local "hospitality", materialised in their heather,
mountain dew, trinkets, and elaborate speech performances. Tapping a
rich scholarly vein,[37] this study finds no fixed imbalance in power relations
inherent between such "hosts" as Kate Kearney's "granddaughter", and
"guests" such as Silloway and Powers. It does not assume that either group
is a monolith or that tourism invariably constitutes a form of colonialism,
even if, especially in travel writing, it is easy to find many efforts to constitute the authority of the tourist over the native in a variety of (often crude)
ways.[38] It reveals considerable scope for inventiveness and agency amongst
hosts and guests, even as they negotiated deep internal cleavages.[39]

Most travel narratives of Ireland embraced more than this one district,
and most found many of the features of Killarney—poverty, beggary, the

artful exploitation of tourists—elsewhere in Ireland. But there was a peculiar *intensity* to the Killarney experience. It was no sideshow, but rather a
main-stage for aggressive hucksters, heather-toting colleens, guides, and
hangers-on. If the writer Clement W. Scott described mayhem at Killarney, he found none at Lake Glendalough, in Connemara, which evoked
the stillness and solitude that led Tom Taylor to declare it the place for
honeymooners.[40] As Scott asked: "What more could any one desire, save
that peace to enjoy scenery, which at Killarney and in a land of anecdote is
apparently impossible?"[41] Even if "half guides, half beggars" infested the
Wicklow mountains,[42] another district of comparable scenic variety, and
a popular destination for travellers, Killarney was an altogether different
specimen. To the American writer Burton E. Stevenson, only the Giant's
Causeway on Co. Antrim's north-east coast, with its evocative myth of
origin and its curious natural features, could equal Killarney in its claims
on the tourist's purse, "[f]or it should be remembered that the Causeway is
as strictly organised for profit and as carefully exploited as is Killarney."[43]
The Causeway's misfortune, Stevenson lamented, was that "its fame is
too great".[44] To many observers of Ireland's most famous tourist destinations—Co. Wicklow, including Glendalough and the vale of Avoca; the
Causeway; and, through the second-half of the nineteenth century, the
western province of Connacht's dramatic coastline—Killarney's supposed
wretched misfortune, as well as its signature draw, was the remarkable
peasant pantomime for which it served as a backdrop. When Stevenson's
travelogue was published on the eve of the Great War, Killarney was both
a place of long-standing pilgrimage to the traveller in search of "beauty
spots", and also a site of intense commercialisation (which he described
wittily in print). Herein also lay a paradox: most tourists on the Killarney
tour were inducted into a web of exchanges that ended in lamentations that
they had departed the Gap of Dunloe with emptier pockets than they had
anticipated, having had their hopes of solitary moments to appreciate sublime mountain landscapes and picturesque sites frustrated and unfulfilled.
They were not reluctant to convey their experiences in print. In so doing,
they disseminated the contours of the Killarney tour. Indeed, generation
after generation of excursionists submitted to similar exactions and irrita-
tions, many professing hopes that they could break free, but later writing
that they had succumbed to a fate that was as abiding as the rocky precipices that flanked the Gap of Dunloe.

PERFORMING TOURISM AT KILLARNEY: SOURCES

In the post-Famine era, tourism had an important role in the Irish economy.
This was signalled by a proliferation of popular holiday travelogues such as
that of Thomas W. Silloway and Lee L. Powers. Some were primarily written as fire-side entertainments to educate the reader on the landscapes of

Ireland and the customs of its people. Others adopted the trope of the holiday but were vehicles for explicitly polemical commentary, including sear-
ing indictments of the landlord class, optimistic appraisals of Ireland's new
potential, and extensive evaluations of the Irish character and Irish society.[45]
While guide-books and travelogues (the latter published as books, in periodicals, and in newspapers—often in serialised format) are the principal texts
employed in this study, the lines between them often blur, not least because
they feature a high degree of intertextuality, incorporating—often *verba-
tim*—earlier and contemporary antiquarian writing, surveys, and fiction.
This textual feature suggests that authors read other accounts and integrated
them within their own writing, producing a metanarrative of place. While
this overlap is an important textual feature of the field of travel writing, genre
had important implications for the narrative of place, too—and particularly
for the relative emphasis on Killarney as a place of natural beauty or a tourist
bedlam. Accounts of Irish travel—whether recreational or otherwise—have
been explored from a variety of disciplinary perspectives, including literary
history,[46] and cultural geography.[47] Their diverse, and overlapping, generic
features have been dissected in detail. And since Erik Cohen's ground-
breaking work on tourist typologies,[48] scholars have elaborated increasingly
complex types and sub-types, associated with different tourist intentions,
resources, and forms of emotional engagement both with home and away;
this was true in the historical development of tourism, too.

In this study, many writers who visited the Gap of Dunloe can be
broadly, though not always exclusively, categorised as: (1) recreational
"excursionists"—men, women, and families who narrated a relatively short
day tour of sites, usually as first-time visitors to the district, often (but not
always) conducted by locals, in the company of fellow tourists, frequently
in a wider journey through Ireland, the United Kingdom, and Europe; or
(2) more serious-minded travellers, whose lenses often focussed exclusively
on Ireland, and whose narratives, often written in tones of pity or despair,
professed to eschew frivolity, and find in tourism and its actors a window
into privation or primitive culture. Some, like Silloway and Powers, professed to slip between frivolous and more purposeful travel. The flows of
people through Killarney included a substantial number of Irish tourists,
brought to the pre-eminent recreational destination as part of clubs, antiquarian societies, working men's associations, and as independent travellers—coming from urban centres such as Dublin, Belfast, and Cork, as
well as smaller locales. The extent to which the categories "tourist" and
"traveller"—terms used interchangeably by contemporaries—have analytic
value is a matter of debate, though many who made their way through Killarney were labelled "excursionists" (especially those in touring parties). In
Killarney the flight from the "beaten track" was the professed intention of
many travellers. James Buzard has identified this trope in his examination
of how the tourist served as a rhetorical foil for self-characterisations of the
tasteful and adventuresome travel.[49] Many writers narrated efforts to escape

the constraints of "cockneyfied" touring conventions and depart from the beaten track—evading both predatory locals and the tourist hordes. Their exasperation at the futility of such efforts, however, became a conceit in the Killarney travel narrative, in which the intrepid traveller admitted defeat and joined legions of tourists as they snaked their way through the defile and submitted themselves to codes associated with this infamous tourist "trap". No doubt readers felt some pangs of sympathy—building bonds of sentiment with the author as they read rollicking accounts of harrowing escapes and misadventures intermingled with lamentations, some humorous, some forlorn, on the despoiling of Killarney.

The printed accounts explored in this study were directed to some extent at a public audience (though some, such as *The Eagle*, a publication supported by members of St John's College, Cambridge, were expressly published for subscribers only, or for family and friends interested in accounts of travel).[50] These travelogues were mainly penned by Anglophone travellers from Britain, Ireland, America, and Canada.[51] They were largely written by those who self-consciously distinguished themselves from the wider touring "public", occasionally through a claimed expertise in archaeology, religion, or history—a connoisseurship which marked their difference from the travelling crowds, and established cultural authority vis-à-vis readers, too. They variously expressed exasperation, sympathy, and affinity with the toured culture. They emplotted travel within several master-narratives—including that of the leisure traveller, whose account was heavily inflected with humour, and that of the touring investigator, but there was inevitable hybridity in many accounts, too.

Many travel writers broadly shared some cultural and social characteristics. A number, including many recreational excursionists, explicitly constructed a privileged socio-economic identity—not only in counter-distinction to locals, but also in contrast to fellow excursionists, by professing to detect deceptions and disguise with greater clarity than the "everyman" tourist (and especially that most indiscriminate and indiscriminating of tourists, the "cockney"). Some travelled under pseudonyms, which dramatised their experience of meeting the wily denizens of a tourist trap and signified their narrative positioning in such encounters ("The Victim"),[52] signalled to readers their identification with the wider body of fellow travellers ("Viator"),[53] or proclaimed confessional identities and (often related) philanthropic motivations ("The Christian Tourist").[54] In most cases, these travelogues were written to circulate widely, and were part of a growing commerce of popular travel literature that privileged the witty and entertaining account. Exaggeration, elaborate characterisations, and dramatisation of Killarney misadventures served this purpose well. Even those writers who affected to leave the beaten track and the strictures of the "regulation route" rhetorically underlined the dominance of "conventional" practices, often in accounts that were leavened with comical anecdotes of the author succumbing to natives' wiles.

Beyond these accounts of recreational travel, Irish travel writing for the commercial leisure market encompassed a constellation of texts. Though it is often overlooked, in part due to the pernicious scholarly stigmatisation of commercial leisure, the tourist guide-book is a complex and valuable source.[55] Its expansion from the 1830s, led by landmark firms, extended the guide-book to Ireland and refined its form. Take, for instance, *Murray's Handbook for Travellers in Ireland*, first issued in 1864 (with maps by "Mr Stanford" and "[a]n elaborate *Plan of Killarney*, on a large scale", at the end of the Introduction).[56] It was subsequently revised and reissued in new editions, and positioned itself in the late-Victorian period, under the editorship of the esteemed antiquarian, John Cooke, as an authoritative guide-book to the whole country. This book was regarded by the travellers who toted it as a signifier of their superior taste, in comparison with such guide-books as John Bradbury's *Killarney and the South of Ireland: How to See Them for Eight Guineas*, which was explicitly aimed at the thriftier and hastier traveller. Bradbury focussed on one region of Ireland, and meticulously enumerated costs of travel, with the purpose of showing that it was open to the frugal traveller.[57] While such volumes did not "direct" the tourist in any unmediated ways, they prefigured travel, influenced destination choice, and indexed and mapped space, constructed hubs and linear routes as *prima facie* tourist places and tourist paths, and also emplotted narratives of space by signifying sites of interest and propounding on their relevance.[58]

Murray's first 1836 guide-book has been described as heralding a new age for the genre.[59] Its present-tense, first-person-plural narrative departed from the voice of the autobiographical travelogues which preceded it.[60] *Murray's* authority rested on the systematic collection of information from experts on the ground, and on continual revisions in successive editions. Rather than the persona of the embodied writer, its authority derived from conventions of collective compilation, revision, and presentation of tourist information with which the John Murray dynasty became associated, and for which their corporate name served as short-hand.[61] As Rudy Koshar has shown, the guide-book also reproduced notions of social and cultural differentiation;[62] this was as true in Ireland as it was on the continent. The *Murray's* volume for Ireland, which began to incorporate Bartholomew's famous maps, came to be conspicuously organised around the knowledge and authority of John Cooke. His preface used the third-person "The Editor", was followed by an extensive introductory section on practical questions of travel, and then offered expansive discussions of history, archaeology, botany, and other topics addressing "the tourist" throughout. While *Murray's* and Adam and Charles Black's guide-books (another of the United Kingdom's pre-eminent series) published Irish volumes, and the latter a volume dedicated to Killarney and the south, the English-language editions of *Baedeker's*, the iconic German series, did not. And *Murray's* narrative structure belied a particular ideological framing of Ireland for tourist consumption. This was not unproblematic, as the nationalist and writer Aodh de Blacam noted in the Catholic confessional periodical *The Irish Monthly* in 1935. Praising the old "bulky red volume"—now long since superseded—for its detail, and noting that "[w]ith Murray at hand, a train journey across the country was filled with instruction," Aodh de Blacam nevertheless asserted that "[t]here were defects" in it. In a critical analysis which anticipated Roland Barthes's reading of the *Blue Guide*,[63] de Blacam argued that these deficiencies proceeded in large part from the way the country was represented for a British travelling public by Cooke, though he was "an Anglo-Irishman who loved his country".[64] His guide-book extolled the culture of the great house, narrated a society unfamiliar to the Irish themselves, and implicitly endorsed the "Protestant order":

> Yet it looked to a public which was largely alien in sympathy (to say no more!), and its image of Ireland was not that which tradition cher-ishes. It did not record things which are dear to Irishmen, the deeds of our patriots. It accepted the Protestant order; Catholic things got only the attention which a friendly person in the minority chances to grant them. Politically and socially, it was strange to us. In every district it gave lists of the "big houses" and their occupiers, often absentee landlords—information which had little interest for Irishmen and reads strangely in the old volumes now, when the big houses have changed hands, and the names once attached to them have passed into inglorious oblivion.[65]

If antiquated narratives of Ireland found in a musty *Murray's* struck this ardent nationalist as peculiar constructions, produced by a scion of an eclipsed order, *Murray's* was firmly associated with not only the British market, but specifically the upper-middle-class British traveller.[66] Not just in narrative, but in its material features—its portable, "hand-book" quali-ties became a signature feature of guide-books—*Murray's* became central to the travelling apparatus of the discerning traveller abroad and at home. Despite the prominence of *Murray's*, the guide-book genre admitted a plethora of sub-sets. Thomas Cook's guide-books, for instance, codified tours according to the firm's own commercial priorities and relationships,[67] as did the railway guide-books which are explored in the last chapter of this study. Both proposed to bind the traveller to transport, accommodation, and touring itineraries which the firms superintended. But they were con-cerned with marketing places as well as their own services: they recognised that in order to carry people by rail, house them in hotels, and shepherd them through regulation routes, the prospective traveller would have to be attracted to the destination. Hence they supplied evocative narratives of place to accompany their tables of transport fares and schedules—accounts that often elided the comedic episodes described in detailed travelogues.[68]

Aodh de Blacam's comments also suggested the extent to which even the most apparently anodyne narrative was saturated with politics and evaluated as a political text. Accounts explored here span the decades from the end of the Famine, when tourism gained pace, especially during the flowering of tourist-development programmes in the 1890s, through to the First World War, which disrupted markets and reduced tourist traffic there. This era encompassed the advancement of nationalist politics, and its many moments of crisis and division, as well as the continuing evolution of evangelical Protestantism (even as Unionism itself was tested by the robust politics of class), the decline of Ulster Liberalism, and the seminal events of the Land War and the Home Rule debates—as well as the balms of "constructive unionism". As we shall see, writers approached these questions with a marked ambivalence that signalled just how uneasily the sector was positioned within discourses of land, nationhood, the state, and tourism.

If guide-books sometimes spoke to their prospective markets with titles that sold for a shilling and promised to show how a tour could be done for less than eight guineas, travelogues were organised around myriad conceits: some proposed how Killarney could be done in one day or one week, using the author's routes as examples, and encouraging the reader to follow in the writer's footsteps.[69] Others adopted whimsical conceits: proclaiming the author had apprehended the *British Isles through an Opera Glass*,[70] for instance, or anchoring the narrative to some vehicular device—whether canoe, aeroplane, or jaunting-car.[71] Others explicitly proposed to reveal hidden Ireland, or elucidate the tragic impacts of Famine, or illuminate the Union's intrinsic inequalities.[72]

In addition to monograph-length travelogues, this study examines several travel accounts published in the burgeoning Victorian periodical press, ranging from venerable publications such as *Chambers's Journal* to more ephemeral titles, and the annuals, monthlies, and other periodicals which aimed to entertain mostly middle-class readers, many signalling this intent with sub-titles suggesting the "amusement" that might be obtained from leisurely reading (with some also boldly proclaiming a confessional affiliation and loftier educative purposes). The history of travel writing's growth is linked inextricably to the expansion of reading markets—and perhaps none was more critical than the fire-side periodical in popularising the misadventures that attended a Killarney tour, making every reader the vicarious companion of travel writers as they navigated perilous paths and baffling customs. The travel accounts contained in this rich literature were tailored to audiences which were defined not only by class and confession, but intersecting age and gender identities, too (as the number of titles dedicated to the leisurely reading of "ladies" suggests).[73] In contrast with the guide-book, these texts were usually single-authored narratives which emplotted the traveller's Irish exploits, replete with evocative episodes that served as dramatic foci for the story of travel and drew the reader into an intimacy and identification with the writer.

In this analysis, which draws heavily on this material to underscore its value as a source-set in tourism history, as much information as possible is included about each author (though publications, especially in periodicals, were conventionally anonymous, or written under *noms-de-plume*, while guide-books were often aggregations of material from a range of sources, edited and revised with each successive edition). Authorial self-presentations are a critical consideration in this study. Whether the narrator was making a pilgrimage to the "homeland", was a clergyman connected to a specific "mission", or was an intrepid traveller desiring to escape from tired touring conventions, self-positioning had important implications for how writers narrated regimes of mobility and sociality.

Newspapers employed in this study include a broad range of British and Irish titles that offer insights into local and national formulations and reception of tourism. Newspapers, which were part of a flourishing local press in the period under study—the Tralee-based *Kerry Sentinel* and the *Killarney Echo*—are valuable in charting complex local debates over tourist-development initiatives.[74] British titles, from the *Aberdeen Journal* to the *Leeds Mercury*, published (often serialised) accounts, often in epistolary form, from travellers to Ireland which illuminate ideological productions of landscapes and cultures. All these periodicals constructed landscapes through a variety of media, including the printed word and illustrations.[75] The political orientations of these periodicals on such contemporary debates as the land question and Home Rule are highly salient to this study, which explores how divisions over the political status of the island were negotiated in tourism.[76] The results are often surprising. Indeed, analysing tourist development as a natural or exclusive ally of unionism fails to account for its ambiguous and ambivalent receptions in many quarters—amongst antiquarians and scholars who despaired of Ireland's "cockneyfication", and also nationalists who condemned tourism's corrosive impact on Gaelic autarky, even as Gaelic Leaguers enjoined Irish men, women, and youth to venture west into Gaeldom's soul.

A few accounts written by Irish excursionists are also included here, including narratives which appeared in *The Irish Monthly*. A more definitive study focussing on Irish travellers remains to be written; after all, they joined, and far outnumbered, other excursionists and travellers on the Killarney tour. It might elucidate the nuanced views of "domestic" travellers in the principal tourist district of Ireland and reveal diverse responses to the imperative issued in the late-nineteenth century for Irish people to travel in their own country to better know it. Yet identifying precise features of the domestic tourist as a "type" is problematic. Cultural identification was often expressed in highly ambivalent ways. Take as an example the novelist Dinah Maria Craik. Craik was the daughter of a Dubliner, Thomas Mulock. He made his way to London and then to the continent around 1820 for a journey of around two years. He returned to Britain, married and, abandoning his family, moved to London.[77] Dinah, his daughter and the namesake of her mother, declared herself an "Irishwoman" in her Killarney travel writing. Like Irish-American tourists whose patronage was so desired by tourist-development promoters,[78] her birthplace did not confer a sense of nationality on Craik. Moreover, the physical distance which many writers travelled did not necessarily diminish cultural identification with Ireland (Irish-Americans were often encouraged to "return home" for holidays, while some Ulster travellers marvelled at the "gulf" between North and South). There are few touchstones that appear to unite the Irish traveller, though it is a subject that would reward the scholar.

The *Irish Tourist*, the self-styled "Official Organ of Tourist Development in Ireland", is used widely in this study, especially in the absence of early minutes and other archival records. The transplanted Englishman Frederick W. Crossley, an indefatigable promoter of the tourist sector in Ireland, founded it in 1894. The periodical was established in the same era as such trade journals as *The Irish Vintner and Grocer* (1904) and the *Irish Draper* (1900),[79] and was published by his Irish Tourist Development Publishing Company, Ltd, in Nassau Street, Dublin. It offers insight into an ideology of improvement within the tourism sector that was grounded in efforts to link economic improvement with enhanced political harmony between "sister" isles. From its inaugural issue through the first years of the twentieth century, the *Irish Tourist* evolved from a periodical largely comprising (as some of its early mast-heads proclaimed) "entertaining and amusing" travel hints, anecdotes, and historical jottings with photographs and profiles of "beauty spots", as well as many advertisements for hotels, railways, and other services, to explicit affiliation with Ireland's representative body of hoteliers and restaurant proprietors, and the official organ of the Hotel Proprietors' Association.[80] It championed such initiatives as the Shannon steamers in which Crossley had a hand—in this case, through the Shannon Development Company and Tourist Development (Ireland) Co., Ltd., a body founded in 1896.[81] The inaugural issue made it clear that the main rhetorical object of tourist development, in its view, was to lure tourists from across the Irish Sea: "[I]t is, in our opinion," the editor, Crossley, declared, "well within the bounds of possibility to make it quite as fashionable among Britons to visit Ireland as it is with them to visit the English Lakes or the Scottish Trossachs."[82] In this respect, it provides valuable insight into how late-Victorian and Edwardian programmes aimed to develop new touring grounds and promote new projects outside Killarney and its principal sites (the so-called "lions" of the district). The periodical assembled a variety of texts, from fiction to short notices to advertisements and photography (especially images from Robert Welch and the firm founded by William Lawrence) to promote Ireland to the prospective traveller, to communicate news with sections of the trade, and to issue a rallying call for Britons to forsake the continent and travel to the "sister isle" instead. As we shall see, this rhetoric had a long pedigree and was associated with those who exhorted people to travel as a patriotic duty—even if their audience, and the meaning of patriotism, were contested.

CONCLUSION

When Thomas W. Silloway and Lee L. Powers braved the Gap of Dunloe, it is certain that they had been schooled in the ways of Kate's "granddaughter" by this vast travel literature. Their astonishment at the indomitable woman's audacity must be interpreted with sensitivity to the disposition with which many tourists approached the Gap tour. Many adopted an ironic tone and a marked readiness for what Erik Cohen has called "playful self-deception, the willingness to go along with the illusion that an obviously contrived, inauthentic situation is real".[83] Their folly, writers lamented, was falling within the woman's mercenary grip. Their assessment of the extraordinary claims, at a time when writers and artists were constructing a vision that conflated purity with periphery on the Western coast, draws our attention to Dean MacCannell's seminal study of tourism as a search for authenticity—that quest reflecting alienation from the perceived inauthenticity of the modern condition. Drawing on Erving Goffman, MacCannell argues that societies adopt strategies designed to "stage authenticity" for the tourist, deterring them from penetrating the dynamic "back" regions of the toured culture, and thereby frustrating the tourist's essential quest for wholeness and authenticity through tourism.[84] MacCannell, acknowledging John Urry, argues that the tourist quest is motivated in part by a second "gaze"—one which critically engages with the ideological production of the first. In "recognizing the misrecognition that defines the tourist gaze",[85] the tourist desires to move beyond it. It is the intuitive sense of the fabricated character of the first gaze that reveals its ideological foundations and ultimately offers emancipation from its strictures. To many post-Famine tourists, Victorian Killarney was a manufactured place, saturated with the features of commercial tourism. Some travellers went along for the ride. Others lamented tourism's malignant effects on the locality and searched elsewhere for "authentic" Ireland. Still others endeavoured to recover a Romantic landscape there. These efforts were often recorded in luminous—even grandiloquent—prose, with many writers affecting a disapproving tone.

Wider processes of "spatialisation" were central to these efforts to release Killarney from the grasp of myriad despoilers: tourists blind to their destructive impacts, rapacious local hucksters, and pernicious landlords who endeavoured to squeeze every shilling from excursionists at ubiquitous toll-gates. Tim Edensor, in work on national landscapes, explores "national forms of spatialisation which interweave to consolidate a strong cognitive, sensual, habitual, and affective sense of national identity".[86] Often these "ideological rural landscapes" are performed as places of purity and permanence—as sites of an ossified primary culture, where natives dwell and where their "traditional" habits of mind and practices endure.[87] Contrasts between the sedentary character of the toured and the sacred places that they inhabit on one hand and, on the other hand, the active progression of the modern tourist through native space, can reinforce a reified reading of the peasant *habitus*. This study explores the dynamic choreographies of tourist encounters and the distinctive narratives of Killarney—and tensions between cultural preservationists, fun-loving tourists, disparaging moralists, and the many local characters, some of them famously age-defying, whom they encountered on tour.

1   The Eclipse of the Sublime

Harry Speight, a Yorkshire local historian and travel writer who penned a serialised travelogue on Ireland for the *Bradford Observer* under the pseudonym "Johnnie Gray", advised readers in 1884 that "[t]o 'do' Killarney, after the modern tourist fashion, is only a matter of about a couple of days, though as many weeks would be little enough to fix all the charms of the place upon the memory."[1] Yet "'the lions'" could be done in two or three days: a visit to Muckross Abbey and the Torc Cascade, an ascent of Mangerton or Carran Tuel, and the requisite drive through the Gap of Dunloe and sail down the Lakes.[2] The latter tour, he noted, comprised a "'regulation route'", with parties being assembled every day at hotels before setting off for a carriage ride, followed by a 14-mile boat trip. With charges for carriage and boat rides, guide and bugler, tips to the boatmen, and lunch bringing the total cost to under 10*s*. per head, Speight declared that "it is one of the finest day tours possible to be had for a moderate sum"; therefore, "everybody takes it."[3] Indeed, thousands of tourists followed Speight's route through the district, making a tour of Killarney the signature Irish tourist excursion, and an encounter with Kate Kearney's "granddaughter" its primary conceit. Aspects of these tourist performances were not altogether novel, for many earlier travellers had discussed, often in disparaging tones, the female beggars and other hangers-on who peopled the Killarney district and cajoled loose change out of travellers. But in the second-half of the nineteenth century their presence was amplified by the growth of commercial tourism, an increase in tourists who visited the district, and new codes of touring which foregrounded the social and diminished the solitary as modes of engagement with the landscape. Travellers deployed a different vocabulary and engaged in different travel practices than their early-Victorian predecessors.

In the decades after the Irish Famine of the 1840s, tourists such as Speight snaked their way through a landscape that was once mainly depicted by travel writers as forbidding and sublime. It now became the setting for a series of extraordinary performances involving tourists affecting disapproval and disbelief at an unruly spectacle led by a formidable hostess at a profitably situated cottage and her entourage of buglers, fiddlers, guides, and a boisterous band of so-called "mountain dew girls" deeper in the Gap. Armed with containers of putatively illicit whiskey ("poitín", or "mountain dew") and fresh goat's-milk, these mountain dew girls served a potent concoction for the tourist to imbibe. It was part of an elaborate carnival that engaged the senses and, over time, became the dominant feature of the Gap tour. The women's inspiration—and, some of them boldly asserted, their direct ancestor—was a legendary local woman, Kate Kearney. Kate was a famous figure in Victorian popular culture whose presence permeated the Gap. She was an increasingly prominent part of the human landscape, as practices of mass tourism displaced those of Romantic travel, and distinctive modes of sociality and embodied engagement became part of "doing" Killarney in the era of crowds and carnival. Doing Killarney now constituted an immersion in a mocked-up world of peasant coquettes, illicit drink, and incredulous tales. Implicitly, it rejected Killarney as a site of authentic cultural experience, and, instead, offered up a site of ludic entertainment organised around narrative tropes of harassment, disappointment, and frustrated efforts at furtive escape from a teeming tourist trap.

On the Gap portion of the Killarney tour, tourists invariably met women who presented themselves as Kate or one of her (apparently numerous) descendants. Guide-books and travelogues playfully disputed their claims, and reminded readers that Sydney Owenson, later Lady Morgan, whose national tales are part of the Romantic-era canon,[4] had given legendary Kate immortal life:

> OH, did you not hear of Kate Kearney?
> She lives on the banks of Killarney:
> From the glance of her eye, shun danger, and fly,
> For fatal's the glance of Kate Kearney.
>
>   For that eye is so modestly beaming,
> You ne'er think of mischief she's dreaming;
> Yet, oh! I can tell how fatal the spell
> That lurks in the eye of Kate Kearney.
>
>   Oh, should you e'er meet this Kate Kearney,
> Who lives on the banks of Killarney,
> Beware of her smile, for many a wile
> Lies hid in the smile of Kate Kearney.
>
>   Tho' she looks so bewitchingly simple,
> Yet there's mischief in every dimple;
> And who dares inhale her sighs' spicy gale,
> Must die by the breath of Kate Kearney.[5]

The Kate Kearney of Owenson's parlour song was an ambiguous enchantress—beguiling and menacing, alluring and dangerous. Penned in the first decade of the nineteenth century, and set to the traditional air "The Beardless Boy",[6] Owenson's melody and lyrics spawned a variety of often comical adaptations. They were nourished by Owenson's other writings and her own parlour-room performances of the fictional Glorvina, "The Wild Irish Girl", of her most famous work and national tale. In these encounters, Glorvina and Owenson merged to produce a figure who occupied what Natasha Tessone has characterised as a "politically ambiguous position" before the English audiences of her embodied spectacle—both affirming and undermining stereotypes of the Irish nation on her parlour-room stage.[7] The colourful exploits of Owenson's other great exotic Irish peasant creation—Kate Kearney—and her putative descendants were recounted in the pages of leading British and American periodicals,[8] and were discussed in widely read travelogues by celebrated writers, including Thomas Carlyle, who toured Killarney in 1849.[9] In addition to transatlantic lyrical and literary incarnations which implanted her within Anglophone popular culture, Kate Kearney became an iconic figure in Killarney—at a time when the district was solidifying its reputation as Ireland's leading tourist destination. At the Gap, tourists were invited to enter a world of illusion and literary allusion, affecting disbelief as they met this icon of Victorian popular culture, entertained her entreaties, and appraised her hallmark beverage.

These social performances were strongly associated with the contours of mass tourism in the post-Famine period, and with the specific ways in which Irish culture was commodified for the touring public, not only at the Gap, but at other sites, too. That era, beginning especially after 1850, codified the Gap tour in ways that embedded it firmly within modern tourist commerce. In contrast, from the mid-eighteenth century through the 1830s, a dominant aesthetic valorisation of the Gap of Dunloe referenced the category of the sublime. However, the dominance of this aesthetic ideal declined, and from the mid-nineteenth century, distinctive sounds, tastes, and social practices became ever-more prominent tropes in narratives of the Gap tour. This did not imply a complete standardisation of tourist practices, or indeed an altogether new tourist practice (Anne Plumptre, writing in the second decade of the nineteenth century, had despaired at Killarney, as at the Giant's Causeway, of the "ingenious devices the people about have, each to pluck a feather out of the pigeon's wing"[10]). Indeed, the undermining of the Romantic-era narrative of the Gap by the post-Famine carnival kept elements of it alive as an ideal way to properly "do" the site—and the occasional tourist reached for the vocabulary of the sublime, if only to wistfully bemoan the eclipse of genteel travel conventions. But mass tourism, and the emergence of a mode of travelogue writing that focussed on Killarney's ludic features, even as a foil for the traveller's claim to taste, also popularised conventions of doing Killarney. These interlaced developments highlighted new features of mobility and sociality which shaped narratives of both the "standard" tour and more subversive ways of doing the Gap, many of which were cast as a recovery of Romantic practices. A cacophonous band of buglers, mountain damsels, guides, touts, and beggars pressing their attentions, services, and wares on excursionists throughout the journey was central to transforming dominant narratives of the Gap from appraisals of it as a site of the sublime, which positioned the tourist as a diminutive and solitary figure in relation to the landscape, and foregrounded their intense, personal mental and emotional engagement with awe-inspiring scenery, to narratives of overwhelming sensorial engagement and intense sociality.

"THIS WONDERFUL SCENE APPEARS A FRIGHTFUL CHASM": THE LENS OF THE SUBLIME

From the late-eighteenth century until the eve of the Famine, the aesthetic ideal of the sublime underpinned many travellers' narratives of a visit to the Gap of Dunloe.[11] The Romantic period was the well-spring of a number of touristic practices which were profoundly influential in framing the site in the pre-Famine imagination. Although it was by no means a complete reaction to the Enlightenment, Romanticism grounded the traveller's relationship to the landscape in terms of powerful, spontaneous, deep, and internally derived emotional responses, drawn from the "liberated imagination" and centred on a range of aesthetic categories such as the sublime.[12] Narratives of travel, domestic as well as foreign, provided a framework for the articulation of these qualities; they often took the form—and indeed the name—of the "picturesque tour", popularised in printed books and in periodicals, even if this was not always the principal focus of travel to Ireland in the early years after the Union.[13] England, Wales, Scotland, and Ireland furnished many English writers with places which they recounted as distinctly exotic, especially as the "Home Tour" became a fashionable middle-class performance from the 1770s and in the first decade of the nineteenth century, when conflict constrained the continental wanderings of many travellers. They discovered Britain and Ireland supplied many exemplars of the sublime, too. Though Romanticism had a transatlantic form, it was also expressed within the parameters of national cultures, which furnished histories, politics, mythologies, and other literary forms and thematic materials through which distinctive national expressions were forged.[14] While there were myriad motivations behind tours, a search for inspiring landscapes was amongst the most prominent. In the rugged mountains of the Scottish Highlands, in Snowdonia, and at the Gap of Dunloe, many tourists satisfied their desire to behold peaks, precipices, and deep recesses which drew out profound sensations of personal engagement with an elemental landscape. Writers explored their personal relationship to a vast natural world, which at once diminished solitary travellers and connected them to some otherwise elusive element of the Deity and its awesome power.

The ideal of the sublime had a long history stretching back to antiquity, and had various late-seventeenth-century, eighteenth-century, and Romantic elaborations. In the Romantic period it was grounded in the individual's encounter with an external object that initially overwhelmed reason and understanding. The resulting intense, inexpressible emotional response hinted at powers that lay beyond the limits of understanding.[15] Qualities of the sublime in nature—the discourse most frequently invoked in descriptions of the Gap tour—were expounded by thinkers such as John Dennis, Joseph Addison, and Edmund Burke; indeed the latter's famous work *A Philosophical Enquiry into the Origins of Our Ideas of the Sublime and Beautiful* (originally published in 1757 with a revised second edition in 1759) was a landmark elaboration of aesthetic theory in which Burke delineated the interactions of cognition, sensation, and the external object which produced the sublime: an ideal rooted in passions evoked by that which is "in any sort terrible" in nature.[16] "The passion caused by the great and sublime in *nature*," Burke wrote, "when those causes operate most powerfully, is Astonishment; and astonishment is that state of the soul, in which all its motions are suspended, with some degree of horror."[17] If "astonishment" was the "effect of the sublime in its highest degree", its inferior effects were "admiration, reverence and respect".[18] The terrible, which evoked fear, assumed primacy in Burke's doctrine of the sublime;[19] indeed terror constituted "the ruling principle of the sublime".[20] The sublime was manifest in the response to vastness, or "greatness of dimension", and also to the qualities of "[d]ifficulty" (as evinced by Stonehenge) and "[m]agnificence".[21] Certain qualities of light and colour might also elicit such a response, with Burke writing that "[a]mong colours, such as are soft, or cheerful, (except perhaps a strong red which is cheerful) are unfit to produce grand images. An immense mountain covered with a shining green turf, is nothing in this respect, to one dark and gloomy; the cloudy sky is more grand than the blue; and night more sublime and solemn than day."[22] Yet Burke also contended that the eye was "not the only organ of sensation, by which a sublime passion may be produced", and wrote that "[e]xcessive loudness", such as that produced by "vast cataracts, raging storms, thunder, or artillery", could awaken the same passions and sensations as the terrible landscape.[23] Sudden and intermittent sound might also have the capacity of producing the sublime, as could the cries of animals; while taste and smell might also have this effect, in Burke's opinion only "excessive bitters, and intolerable stenches" were productive of truly "grand" sensations.[24] Burke's ideal of the sublime, then, was very much grounded in responses to the visual. Techniques associated with contemporary landscape evaluation according to another ideal—the picturesque—implicated technologies such as the Claude Glass in practices which framed the external world as a composition.[25]

Many travellers in Killarney found the Gap of Dunloe to be an exemplar of the sublime. The surrounding mountainous district, largely given over to pastoral farming of cows and sheep by cottiers in cabins, and extensive woodlands, including large coverage of the native arbutus, dramatised the grandeur of the landscape. It engendered parallel explorations of the interior emotional landscape. These Romantic tropes continued to exert power over the imagination—and pens—of travellers in the post-Union period, even if such terms as "sublime" and "picturesque" were more loosely applied than some of their their eighteenth-century expounders intended. At the Gap in particular, travellers employed the language associated with the sublime widely in early-nineteenth-century travel writing as they reflexively engaged in protocols of "tasteful" travel. The prolific author Sir Richard Colt Hoare, in his 1806 *Journal of a Tour in Ireland*, described Killarney as offering a varied, visual feast.

> I have seen no spot more adapted for the school of a landscape artist than KILLARNEY; and where he may study all the component parts of a fine picture with greater advantage. The rocks that bound the shores of MUCRUSS and the Lower Lake, with their harmonious tints, and luxuriant decoration of foliage, stand unrivalled, both in form and colouring. The character of the mountains is as grand and varied, as the lakes in which they reflect their rugged summits; and the inconstant state of the climate subjects each to the most sudden changes, and produces the most admirable effects of light and shade imaginable. Here, in short, in this western *Tempe,* the artist will find every thing he can possibly wish: the *beautiful* in the Lower, and MUCRUSS Lakes; the *sublime* in the Upper Lake; *variety* in the river that connects the lakes, and the *savage* in the mountains that form the Pass of DUNLOE.[26] [Italics and capitalisation as in original]

Critical to this visual framing of the Gap was the identification of "views" offered at specific stages on an excursionist's journey through the pass—a device common to tours in the late-eighteenth and early-nineteenth centuries, especially amongst those inclined to mimic the conventions of picturesque travel propounded by such aesthetic theorists as Rev. William Gilpin. These narrative strategies, and allied travel practices, were reproduced in early guide-books to the district, and bear testimony to the influence of these aesthetic categories over the print accounts of Irish travel. In 1822, for instance, George Nelson Smith produced a guide to the district of Killarney divided principally into "stations", a convention that promised especially pleasing and panoramic views of scenery. He represented the "Gap of Dunlow" [sic] as awe-inspiring, wild, and savage.[27] Awe and expressions of fear were signature emotional responses to the landscape in other accounts, too. As to how excursionists could not only emotionally, but also physically, navigate this site, writers urged caution, noting that even mountain goats risked death on its precipitous walls. One writer rhapsodised about the "wild" character of the scenery, which could prove treacherous to the traveller, in the periodical *The Day*:

> Though having every disposition to linger o'er the scene, yet our stay being unfortunately limited to the short space of two days, we resolved

at all events to extend them to the utmost limits which the season
afforded. With that end, we were early on foot next morning, and having the aid of hardy, sure-footed Kerry ponies, pursued our way towards
the Gap of Dunloe. This is a wild mountain pass, formed between the
hills, which on both sides are quite precipitous, with immense masses
of rock lying about in every direction, and frequently threatening to
interrupt the path of the traveller.—

"Crags, knolls and mounds, confusedly hurled,
The fragments of an earlier world."

We have never seen Glencoe; but assuredly Glencoe presents nothing to equal the dreary sublimity of the scenery through which we now
passed. A gloomy pool attracted our attention at a part of the rugged
road, where, had we not possessed the most unlimited confidence in
our sturdy ponies, the dread of being precipitated into these dreary
waters, would have quickly dispelled our ideas of the sublime: as it was,
the slight idea of fear served but to increase the feeling produced by the
surrounding grandeur of the scene.[28]

Romantic travel foregrounded deeply personal engagement with the landscape. Thus narrators often adopted the voice of the solitary traveller, even
when accompanied by others on the tour.[29]

Not all narratives placed the tourist alone in the Gap, however, or narrated it as a solitary experience. In fact there were multiple "readings" of
the Gap which invested it with different degrees of emotional power, and
which variously acknowledged or elided the human element there. William
Reed's reflections on the Gap mixed his own assessment of its exceptionally
sublime features with commentary on the barrister and travel writer (later
Sir) John Carr's famous account of an 1805 tour in southern and western Ireland when, upon seeing the Gap, he declared no "indisposition to
quit this desolate region and return to Dunloe castle".[30] In contrast, Reed
offered this evaluation of the site, in which he described some features of
human habitation that other narratives often elided and assimilated them
within his evaluation of the sublime scene: "The Gap is not destitute of
inhabitants. On some of the broad projections of the rock, at a considerable elevation from the road, a cabin, and in some places a small group of
cabins, is seen surrounded with plots of grass and garden-ground."[31]

However much it was celebrated as an exemplar of the sublime, it was
on their emergence from the Gap that tourists were sometimes promised an
even finer specimen of such scenery. According to the author of *Picturesque
Scenery in Ireland*, the Black Valley onto which it opened was a "wide and
desolate hollow, surmounted by the finest peaks of this mountain range".[32]
The dark and savage valley, the author remarked, "is considered by many
more striking than the Gap of Dunloe". Indeed, in his celebrated account
of Ireland in 1834, the Scottish travel writer Henry David Inglis had made
the same observation.[33] The textual field that propagated this landscape

aesthetisication was not limited to the printed word. Similar techniques for representing the otherworldly character of the sublime were evident in contemporary landscape painting. While sites in Killarney had been subjects for painting since the eighteenth century, frequently assembled in collections which highlighted "scenic spots", or panoramic views of the Lakes,[34] the Gap was often represented by visual artists in ways which complemented renderings of it in travel accounts—a solitary and majestic site in which watercolourists such as George Robson employed light to dramatic effect, and inserted a lone figure in the landscape, a technique which also dramatised the grandeur of the place. This image of what Carla Briggs has described as "figures diminished" by the "vastness" of the Gap was a recurrent theme.[35] They echoed prose narratives of the solitary traveller facing a grand, elemental landscape.

Although its sublimity supplied a rhetorical conceit within which the Gap landscape was appraised, its suitability was contested. Some depictions invoked picturesque qualities, alongside the sublime. Others disputed the sublime character of the Gap altogether, using the occasion to claim authority as widely travelled narrators. In a series of letters on travels published in 1827, for instance, Nathaniel Hazeltine Carter, recounting his tour through Europe, opined that the Gap did not evoke fear, or indeed the range of raw emotions expressed by other writers. Indeed, in an assertion of the superiority of the New World over the Old, Killarney offered no more than diminutive versions of other sites:

> In the exaggerated descriptions of the scenery about these lakes, it is stated among other things, that persons have entered the gap of Dunloe, and were so terrified at the precipices overhanging them, as to retreat without venturing through. They must have had weak nerves, if there be the least foundation for the report. We experienced nothing like terror. The scene is grand, but cannot be considered awful. In sublimity, it is far inferior to the Notch in the White Hills of New-Hampshire. The Saco is a much finer river, than the streamlet hurrying down the rocky pass of Dunloe, and M'Gilly Cuddy's Reeks and Purple Mountain are mere mole hills, in comparison with Mount Washington.[36]

Efforts to appreciate the scene within the conventions and discourses of Romantic travel were often frustrated by the disruption of local men and women who pressed themselves upon the traveller, offering articles and services, and intruding upon the tourist's gaze. As one traveller, "J.K.", whose accounts of travel in the south of Ireland 1836 were serialised in the *Ulster Times* in 1837, wrote: "The only alloy to this glorious scene was the sight of the miserable peasantry, who, seeing our boat passing over the Lake, had run down from Mangerton and the other hills, to offer us goat's milk and 'poteen.' They seemed poor and wretched in the extreme, and formed a melancholy contrast with the heavenly spot they inhabited."[37] This disruption was to become a dominant theme in travel accounts in the post-Famine period, and eventually became the principal conceit of the tourist's excursion narrative. It reflected how John Urry's "romantic gaze" became destabilised, and ultimately displaced by a mode of apprehension in which new sights and sensations came to define the Gap as a tourist place—and foregrounded the carnivalesque features of the Gap tour.[38] The frustrated recovery of the Romantic narrative remained an imperative underpinning many travel accounts—and writers used encounters with Kate Kearney's "granddaughter" to critique the raucous circus that prevailed at the Gap of Dunloe.

"YOU SEDUC'D EVERY THOUGHT EV'RY WISH OF MY SOUL": THE ROMANTIC KATE KEARNEY

Pre-Famine Romantic framings of the Gap's scenery were propounded not only by the picturesque travelogue and guide-book, but also by poetry, fiction, and photography—and not all of them were entrenched within the aesthetics of the sublime. As one of the best-known districts in Ireland, lauded by poets and popularised internationally as a tourist centre by writers, etchers, and painters, the Lakes of Killarney were often, if not exclusively, a district for pilgrimage for tourists wishing to see landscapes that inspired Thomas Moore's ode to "Sweet Innisfallen" (one of the most quoted works in travelogues and guide-books). They were also drawn there by the works of Poets Laureate William Wordsworth, Alfred Lord Tennyson, and other poets, librettists, and novelists; they extolled picturesque landscapes found only a short distance from the savage mountains that gripped the imaginations of other travellers.[39] In the pantheon of Killarney's panegyrists, Sir Walter Scott's brief visit to Killarney in 1825, in the company of Maria Edgeworth, attracted great contemporary interest. In the interpolation of literature and landscape, Sydney Owenson's poem and its protagonist became intimately associated with the district (Henry W. Longfellow accorded "Kate Kearney" a privileged place in the Irish volume of his *Poems of Places* under the section "Killarney, the lakes"[40]). But there was an equally critical expansion in the textual field that addressed a new Killarney tour. In particular, the recreational travelogue pivoted from a narrative largely concerned with the physical landscape to one that detailed and evaluated the human landscape—often with comedic effect. The performance of the narrator as a figure engulfed by commerce and carnival challenged Romantic tropes; many visitors now lamented the grubby commercialisation of the district. In this way, in proliferating accounts of travel, many penned in popular fire-side periodicals and travelogues, writers affected to distance themselves from the conventions of mass tourism—the standardisation of tourist performances and various commodifications of Irish life that attended it—and refashioned the "epistemological quest" as a search for that authentic rural space that lay beyond the nakedly inauthentic realm of Kate Kearney. They endeavoured, with frustration, to depart from a script over which this figure had tightened her grip. As a writer styled "The Victim" recounted in the pages of *The Idler Magazine*:

> King Midas touched an article and it became gold, a most useful accomplishment to possess when times are pannicky [*sic*]. Literary kings have the still greater power of bestowing immortality on those they touch. Thus Burns immortalized the name of Glencairn, and made it so celebrated that it was considered good enough to designate a brand of whiskey. Three generations ago, a poet wrote of Kate Kearney, and she will be famous from now till the end of time.[41]

There was political significance in the demarcation of this space as the realm of Kate—and great commercial advantages to be enjoyed by its denizens, too. Indeed, by the mid-Victorian period myriad women tapped both growing interest in Killarney as a tourist destination and the growing popularity of Kate Kearney as a figure in Anglophone popular culture.

Owenson's song, in contrast to many literary works which extolled Killarney, but in common with works by writers such as Sir Walter Scott and others who shaped literary landscapes in other districts in the United Kingdom, made a beguiling peasant girl the emblem of the region's wildness and allure. Kearney's popularity harnessed the romantic sentimental literary tourism generated around female figures during the nineteenth century—including Scott's 1810 *Lady of the Lake* and R.D. Blackmore's 1869 *Lorna Doone*. In Scotland, Loch Katrine and the Trossachs gained international fame as the setting for Scott's poem about the sixteenth-century, ethereal Ellen, Lady of the Lake, and her suitors, set against a backdrop of conflict between clansman and Royalists. Subsequent embellishments of the tale, with the complicity of a local landlord, who erected a "summer house" on "Ellen's isle" in the lake, sign-posted this romantic Scottish topography to legions of visitors.[42] Indeed, much of the romance that surrounded Kate Kearney's narrative seemed to derive from the Scottish canon, perhaps a consequence of what some judged to be the comparative paucity of literary associations with Killarney, in comparison with Scotland's Highlands.[43] As C.P. Crane declared in *Kerry* (part of "The Little Guides" series): "On the whole . . . Kerry is not rich in literary associations. The county has produced no great poet and no great dramatic historian like Sir Walter Scott," though it had "materials enough" for someone possessing "the gift of interpretation and the power of turning into glowing romance all the mass of historic fact and legend".[44] Crane joined a chorus of guide-book writers and tourist-trade promoters who looked jealously to Scotland and lamented that Ireland's tourist sector had no Scott to work his "magic wand" and produce an oeuvre which would compel the tourist to make a pilgrimage to the sites of his work. Still, Kate Kearney furnished the district with one of its best-known figures. The search for her, and bitter disappointment at beholding an ugly, putative descendant, became an enduring feature of Gap tour narratives, and a signal of how locals sought to tap the rich vein of tourism, just as landlords had long endeavoured to do.

In other parts of Ireland, before the eras in which William Butler Yeats and James Joyce were mobilised to promote specific literary places, efforts to "brand" districts for the literary tourist did not achieve the desired goal of implanting them as firmly in the public imagination as comparative districts in England and Scotland. An 1898 piece in the *Irish Times*, for instance, trumpeted a district of the Shannon encompassing several counties as "'The Goldsmith Country'". There, tourists could visit Lissoy, in Westmeath, the "Auburn" of Oliver Goldsmith's famous work *The Deserted Village*; Goldsmith's boyhood home was now "represented by roofless walls and a smokeless chimney-shaft" (not far away visitors could pay a pilgrimage to the birthplace of the poet in Co. Longford). "This", it contended, "is the Irish counterpart of the Stratford-on-Avon district of England, the Mecca of English poetry."[45] But any comparison with that shrine to England's bard only highlighted Ireland's deficiencies. "A little interest," the author asserted, "a limited share of thoughtful care on the suggestion of those whose energies are so well directed to promoting the tourist industry of this country might be well applied to this shrine land of Irish genius. Think only of what has been done in the sister countries to honour and preserve the memories of their poets and scholars! Think only of the homes of Scott and Burns, of Wordsworth and Southey, and of Stratford—the pilgrim place of the world's votaries of song! Can Ireland not follow suit even in a remote way[?]"[46] If so, the result would be welcome contrast to the "loquacious fund of knowledge with which the ciceroni of Wicklow and Killarney regale their patrons". There were no celebrated homes of writers to be visited in Killarney, though tourists could ritually follow in the (often fleeting) footsteps of some esteemed literary visitors, including Scott. Even so, with the exception of Thomas Moore's work, the Killarney was dominated by lesser known writers and by minor poets such as Thomas Gallwey.[47] His 1871 *Lays of Killarney Lakes, Descriptive Sonnets, and Occasional Poems* was recommended by the *Irish Times*, though Gallwey's lays compared unfavourably with those of Sir Walter Scott, in the reviewer's assessment, and were also inferior to his accompanying sonnets. However, "[r]ead *in situ*," the review remarked, "its legends and fairy lore would add a new pleasure to that afforded by the scenery, and would certainly be a most desirable substitute for the stock of threadbare and childish elucidations of the local guide".[48] The idea that fictional writing and poetry offered a counterweight to such fantastical stories reflected how the "tasteful" tourist affected disdain at patently absurd local tales, and also established distance from other tourists who presumably hung on his every word. But, over time, a popular "literary" element of the Gap tour became central to mass tourism—and the Gap tour generated its own distinctive form of travel writing, laden with specific conceits, including accounts of the garrulous local guide and his entertaining legends, propounded by authors of humorous periodical "jottings" and longer printed travelogues, in which Kate Kearney, dubbed by the poet John Clare "The Irishmans [*sic*] Queen", featured prominently.[49]

While apparently it could boast no literary genius to compare with Shakespeare or Scott, Killarney had Kate Kearney, and she became closely associated with the Gap of Dunloe, even if Owenson did not identify the pass as her home in the popular parlour song. The early inspiration for Owenson's song is evident in her *Twelve Hibernian Melodies*, a collection of works purportedly drawn from the "Ancient Irish Bards" which was published in the first years of the nineteenth century.[50] It included a song, "Oh tell me sweet Kate, or Cathleen O'Tyrell", which reads very much like a precursor to the popular nineteenth-century song:

> Oh tell me sweet KATE by what magical art,
> you seduc'd every thought ev'ry wish of my Soul;
> oh! tell me my credulous fond doating heart,
> by thy wiles and thy charms, from my bosom was stole.
> Oh whence dangerous girl was thy sorcery tell
> by which you awaken'd loves tear and loves sigh,
> in thy voice in thy song lurks the dangerous spell
> in the blush of thy cheek or the beam of thine eye.[51]

Drawing on similar language, and the same figure of Kate as a bewitching seductress, Owenson's popular song placed Killarney squarely on the literary touring map. A wood-cut image accompanying a subsequent publication of the song featured a buxom, "doe-eyed" creature with basket in hand: it was to become a template for many subsequent visual representations of Kate Kearney.[52] But local lore placed her specifically in the Gap— and it became the stage for tourist performances centred on her hospitality over many generations.

Kate was not a unique literary-cum-tourist figure; many similar characters had arisen from the waters of the United Kingdom's lakes. In the pantheon of tourist "lake ladies", amongst whom Kearney surely deserves a place for her associations with the Killarney Lakes, particularly instructive British comparisons may be drawn in this era with the Lake District's Mary Robinson, the "Maid", or "Beauty", of Buttermere.[53] First popularised by Joseph Budworth as a dark-haired "Lavinia", her plight as the deceived wife of the imposter John Hatfield captured the attention, and inspired the pens, of William Wordsworth, Samuel Taylor Coleridge, and Thomas De Quincey.[54] Robinson's parents' inn, where Budworth had first encountered her as a young girl, became a site of tourist pilgrimage in the Lake District, well before Hatfield's fraudulent marriage to her. Thereafter her fame grew. Like Kate Kearney, Robinson's physical attributes attracted a range of appraisals, and like Kearney, the tourist's narrative of an encounter with her was inextricably bound up with the rural landscape that she inhabited. But unlike her, the "Beauty of Buttermere" was a living figure at the height of her fame, whereas Kearney was an accretion of legend, song, image, and lore whose lineage was diffuse and whose real-life inspiration, if there was one, was shrouded by the mists of time. And in contrast with Loch Katrine, where no excursionist expected to encounter any figure from Scott's poem, the Gap of Dunloe served as a backdrop against which tourists met Kate, the incarnate "Lady of the Killarney Lakes", at many points on their journey. Indeed, meeting her supposed "granddaughter" became a central conceit of doing the Gap, even if many tourists bemoaned her insidious presence, and lambasted her deception.[55] In some narratives, Kate Kearney was also conflated with another iconic literary and theatrical figure associated with the district, "The Lily of Killarney", heroine of Sir Julius Benedict's opera, which premiered in 1862 and was based on Dion Boucicault's melodrama *The Colleen Bawn* (which was, in turn, an adaptation of Gerald Griffin's 1829 novel *The Collegians*). Although the story of the Colleen Bawn was loosely based on the documented murder of 15-year-old Ellen Hanley in 1819, by John Scanlan, a man with whom she had eloped, and Scanlan's servant, which had occurred around Cos. Limerick and Clare, Griffin based his narrative on the tragic death of "Eily O'Connor" in the Killarney district. This restaging of the tale was part of a wider reworking of the story in the interest of the dramatic narrative, which now located the events in a romantic landscape near the ruins of Aghadoe and with a distant view of the Lower Lake.[56]

Over time, the Colleen Bawn became firmly associated with the area and, much like Kate Kearney, with whom she was frequently conflated or confused, the Colleen Bawn's story was worked and reworked and adapted for stage and screen, through the course of the nineteenth and early-twentieth centuries. Images and written accounts of Kate Kearney and the Colleen Bawn merged in many accounts of the Killlarney tour to produce a hybridised narrative, and a touring district sometimes promoted as the "[c]ountry of Kate Kearney and the Colleen Bawn".[57] The Gap itself was, for instance, identified by the New York-state-born Sarah Jane Clarke Lippincott, under the pseudonym "Grace Greenwood", as the site of "Eily Connor's [sic] honeymoon and tragic taking off".[58] A writer in the *Irish Tourist* declared that Kearney's Cottage was "as celebrated as the lakes themselves", while also remarking on the nearby "cottage" of the Colleen Bawn, "dear to every reader of Gerald Griffin's pathetic story".[59] In testament to the influence of tourist literature in "mapping" the Gap as the stage for an encounter with Kearney, and also to the conflation of these literary icons of Killarney, one railway guide-book placed the original Colleen Bawn's Cottage in Killarney, mistakenly credited Kate Kearney's fame to Thomas Moore, and explicitly asserted that "the memories of beautiful Kate Kearney mingle with those of the comely Colleen Bawn" in the district.[60] The narrative of Kate's life was spun into a romantic, if occasionally confused, narrative of unrequited love and profound grief as local lore developed around her, and she established a beach-head at a site near the Gap of Dunloe over which her "granddaughter" symbolically extended authority as a custodian of the pass.

"THE QUEEN OF GRIEF": PRODUCING KATE KEARNEY(S)

If parlour songs and the London stage contributed to elaborating the story of Kate Kearney, implanting her within popular culture and mapping the Gap of Dunloe as a literary landscape, local guides embellished her life-story before sceptical, but entertained, tourists. In the chapters that follow, we shall see how guides were important agents in the articulation of "place", but they themselves were celebrated in, and in part produced by, literary narratives. As one 1859 guide-book declared: "Those who visit Killarney go to stay at least two days; and their best 'guide,' when a survey instead of a glimpse is contemplated, is, not a book, but one of the men who hire themselves for the day to describe the beautiful neighbourhood."[61] Illustrating the extent to which the human guides were accredited by writers, the guide-book declared that "[t]hese constitute a numerous class, some clever, ready, and intelligent, and some possessed of qualities which, through the books of literary tourists, have rendered themselves famous."[62] As interest grew, the guides were keen to share their repartee and knowledge of the Gap's celebrated lore. The story of Kate Kearney distinguished the Gap of Dunloe from Glen Coe in Scotland (with which it was sometimes compared); violent events that were deeply etched in the national consciousness made the Scottish pass a more overtly politically contested site.[63]

Whether framed by pleasure-seeking or social investigative motivations, the very acts of travel and of travel writing to Ireland, to Co. Kerry, and to Killarney, were also political: writers selected scenes and composed narratives, using specific genres, with particular ends in mind, sometimes as overtly polemical attacks on the system of land proprietorship or on the character of the peasantry, while others enjoined tourists to follow in the authors' footsteps in acts of recreation. Lyricists, poets, and prose writers penned works that portrayed the Gap as a place of grandeur and romance in narratives in which Kate's tragic life touched on key contemporary themes— emigration, rural depopulation, and the collapse of cultural realms of the peasantry—in an elegy to an Ireland of legend and lore. The expanding generic field of post-Famine guide-books and travelogues referenced this lore, just as another key tourist site in Ireland, the Giant's Causeway in Co. Antrim, was firmly embedded within popular imagination as a place of heroic legend, and of common Hiberno-Scottish cultural origins.[64] "Viator", writing in the *Irish Tourist* on some memorable jaunting-car rides, noted the similarities in the landscape between the Glen of St Columbkille in Co. Donegal, the Gap of Barnsmore [*sic*], the Gap of Dunloe, Keim-an-Eigh in Co. Cork, and the Devil's Bit in Co. Tipperary, noting also the "striking parallelism in superstition between the last named and the yawning fissure through which I was now jolting [Glen of St Columbkille], since on the summit of the overhanging mountain, on one side, there is a lake, at whose bottom is perpetually imprisoned no less a personage than the devil's mother!"[65] "Viator" proceeded to describe how the Devil's mother had been transformed by St Patrick into an "enormous red eel" after she had passed through the Gap, that passage having been effected by the devil's teeth biting through a mountain, which he subsequently deposited at Cashel. Exposing the currency attached to fantastical lore in the presentation of the Gap as a repository for a cultural world that was both primitive and captivating, the *Illustrated Handbook to Cork, the Lakes of Killarney and the South of Ireland* noted: "The local histories in connexion with this wild pass are fraught with romantic interest, and the historians are, of course, proportionately enthusiastic and rapturous."[66] One legend surrounding its creation held that Finn-ma-Coul had created the pass through the mountains with a strike of his sword.[67]

The Gap of Dunloe was far from the banks of Killarney, yet it became the undisputed popular haunt of Kate's many pretenders. Legend obliged by placing her there, too—and it circulated through the pages of newspapers and fire-side periodicals. Take a piece on Kate Kearney that appeared early in the nineteenth century in the pages of the *Morning Chronicle* in 1812. The author noted that while Lady Morgan had written of Kate's fatal beauty, she had elided "the strong features which marked the mind and misfortunes of this female, whose heart, though one in which all the tender susceptibilities were mature even to luxuriance, was too much oppressed by feelings of another kind, to cherish those of love".[68] The subsequent story, the author contended, relied only on oral authority, and "has a great deal of the fabulous in it, which can be accounted for by the romantic spirit of the people of Ireland, and the ignorance of that part of them who lived in the interior of the country, upwards of two centuries ago".[69] It centred on Kate and her widower father, with whom she lived on the Lake of Killarney. There, she indulged in singing and fishing. One day, when her father had not returned from fishing, 15-year-old Kate set off on a skiff, and to her horror, found his empty boat. After a frantic and unsuccessful search, she fell into an inconsolable state, and for a long time thereafter refused all food, earning her the moniker "The Queen of Grief" from locals. Under the care of an elderly woman, Kate's "affliction was by time mellowed into a kind of constitutional melancholy".[70] As for the figure in Owenson's song, "[t]here is no proof," the author related, "or even report, that she was at that time distinguished for a levity which has been attributed to her by the present panegyrist of her beauty, who has also ascribed cruelty and inconstancy to her."[71] Three years passed, and Kearney sought the advice of a visiting woman who was reported by some to be a witch, as the loving daughter had always believed her father had been carried away by supernatural means. She was told that her father was still alive, trapped in the clutches of the divinity of the Lake, "the hoary Killarn". Kate could see him if she visited the bottom of the Lake. She resolved to do so. Emerging from its depths, she announced that she had indeed seen him, and was returning there. With that she plunged back into the water and was never seen nor heard from again. This fantastical genealogy lent an air of other-worldliness and romance to Kate's Gap home, affirming the observations of a visitor from the British and Irish Baptist Home Mission in 1872, who wrote of Kate Kearney as a "weird, half real, half mythical character" who was the chief figure in legends of Killarney: "If such a person ever lived, it is certain that she never dies."[72]

The romantic image of Kate produced by lore was malleable and evolved within the changing framework of commercial tourism. Indeed the very persona of Kate changed markedly and became entrenched within a narrative of the carnivalesque—an index of the shifting master-narrative of Killarney travel from one centred on a Romantic landscape to one focussed on the comical figures who peopled it. By 1903, the Kate Kearney of legend was less a mournful siren than a rambunctious, loquacious figure who more than faintly resembled the local woman who now claimed her famous mantle at Kate Kearney's Cottage. In that year, the *Kerry Sentinel* published a piece entitled "Recollections of Killarney. The Two Hurlers", which began by describing a "heather-thatched cot" that stood "many years" ago in the Serpent's Lake in the Gap of Dunloe, where the tourist "could sit at ease far away from the busy throng of towns and cities, breathe the exhilarating air, and imbibe his draught of mountain dew for which the 'Gap' is celebrated".[73] The "good hostess" at this abode was Kate Kearney, "who was possessed of a larger fund of legend and anecdote than even the loquacious 'Gap guides,' the famous Stephen Spillane himself not excepted". In this cottage the widow Kate lived with her "brawny son Mick". The newspaper recounted how, after a hurling match played with his cousin Jack Dowd against "the stalwart men of Templenoe", whom the two cousins defeated, Jack resolved to return home to Cromaglen by way of the Tomie Hill, rather than the Gap, as was his wont. The two set off together, and as darkness fell across the enchanting scenery from the top of the Hill, they caught site of a "snow-white steed bearing a rider", whom they took to be the legendary The O'Donoghue. Pursuing this apparition, they happened upon lake-dwelling men dressed in tights for a hurling match and were enlisted by The O'Donoghue to aid him in this sport, against the rivals in a fiercely contested match, for which he provided them with magic slippers to prevent them sinking into the waters. When at last Mick and his cousin awoke, there was no sight of these legendary figures; the account ended with the following wry comment: "Philosophic thinkers may say our two hurlers had been dreaming, through the effects of the bottle, but Mick and Jack would stoutly combat such wild metaphysics, contending, not without much argument, the impossibility of both dreaming the same thing."[74]

When themes of loneliness and immiseration, rather than tones of sly humour, featured prominently in texts, they buttressed the master-narrative of wistful romance in which Kate figured as a protagonist in a tragedy of exile. While not identifying Kate Kearney specifically in his song "The Gap of Dunloe", the lyricist Clifton Bingham depicted it as a place of enchantment, where a lonely, barefooted woman "watches the black valley daily alone" in the hopes that her love "far o'er the waters" will "come back one day to the Gap of Dunloe".[75] As Leith Davis has noted, such nostalgic, elegiac tones characterised many songs in the nineteenth century; Irish-American song sheets also tended, through visual iconography, to associate Ireland with the feminine: the popularity of female images, including Kate Kearney, on these sheets, attests to this association, which was often framed by the "departure" of the emigrant male from feminine Ireland, to seek what Davis describes as "a more mature masculine and progressive state of modernity".[76] In the poetic vein, the celebrated English poet John Clare penned a poem entitled "Pretty Kate Kearney", which elaborated the story of this beguiling figure, making her emblematic of a feminine nation:

> Kate Kearney is bonny the queen o' ould Erin
> The gem o' the emerald Island so green
> By the lake o Killarney the morn sun appearing
> Is nothing more bright than the bonny young queen
>> She blooms like the morning
>> The mountains adorning
> Sweet Kittys [*sic*] the gem o the mountain so green
> Oh Kitty's as fair as the rose wet wi e'ening
> And sweet as the apple just pulled from the tree
> While her beautiful head on her white hand is leaning
> She's just the choice Angel to bother poor me
>> Her eyes diamond lustres
>> Her dark curls in clusters
> Went nigh to the death and the finish o' me.
> I sat down and sigh'd by the lake o Killarney
> When bonny Kate pass'd wi such life in her face
> She turn'd round and laugh'd and called it a blarney
> That a man should be sitting alane in that place
>> Sae I ventured to meet her
>> In love words to greet her
> And sweet were the smiles that she left in my face
> I went on beside her the pretty Kate Kearney
> And call'd her my hinney my darlint & dear
> She says my young man are you bent on a journey
> I muttered excuses and look'd rather queer
>> And she went on smiling
>> And look'd so beguiling
> I spake bold and won her when no one was near[77]

In addition to renderings of the Killarney beauty, seductress, and mountain queen, narratives embellished the narrative of Kate's life and her romantic exploits. In *The Zenana and Other Poems*, the poet Letitia Elizabeth Landon, whose young death by suicide at the age of 36 capped a life marked by prolific writing and controversy,[78] wrote of a forlorn woman (perhaps in her image?), and included at the end of her short poem a note: "The romantic story of Kate Kearney, 'who dwelt by the shore of Killarney,' is too well known to need repetition. She is said to have cherished a visionary passion for O'Donoghue, an enchanted chieftain who haunts those beautiful lakes, and to have died the victim 'of folly, of love, and of madness.'"[79] Similar renderings of Kate Kearney appeared in the play entitled *Thierna-na-Oge*, peopled by fairies, which told the story of a man, Dan O'Reilly, and his unrequited love for Kate, who was being pursued by another suitor, Lord Glencar, in the guise of a peasant. Acting on the advice of O'Donoghue, O'Reilly pressed his claims on Kate, but then found himself in conflict with Glencar, and, giving up hope, left gold coins for her and Glencar to enjoy together. Kate, fleeing the peasant now revealed as Glencar ("a sort of Irish Don Giovanni"), jumped from a rock into the depths of the Lake, but through the offices of O'Donoghue, she was eventually reunited with Dan O'Reilly.[80] These tales were disseminated through opera, song, anecdotes, and legends recounted to tourists by Killarney's guides, who were notorious for engaging in elaboration and exaggeration. Whether they constituted a kind of "fakelore" designed to supply the tourism sector with a ready-made romantic heroine enveloped in legend is difficult to assess, given that so much that was written about her was attributed vaguely to oral tradition, and also given that the distinction between "fakelore" and "folklore" is far from clear-cut.[81] Still, tourists eagerly, if sceptically, consumed the lore as a requisite part of an entertaining tour of Killarney.

Romantic features of the Gap were also expounded in narratives of depopulation and poverty that assumed particular salience in the mid-1840s, when the Famine accelerated interest in documenting Kerry's experience of privation, and the pastiche world of Kate Kearney attracted less attention. Here, too, generic conventions shaped the narrative of place, the proportional focus on ludic elements of travel, and the relative focus on Killarney and outlying districts. Travelling west of Killarney in 1845, *The Times*'s self-described "Commissioner", Thomas Campbell Foster, commented on districts seldom visited by tourists, where agriculture prevailed and an "infinitely subdivided and pauper tenantry, who (excepting a little butter, which they manufacture to pay their rents) create nothing beyond their consumption".[82] In these mountainous areas, Foster described wretchedly impoverished people, exploited by middlemen and ignored by landlords, without knowledge to effect agricultural improvement and with defects of character—a "natural bent of mind" directed to "cunning" rather than to "ingenuity", along with "want of enterprise",[83] which conspired against their material improvement. In the second-half of the nineteenth century, these farther reaches of the county continued to attract attention as a place of congestion and poverty—where peasants were depicted as victims of impoverishment—in altogether more distressing circumstances than their Killarney compatriots. Decades after Foster's tour, a "Special Commissioner" from the *Journal des Débats* in 1886 also reported on widespread poverty (observing "frightful misery" in one peasant hovel), as well as on the high level of land agitation in Killarney.[84] Indeed, writers—amongst them the labour leader James Connolly—described acute poverty in Co. Kerry in the 1890s,[85] though the tourism industry had long been credited as sparing Killarney in particular from the worst ravages of distress.[86] The tourist's Killarney was decoupled from these narratives of immiseration and insurrection, which foregrounded squalor and instability—and Kate's story, which encoded them in ways that supplied divergent political meanings. To some frustrated commentators, the "land question" was obscured in the tourist landscape of Killarney until the early-twentieth century, as writers constructed it as a place of recreation and light-hearted amusement, leavened with the occasional Romantic allusion, but offered few such references in narratives of a country respiring heavily under the weight of poverty and oppression.

In the wake of the defeat of Gladstone's first Home Rule Bill in 1886, and in a striking example of the tension generated by two master-narratives of travel, an early voice of Protestant Dublin nationalism that was to become in short order a tribune of unionism, the *Irish Times*, castigated a correspondent for the *Daily News* who, travelling through Kerry, had, in the *Irish Times*'s view, "apparently committed the common mistake of his journalistic fellows who come to Ireland upon a 'special mission.' He has derived his views altogether from one side".[87] The correspondent was criticised for exclusively giving expression to tenants' grievances (the injustice of the land system was a frequent subject of polemical travel writing). Instead, the *Irish Times* remarked that he was "much more impressive when he talks about the scenery, which is much more interesting and not so stale a theme". The master-narrative of a scenic district was more palatable to the newspaper's vision of a peaceable kingdom than the "stale" account of an impoverished countryside teeming with aggrieved tenants harbouring potentially sinister intentions. This was a tension apparent in many renderings of Killarney as a site of entertaining native performances, and those that portrayed the wider district and county as regions of deep privation.

Contentious accounts of local poverty were articulated in travel writing by authors who self-consciously positioned themselves as social investigators, rather than pleasure travellers. They were framed by, and entwined with, debates over Ireland's political status as the heady days of the pre-Famine campaign for Repeal gave way to fierce internecine contests over visions of the Union, autonomy, and independence. As these ideological positions found institutional expression in parliamentary and extra-parliamentary forms—the physical-force Irish Republican Brotherhood, Isaac Butt's Home Government Association and Home Rule League, Charles Stuart Parnell's

Irish National League and Irish Parliamentary Party—the Irish tour became a vehicle for the articulation of the "state of Ireland", and prescriptions for its remediation. If some travellers to south-west Ireland found evidence of poverty and the punitive effects of the Coercion Acts in the 1870s and 1880s, recreational travellers presented Killarney as an oasis of tranquillity.

Local immiseration was largely suppressed from recreational narratives of the whimsical realm of Kate's Killarney. Most also elided associations between the district, political violence, and even the moderate nationalist politics associated with the most prominent son of Kerry soil. *Murray's* had, after all, been pilloried for its "big house" narrative after the Free State was formed.[88] Most guide-books mentioned only fleetingly that "The Liberator", Daniel O'Connell, was born at Cahirciveen,[89] and that Derrynane House had strong associations with his family. Scanter mention was made of such episodes as the Fenian uprising of 1867, which saw rebels flee through the Gap of Dunloe, and the murder nearby of the caretaker of the Herbert Estate in 1881,[90] at the height of the agrarian outrages that rocked the district in Parnell's Land War. The "big house" travel narrative also suppressed ongoing struggles over evictions by the Kenmare estate (in particular the deepening estrangement between the fourth earl and his tenantry after his succession to the title in 1871, growing local support for the Land League and Home Rule movements, and the parlous condition of the two dominant local estates, which left both in trusteeship in the last decades of the nineteenth century).[91] Despite the relatively healthy position of the Kenmare estate in the wake of the Famine (an era that washed away many of Ireland's landlords, whose property was to be liquidated through the Encumbered Estates Court), by the 1870s local grievances against the estate crystallised in the humiliating defeat in 1872 of the Liberal earl's favoured successor, a relation, by a Home Ruler in the election for a county MP when the sitting member, Lord Castlerosse, succeeded to the earldom on the death of his father. The other major landholding family, the Liberal Herberts, maintained a lock on the second county seat for most of the nineteenth century. The Plan of Campaign, a co-ordinated assault upon the institutions of "landlordism" that revived the animus and many of the tactics of the Land War of the early 1880s, visited upon Killarney what T.W. Russell, in a letter to *The Times* in 1889, described as "a tempest of crime, demoralization, and violence more terrible than has visited any other part of Ireland"; he enumerated the grim evidence of unrest, including "no fewer than six brutal murders" committed within the Killarney police district between 1885 and 1888.[92] At one point the earl of Kenmare fled his local residence—his agent Samuel M. Hussey having engendered antagonism towards the estate. The estate, suffering the vicissitudes of agrarian crisis, was now burdened with heavy debts that left it after 1882 in the hands of trustees of the leading mortgagee, the Standard Life Insurance Company. As we shall see, Kenmare sought to redeem his status and secure his local stature through conspicuous patronage of the tourism sector —his slide into insolvency making him ever-more reliant upon such tools of "soft diplomacy".

CONCLUSION

The visit of the reigning Queen to Killarney, from Monday 26 to Thursday 29 August 1861, following on a tour taken by the Prince of Wales three years earlier, was a landmark event in Killarney tourism—and reproduced many Romantic-era travel practices. By then, the tourism sector had expanded beyond the aesthetic and commercial parameters of the pre-Famine era, and Kate Kearney had assumed new salience, and form, in the context of an elaborate tourism network. Few travellers claimed to find solace or solitude amidst the mountain fastnesses or picturesque lakes. Only royalty, it seems, ferried from one picturesque station to the next and insulated by a retinue of retainers, could contrive to recapture that world of late-eighteenth and early-nineteenth-century travel, when a modest stream of travellers reached vantages unperturbed and wrote of solitude and savage landscapes. Although—or perhaps because—during her long reign Victoria spent little time in Ireland, preferring her Scottish estate when she ventured to her "Celtic" kingdoms, newspapers of diverse political orientations reported on her progress through Killarney breathlessly.

Through her tour, the Queen's *imprimatur* extended the marks of both fashion and royal favour to Killarney. Neither imprint was as lasting as that left by her son: the route he took from Glengarriff to Killarney was popularised as the "Prince of Wales' Route" (a third future monarch, the Duke of York, late George V, lent his name during an 1897 visit to a similar, but much less successfully marketed, "Duke of York Route" along the Shannon). With the exception of an eponymous pier, Queen Victoria's tour provided great contemporary excitement, but supplied little in the way of an indelible "marker" that, for instance, King George IV's visit to Edinburgh furnished with his colourful and highly influential visit of 1822, under the meticulous choreography of Walter Scott.[93] James H. Murphy has argued that the Queen's 1861 tour, and the preceding visit of the monarch and Prince Albert to the 1853 Dublin exhibition of industry and arts, represented conspicuous endorsements of an effort to incorporate Ireland within a political framework grounded in ideas of progress and scenery. Killarney offered an opportunity to insert the Crown within the country's premier touring ground and win the approval of those nationalists impatient to gain her *imprimatur*. Their O'Connellite inheritance was signalled, if not by the deep personal affection for the Queen which O'Connell often evinced, than by a hope that the monarch's affirmation would prove politically expedient to their project aimed at building a new political framework to accommodate their ambitions for Ireland.[94]

Victoria's visit, during which she was entertained by the leading landed families, the Kenmares and the Herberts, at Kenmare and Muckross House respectively, provided occasion for newspapers ranging from the *Freeman's Journal* to the *Irish Times* to hail the charms of Killarney—alleged to have been long-neglected by recent monarchs. The nationalist *Freeman's*

Journal noted in describing her tour of the Lakes: "For the first time since the sway of native monarchs ceased a Queen glided in peace and confidence along Killarney's Lakes."[95] The occasion was one of great pageantry, as Victoria ceremoniously traced the beaten track, albeit with a large retinue in tow, and with no encounter with claimants to Kate Kearney's mantle. The party included not only leading members of the royal family, including Prince Albert and the Prince of Wales, but a much larger party of courtiers and officials, representatives of the British press, and celebrated local figures associated with the district's tourist sector, whose credentials were burnished as they supplied exotic ornamentation to the scene as the Queen's boat glided along the Lakes. Indeed, on one of Lord Castlerosse's two oak barges Stephen Spillane stood at the helm. The *Freeman's Journal* described him as "the well-known, intelligent, and humorous Chief of Killarney guides"; as the royal party toured by boat, including a circumnavigation of "Sweet Innisfallen", Castlerosse and Spillane provided "a graphic outline of its history, traditions, and principal legends".[96]

The tour also provided occasions to patronise markers of the gentry's local engagement in the tourism sector. So doing, it reproduced a culture of travel that was often described as elusive by travellers to Kate Kearney's raucous realm. The party stayed at the homes of the two largest landlords, and enjoyed a stag hunt. During its tour of the Lakes, the party alighted at Glena Bay. At rustic Glena Cottage (built by Lady Kenmare) the visitors found an illustrious station that afforded a vantage point of the Lower Lake. The cottage, built as a refreshment stop, provided an opportunity for the Queen to behold an Irish building in a putative vernacular. Whereas the royal party had bypassed Kate Kearney's eponymous cottage, Glena Cottage provided a focus point for the *Freeman's Journal* to extol "one of the handsomest structures of the kind ever designed": with "overhanging eaves of tastefully-designed thatch, supported all round on the trunks of arbutus trees", the cottage was surrounded on three sides by "a handsome tesselated pavement" with floral ornamentation, boasting an interior furnished with white chintz with floral pattern, and a large apartment where the royal party enjoyed an extensive "*dejeuner*, served in princely style", whose elements bore no resemblance to the whisky and goat's-milk which featured as the core gustatory element of Gap excursion.[97] While the brief royal visit attracted considerable attention in the London and Irish press—Victoria displacing, however briefly, Kate Kearney as "Queen" of this realm—it signified a mode of travel which persisted only in the long shadow of the carnivalesque, in which heavy doses of irony were dispensed as promiscuously as the flattery of locals and servings of mountain dew.

2   Creating and Contesting Ireland's Tourist Movement

In 1852, in the Famine's wake, the Great Southern and Western Railway and the Chester and Holyhead Railway made plans to lure English visitors to Ireland's shores. The geographic compass of "Killarney Tickets" would be expanded from the previous year to include originating stations throughout Great Britain (rather than only London, Birmingham, and Manchester). The rechristened "Irish Tourist Tickets" would now ferry tourists across the Irish Sea to Dublin and thence to Cork or, alternatively, to Mallow and then the Killarney Lakes. After a tour of the Lakes, carriages would convey them along a route embracing Kenmare, Glengarriff, and Bantry, before they were transported by train to Cork.[1] In describing these arrangements, the *Freeman's Journal* noted that the inn at Glengarriff was undergoing expansion, while Killarney was soon to boast a first-class hostelry under the proprietorship of Mr Roche. The newspaper also noted that prospective tourists enjoyed a range of ticketing options, which allowed them to explore Ireland beyond the well-known scenery of the South and the well-beaten path to Killarney: on presentation of the ticket in the Dublin offices of the Chester and Holyhead Railway, they could obtain tickets for a four-day tour of Co. Wicklow, and reduced return fares to Belfast and Galway. In Wicklow the magistrates had undertaken to suppress "that greatest of all plagues and annoyances to tourists—beggars", and H.A. Herbert had urged similar action upon fellow magistrates in Killarney.[2] The *Freeman's Journal* also highlighted the publication of the *Illustrated Irish Tourist's Hand Book* and proclaimed that with a comparatively low charge for lodging and the benefits of these tickets, English visitors would now discover that they could travel to, and tour, Ireland, for the price of a Lakeland or Highland holiday. Moreover, travellers (comprising, in the main, "mechanics and small tradesmen") had the additional option of joining one of three Cook's "monster" excursions to Dublin and Killarney during the course of the tourist season.

These arrangements signalled significant developments in the scale and organisation of tourism, not only in Killarney, but in Ireland: railways were now offering a range of transport options, some in partnership with other firms. Thomas Cook was establishing a presence in Ireland, and his tours embraced a broader social base and wider geographic compass. Hotels were expanding and improving. The conceit of leaving Killarney for places farther afield (including the West) was becoming a prominent feature in tourist promotion. As for travellers to Ireland's most famous tourist destination, in the face of the eclipse of Romantic travel practices, unbearable congestion, and rampant, vulgar commercialisation, travellers asked: how were they to "do" Killarney? Poles of the Romantic and the carnivalesque supplied duelling narratives of the Killarney tour. Indeed, in the mid-1840s, the *Parliamentary Gazetteer of Ireland* cautioned readers that writers who extolled the scenic glories of Killarney on one hand, and those who described bedlam on the other hand, both conspired against a tasteful traveller's autonomous appreciation of the district:

> [W]e would strongly recommend all persons intending to visit the lakes, to acquaint themselves beforehand, by means of map and description, with the plain, unpoetic, matter-of-fact topography of the Lakes' basin,—to shun or forget the twaddle and rhapsody of the herd of scribbling tourists in their affected depicting of the scenery,—to form a vigorous resolution, of deaf-and-dumb indifference to the marvellous stories of waiters, ostlers, fiddlers, buglemen, boatmen, and guides,—and, on arrival at Killarney, to commence and prosecute the tour of the lakes with the simple appliances of boat, poney [*sic*], and bugle. Whoever goes thus rationally to work will see Killarney as it really exists, and carry away such correct images of it as might be transferred to canvass; but whoever adopts the contrary and too common method, will see the place in a daydream, and obtain nearly as many and bewildering reminiscences of it as if he were to gaze all the while upon a phantasmagoria. The Irish Killarney, the English Derwentwater, and the Scottish Loch Katrine, have all, though in different degrees, suffered gross vulgarization by having been "written into fame;" and the consequence is, that even an educated person of considerable taste, is in some danger, if he be not on his guard, of following the rush and acclamations of the mob, instead of treading the calm path of his own observations and reflection.[3]

Queen Victoria's 1861 tour, with the pageantry of liveried coaches, her retinue of attendants, and a lengthy and luxurious repast at Glena Cottage, reproduced Romantic-era practices—using royal patronage to draw Killarney conspicuously within the orbit of the United Kingdom's other leading holiday-grounds. It evoked opulence and gentility—features which most tourists found elusive as they encountered troupes of beggars and colourful local characters, as well as hordes of excursionists.

"KILLARNEY NO LONGER BOUNDS OR LIMITS THE TOURIST'S OPPORTUNITY": THE EXTENSION OF MODERN IRISH TOURISM

By the 1860s, the Killarney tour was a far more democratic exercise than the Queen's journey might suggest—and it signalled not just Killarney's, but Ireland's, growing prosperity, as well as the widening reach of tourism.

Rising incomes, improved technologies of transport, and extensive local and national commercial development in the sector extended the tourist's reach. It won broad endorsement from all political quarters—from nationalists as a marker of Ireland's status (they exhorted domestic tourists to demonstrate "loyalty" by expending their hard-won pounds on Irish soil), and from unionists who saw tourism as an engine of economic and political integration. With the injection of private capital, the sector became more firmly entrenched in international commercial tourist enterprises which linked it to national and transnational markets by rail and sea, including the Rosslare-to-Fishguard route, a collaboration between the Great Western Railway and Ireland's Great Western and Southern Railway, which opened in 1906. Piers and light railways were added under the aegis of the Congested Districts Board from the last decade of the nineteenth century. The acceleration of tourism was enabled by the development of a rhythm of holiday time, though this was more haphazard than any narrative of the inexorable and democratic rise of the Bank Holiday would suggest. But before this period, the extension of the railway and the elaboration of new tourist routes (such as the "Prince of Wales' Route") contributed to the development of the sector.

As the "Iron Horse's" reach extended, so too did that of the coach (though the condition of many of Ireland's roads continued to draw disparaging comment). The country's tourist network expanded in the post-Famine years, as the sector embraced a broad range of travellers. Coastal resorts such as Blackrock, Co. Dublin and Bray, Co. Wicklow, which were within easy reach of the Dublin day-tripper, became centres of fashion, with an infrastructure that supported popular practices such as bathing, and expansive and comfortable hotel accommodation.[4] Long-standing and newly developed spa towns, many serving regional markets, such as Buncrana and Portsalon in Co. Donegal, Holywood, Newcastle and Bangor in Co. Down, Tramore in Co. Waterford, and Salthill in Co. Galway, as well as such well-known spas as Kilkee and Lisdoonvarna in Co. Clare, and Lucan in Co. Dublin, lured visitors who were drawn by their amenities and by improved transport links and heavy promotion.[5] Indeed, the expansion of the transport network—especially rail and then light rail in the 1890s, and the development of large railway hotels and others organised on the joint-stock principle[6] in main tourist centres (such as the Great Northern Hotel in Bundoran, Co. Donegal, a place also famous for its golf links, and the landmark Royal Marine Hotel in Kingstown, Co. Dublin[7])—meant that the guide-book editor John Cooke could speak with both optimism and authority when he remarked in 1907 that whereas once Killarney, Co. Wicklow, and the coast of Co. Antrim had numbered Ireland's principal tourist destinations, now "many spots rivalling Killarney in one or more special attractions will be found by the tourist who takes trouble to explore off the beaten tracks."[8] That beaten track became all the more alluring, and the practices of independent travel more democratic, with the advent of the bicycle, which carried tourists to new reaches, and liberated them from the strictures of the organised tour and the prescriptions of the rail-lines.[9]

While the network of tourist sites grew, extending into areas once off the beaten track, incorporating a range of sports, and signalling the dynamic expansion of the sector to meet growing domestic and international demand, the Irish West was constructed as a peculiar topos—a place of "unspoilt beauty" and a repository of a culture of political consequence both for those who identified it as a site of cultural purity, and for those who advocated its reform. Achill Island, where Protestant missionary activity was accompanied by extensive commercial tourist activity, was an especially prominent site for such contested projects. Because it furnished the popular imagination with iconic images of the Irish peasantry, Achill was seen as a site where visitors could behold Ireland's "traditional" rural culture. In an account of a "Holiday in the Far West" published in 1894, A.J. Hayes drew comparisons between the peasantries of Achill and Norway; Hayes found parallels between their agrarian livelihoods and their home wool dyeing, spinning, and dress.[10] Many writers portrayed the islanders as custodians of Irish folkways, and integrated them within a picturesque island landscape. Tourists were encouraged to adopt the gaze of prominent painters such as Alexander Williams and Paul Henry, and writers such as J.M. Synge, and emulate their western forays.[11] A tourist feature in the *Irish Independent* in 1912 contended that "[o]ne can explore the wilds and study the people of Connemara and Achill."[12] As they were active participants in regimes of seasonal migration to Scotand, where they were employed in agricultural work, Achill's households were seen as disciplined within British labour systems, enhancing their appeal to many commentators. The 1900 Midland Great Western Railway of Ireland guide-book argued that migratory labour was lucrative to Achill islanders, who are "relatively better off than many of their compatriots in the Wild West".[13] Yet if Achill manifested such salutary signs of improvement, its peasant culture was described as resilient, their habits and their cabins showing "very little change in spite of the introduction of a good many articles of manufacture which a generation or two ago were quite undreamt of".[14] The guide-book also described "queer little public-houses", which, "however aboriginal", nonetheless stocked a vast array of liquors, including Martell and Hennessy, "such as a fully licensed inn in England could not show".[15] These images of Achill's tourist amenities—at once quaint and modern— juxtaposed the exotic and the familiar. They promoted its attractions and comforts to the tourist.

If Achill Island offered commentators a case study in tourist development, so too, in a very different way, did Ireland's north-east, where Killarney tourism's self-appointed guardians cast a nervous eye. That region, site of the only Irish city that could claim to be an industrial urban centre on par with Glasgow and Manchester, supplied a ready tourist market, but also sites such as the Giant's Causeway. A proliferating number of resorts on the Co. Down coast, as well as Portrush, Co. Antrim, and Portstewart,

Co. Londonderry, and, farther west, places in Co. Donegal such as Bundoran, lured the traveller. As tourism grew in scale and complexity, thicker, revised versions of the iconic *Murray's* and other guide-books signalled the extent of hotel renovation and construction. Their pages embraced a much wider range of tourist destinations than the "lions" of Killarney, Co. Wicklow, and the Giant's Causeway. This era also witnessed the growth in numbers of excursionists, drawn from the ranks of artisans, factory workers, and Irish agriculturalists, whose increasing real incomes made recreational activity affordable.

If the social base of tourists broadened, the organisation of travel and sightseeing became more varied, ranging from individual tourism to excursion during which tourists, sometimes strangers to each other, were shepherded in large groups from site to site.[16] Often, a tourist embraced both systems as well as a diverse range of recreational practices, not all of which had firm roots in Killarney. Many popular contemporary modes of tourism in Ireland, for instance, centred on the curative properties of climate or bathing, as well as devotional practices. An 1888 publication on the subject of health-resorts and watering places in Ireland—which were increasingly promoted as alternatives to the congested spas of the continent—asserted that at Killarney "[a] well-appointed hydropathic and winter-resort . . . could not fail to command a substantial amount of patronage during the summer and autumn months."[17] It was a signal of the importance attached to climate, and the quality of waters, with their allegedly therapeutic effects (including well-known mineral waters at places such as Lucan, Co. Dublin); D. Edgar Flinn, in publicising them, hoped he might draw not only visitors to Ireland shores, but also induce more home tourism.[18]

What this appraisal of amenities also reveals is the extent to which Killarney was no longer Ireland's unquestioned tourist destination. The compass of Irish tourism expanded, and the Irish tourist "product" became a source of increasingly sophisticated commercial development and differentiation. Now Killarney competed not only with sites of international celebrity such as the Giant's Causeway, but also with attractions in neighbouring areas of Cos. Kerry and Cork for the tourist pound. In the 1890s this included districts of Co. Kerry, including Waterville and Valentia; the *Kerry Sentinel* proclaimed that railway extensions through the country in the late 1890s helped to "bring the wildest parts of Kerry within easy reach of London".[19] The railway network in south-west Ireland had expanded to an extent that, as the *Irish Times* declared, "Killarney no longer bounds or limits the tourist's opportunity." [20] Moreover, Killarney's unenviable reputation as the "El Dorado" of beggary, with Kate Kearney's "granddaughter" as its doyenne, served as a foil for districts in which the tourist might avoid vexatious beggary. In "Unexplored Kerry", for instance, a travel writer argued that the tourist could apprehend the exotic Irish peasant in his natural state—which the writer implicitly contrasted with the fakery of Killarney:

Certainly one marks in the dark Spanish faces of the men about Car-
hirciveen, or in the blue eyes that are commoner father east at Kenmare, little evidence of deep discontent. One might think better of the
people if they cleaned their hovels, and partitioned off half their living
space for the exclusive occupation of their live-stock, just as one would
respect them more did they not address every decently dressed person as "your anner." But he who would measure the adaptation of the
Kerry crofter to his environment must not let the dirt get in his eyes.
Look in at the door of a thatched cottage. The pig may obstruct your
entrance, and perhaps you would hardly care to brush past the rate-
payer and set even the most gingerly foot on the earthen floor. But it is
a clean-faced man that comes out to bid "your anner" good-day, or a
neatly, nay gaily clad, if barefoot "colleen," and granny, who sits in the
ingle-nook, must be at least eighty. Centenarians are as thick in these
parts as the fairy tales of a Killarney guide.[21]

The contrivances of the Killarney tour, its exorbitant costs, and the large,
boisterous crowds of both locals and travellers served as a foil for this taste
of "authentic" Ireland. In response, Killarney's tourist association intensified its promotional activities, opened offices in London and Manchester,
and erected fingerposts giving directions and distances. This taxing ros-
ter of activities resulted in two straight years of deficits, and participation in the body, initially enthusiastically embraced by the local estates
and local businesses as an agent of improvement, dwindled. Eventually, it
became defunct, although it would be revived again in the first decade of
the twentieth century, in part to counteract vigorous promotional efforts
in the North.

Within the context of this expanding network of tourist destinations in
Ireland, Killarney's quixotic *niche* was to be found in its especially dynamic—many would say irksome—informal economy, centred not on resorts,
bathing sites, or ruins, as much on human encounters. A broad range of
services supplying tourists and grounded within more formal aspects of
commerce also grew. Fleets of jaunting-cars were engaged by hotels as well
as Thomas Cook and Son to ferry their customers to the Gap. While Susan
Barton and John Walton have lately dethroned Thomas Cook from the
pantheon of tourism pioneers (where a lamentably uncritical historiography had until recently placed him),[22] his firm nonetheless had a strong presence in Killarney dating to the years immediately following the Famine.
Indeed, an 1852 report in the *Freeman's Journal* reported on the company's
plans for three "'monster'" excursions from the whole of the midland districts of England to Dublin and to Killarney.[23] Each of these excursions was
expected to bring 500 people to Killarney, and signalled commercial inno-
vation in the sector, including joint initiatives by British and Irish railway
companies to develop touring tickets—an enterprise that was accompanied
by the publication of the *Illustrated Irish Tourist's Hand Book*.[24] In 1872

the firm flexed its muscle during a heated dispute with the Great Southern and Western Railway regarding charges and the class of carriages used to convey passengers from England and America—by abandoning ambitious plans for excursions.[25] Thomas Cook and Son did not enjoy the firm grip over the trade to which they aspired, however, since the firm vied with religious, working-men's, employers', and antiquarian societies, and other groups in organising excursions. It faced direct commercial competitors such as Henry Gaze's firm, and also local agents and local providers of services who offered car-rides, pony-treks, and guides to tourists on an *ad hoc* basis. Still, Cook's maintained an office in Killarney throughout the last years of the nineteenth century, having established it in 1893 under the superintendence of J.E. Bethrey.[26] In 1900 its tour of the Gap of Dunloe, followed by a boat tour of the Lakes, was so popular that a correspondent to the *Killarney Echo* contended that the posting contractor for Thomas Cook and Son was required to keep 90 to 100 horses on the road every day to service all of the company's popular tours.[27] Of course none of this would have been possible without the rapid increase in real incomes that, notwithstanding periods of significant agricultural and industrial depression, saw Ireland emerge in the second-half of the nineteenth century as a more prosperous place—at least for those who remained there. But émigrés did their part for the sector, too. The sentimental lure of the homeland as a holiday destination was heightened by marketing campaigns aimed explicitly at them. In the years before the Great War, for instance, the *Irish Tourist* even mooted schemes to attract Irish-Americans through a "Home-Coming Movement" centred on towns and villages from which emigrants left. It might entice them to stay longer than the usual rapid-fire journey "through Dublin, and a glance at Killarney and Cork".[28] The turn of the twentieth century also witnessed concerted—and contested—efforts to lure tourists from Britain.

A leitmotif of late-Victorian tourist development was guarded optimism for the sector's prospects, though not all observers believed that tourism would cure Ireland's ills. Some commentators asserted that tourism could erode the essential qualities of Irish culture. In fact, in expressing anxiety centred on tourism during the purported "Celtic Twilight", many commentators heaped scorn on mass tourism, while other leading nationalists embraced it as a means of economic modernisation. Both groups found its apotheosis, for good or ill, at Killarney.

"WHEN THE PURSE IS HEAVY AND THE HEART LIGHT": TOURISM AND PATRIOTISM IN THE POST-FAMINE ERA

As Killarney became more accessible to ever-larger crowds, it engendered narratives of the polluting ravages of the cockney tourist—a representative type produced in discourses of taste and leisure as a figure who sought familiarity and diversions, rather than the more exacting rewards of travel. The rhetorical cockney tourist accepted as authentic the patent contrivances of the tourism sector, and consumed its products as an unironic distillation of the "real" Ireland, conveniently packaged to meet his limited capacities, timeframe, and means. For some who eschewed the "mere movement" associated with cockney travel and instead projected the persona of the cultured traveller who either professed disdain for, or knowing consumption of, a cultural product, an Irish tour constituted a performance of charity towards the benighted partner in the United Kingdom, which was wrapped in the language of (albeit patronising-sounding) patriotism. Amidst the fluid ideological positions of nationalism and unionism (and the imperial incentive which could variously anchor strains of both), "patriotism" could serve as a rallying cry for Irish men and women, as well as Britons, to come to "know" Ireland in a demotic epistemological exercise that was dramatically different from the surveys of the early-nineteenth century, but which nonetheless encoded similar imperatives. *The Times*, for instance, encouraged readers to divert their holiday planning from popular places such as the Spanish Peninsula and turn instead to Ireland, where a tour would "combine a duty and a charity with a pleasure".[29] "Why should not our poor Irish fellow-subjects benefit by the careless expenditure which takes place when the purse is heavy and the heart light?" it asked, even if the innkeeper and the mendicant might be the first immediate beneficiaries: "We refuse, however, to argue such a question upon strictly economic principles. Ireland just now wants a moral fillip. A little stir and bustle would do the country good, and set heads-a-planning and hands-a-working, that but for such an impulse might have remained idle and unemployed." Citing two frequent comparators that buttressed the writer's authority as someone who was widely travelled,[30] the piece noted: "See what tourism does for Switzerland—remember what it did for the Scotch Highlands after the publication of the *Lady of the Lake*, and still more when the Scotch novels appeared." A "Home Tour" embracing Ireland naturalised the Union, and would reap dividends for the tourist, too—offering an opportunity to appraise the country and reassess the stereotypes that surrounded it, even if the philanthropic tourist exercise involved an immersion in the commodified world of Kate's Killarney.

The immediate post-Famine era led writers of myriad political persuasions to assess the potential for "improvement" with enthusiasm, assimilating tourism within broader narratives of development, interweaving a recreational master-narrative with assertions that travel might achieve some loftier end. To some, tourism served the salutary purpose of knitting the isles more closely together, promoting Ireland's social union, and political integration within the Union. The noted Scottish agriculturalist James Caird's observations on the potential for wider improvement in parts of the West of Ireland helped to make him famous in Ireland (he would later become a prominent parliamentarian and receive a knighthood in a distinguished career).[31] But they earned him the wrath of the *Freeman's Journal*, which objected to his laudatory comments on some Irish landlords. Yet even that moderate nationalist organ endorsed Caird's view that the Herbert Estate in Killarney had done much to improve agriculture without evictions, while Caird hoped that with the coming of the railway, access to the scenic district would no doubt be enhanced.[32] In a similar vein, an article in the *Daily News* trumpeted the emigration of the "Celt" from Ireland and the arrival of the "Saxon" there. The concomitant growth of the railways heralded a new era: "An enterprise and an energy are arising in Ireland, such as have not been witnessed since the fabulous years of her history."[33] Glenn Hooper's claim that social and economic commentaries on the Famine years articulated a new master-narrative of the country's potential is borne out by many enthusiastic endorsements of tourism as an engine of prosperity and renewal. The recreational "Saxon" could also effect such salutary changes, even if his tour took the fleeting form of a summer holiday, and was centred in a place such as Killarney, where naked fakery reigned as supremely as the Gap's "Queen Kate".

But if Ireland was to attract tourists for such purposes, its infrastructure required improvement. National and district tourist associations and actors such as Thomas Cook and Son championed development to service the demands of mass tourism. Others saw it as a decidedly derivative benefit to more substantial investments in Ireland's commercial, agricultural, and industrial sectors. In advocating such a pragmatic approach to tourism, couched in far more prosaic language than F.W. Crossley and *The Times*'s framing of tourism as a patriotic duty, nationalist organs such as the *Freeman's Journal* and the *Kerry Sentinel* embraced it as an engine of rural economic prosperity. Local development bodies in places such as Killarney also subscribed to many of the prosaic, if not the political, precepts of "tourist development" which gave life to the island-wide Irish Tourist Association (ITA), founded in the middle of the 1890s as part of a series of "practical" measures championed by leading figures such as the Lord Lieutenant.[34] The ITA promoted initiatives from hotel improvement to game and piscatorial management to levying local fees to promote watering-place and resort development. The syndicate with which it was closely associated, Irish Tourist Development, Ltd., as well as the national association of hotel proprietors and restaurateurs, were active in enacting programmes of infrastructural development and place-promotion which aimed to enhance Ireland's reputation as a tourist destination, especially in the British market. In so doing, these groups propounded discourses that emphasised the broader social and political advantages of tourism to both Ireland and the United Kingdom. Indeed, Crossley and several others believed that a shared infrastructure was foundational to communication across the Irish Sea, and ultimately to the potential resolution of the "Irish Question" (in the 1890s this took the form of resurrecting the lobby for a quixotic and long-mooted proposal for a rail tunnel under the North Channel linking Scotland and

Ireland[35]). It was not coincidental that the tourist-development movement assumed firm institutional form in the mid-1890s, after the defeat of the second Liberal Home Rule bill and the return of the Tory Lord Salisbury to power. What is more striking is that it did not become a vehicle for any one ideology and continued to draw, as it had in the 1860s and 1870s, on an eclectic group of patrons who found little convergence of views in other domains. Indeed, the concept of "tourist development" was remarkably flexible, as nationalists and unionists alike incorporated it within shared and competing discourses of patriotism and improvement. Here again tourism was an index of other political-cultural concerns and developments, not least the albeit fragile all-party consensus that emerged in the 1890s over the Recess Committee and the Congested Districts Board, and the capacity for political opponents to coalesce in support of measures that extracted money from the Treasury.

For many advocates of Irish tourism, especially those who perceived its instrumentality in strengthening union, Scotland set a worthy example of modernisation. The Highlands were the focus of their praise. They extolled the Scottish district as an inhospitable landscape improved by the tourist and sportingman's purse, where Britishness seemed to flourish amongst Otherness and where recreational tours bore none of the heavy imprint of colonialism. A superior infrastructure enhanced Scotland's reputation as a place of cleanliness and comfort, and explained how Scotland had gained advantages over Ireland as a holiday-ground. Its literature drew tourists. So did its reputation for efficiency. Surveying Scotland, the *Kerry Sentinel* declared in 1899 that "[a] saint never sat down by a holy well in the western highlands, but there is a canal boat running to the place and historical accounts are put into your hand for sixpence, and relics and the like sold for anything you offer. Every bend of the road is made to pay in the bonnie land of the Oaten Cake."[36] By contrast, the writer noted, Ireland offered shoddy and often impractical transport services. A "Yankee" landing at Queenstown and travelling across Ireland by water and land to visit Killarney and other popular districts would be compelled "to treat with about twenty different companies and agencies, and tips and inquiries, missing luggage and importuning porters and baggage-bearers". "In Scotland", in contrast, "a clear itinerary is handed to you, you get a dozen tickets, and off you go."[37] Yet Scots, turning their eyes westward in the same era, also lamented that they had no comparable national tourism movement to the one that received such conspicuous patronage in Ireland.

The Irish movement seemed to achieve a meeting of minds across a broad political spectrum, including energetic proponents of Home Rule—the viceroy Lord Houghton—and also strong opponents, including Houghton's immediate successor, Lord Cadogan. Indeed, the movement did not reproduce cleavages from the Home Rule debates, though it tended also to obscure differences on the meaning of tourism to Irish national identity. In 1885, for instance, the *Freeman's Journal* expressed support for the patronage of the "English health-seeker".[38] At the same time, it cautioned against the misapprehension, especially propagated by the English press, that "the Irishman's nationality can be bought off by a little tourist patronage in the autumn"—a proposition that, it declared, "is about as profound and as wise as any other theory put forward by them for curing the ever lasting Irish problem, and English visitors, it may be taken for granted, have not crossed the Irish Channel with any such idea". Others, drawing, and indeed elaborating on, a discourse that had deep roots in the pre-Union curiosity in exploring Britain's sister kingdom and in the post-Famine enthusiasm for patriotic-tourism, endorsed sentiments expressed in the *Pall Mall Gazette* in 1896. It argued that enhanced interaction between the English and Irish "races" could effect a closer political affinity, too,[39] even if some nationalists believed this reconciliation to be the precursor to Home Rule. Noting that the ITA comprised "all sections of Irish opinion", including the arch-Tory Lord Londonderry and the nationalist Irish Parliamentary Party parliamentarian John Redmond, the *Daily Telegraph* opined that "the sagacious promoters of this association have seen 'with half an eye' that what England and Ireland need is chiefly to know each other better", and that this could be achieved through increased tourist flows, which would allow English tourists to "become more acquainted with the generous, bright, witty, and oft times delightfully unreasonable Irish people".[40]

Travel, thus cast, was an act of patriotism. Indeed, the patriotic impulse served as a counterweight to Home Rule—the fault-line for unionist-nationalist divisions, and offered a malleable rhetoric into which travel and economic development were folded. F.W. Crossley and the *Irish Tourist* expressed this view in 1909, in a leader entitled "An Irish Welcome. The National Aspect of the Tourist Movement". It argued that while the commercial and financial aspects of the tourist movement had received much attention, ineffable and incalculable advantages of a strengthened union would be its greatest legacy. Travel to Ireland by Britons enhanced bonds with Britain. It redressed a mutual misunderstanding which nourished views of Ireland as a "hot bed of sedition and disturbance"; tourism thus effected a "wonderful change".[41] Over 15 years, means of communication had improved, and travel across the channel had developed. Now the British tourist could appreciate, as John Redmond had declared, just how "fine a country Ireland was, and how kind a people were the Irish", enabling greater co-operation in the bid to check emigration and improve the material conditions of the peasantry.[42] Crossley's rallying cry to British tourists to enact a pilgrimage to the sister isle echoed calls by the staunchly unionist organ *The Times* in the post-Famine years for Britons to make such tours. In both cases, travel became an act of patriotism with incalculable social, economic, and political benefits. But such constructions of patriotic-tourism were not monopolised by the British press. The *Freeman's Journal* enjoined Irish people, "who in the matter of holiday excursion leave Ireland to everybody but the Irish", to eschew their travels abroad and perform their own patriotic tour of the Irish homeland.[43] "Shall we continue to force the cry of 'Ireland for the English,' about which we hear so much? Heaven knows they and all the world are heartily welcome to our shores, and the more the merrier." But, the newspaper intoned, could Irishmen not follow their example, and enact a "Home Tour" as a form of Irish patriotism?

F.W. Crossley's formulation of the patriotic-tourist creed was in a narrower vein, lacquered with the platitudes that attended officialdom's pronouncements on tourism's benefits, but endorsing specific schemes in which the ITA's allied development body had a pecuniary interest: amongst its prominent failures was the Shannon tourist steamer (though notable achievements included Crossley's effective advocacy for special taxation powers to promote resorts).[44] Certainly, from Gerald Balfour to the earl of Dunraven, the tourist-development movement attracted the support of key figures who were engaged in wider efforts at reconciliation and pacification during an era of Conservative ministries (the dominant political force between 1886 and 1905, with the Liberals under Gladstone and then Rosebery forming the government between 1892 and 1895), which some historians have characterised as a period of "constructive unionism". They had antecedents that crossed party-political lines, as well as wider ideological divisions over the political status of Ireland. Where might tourist development, its discourses and infrastructural enterprises, figure into this wider political landscape, and how was it nourished by the epistemological project of "knowing" Ireland through tourism? At first glance, it is easy to see how they may be placed alongside initiatives which are often seen as a coherent, programmatic effort at social and economic reconstruction.[45] They included the Congested Districts Board (1891);[46] the light-railway schemes; Labourers' Acts; the expansive transformation of local government (1898); the establishment of the Recess Committee under Horace Plunkett (erstwhile unionist MP, pioneer of the co-operative movement, and a leading force behind the establishment of the Department of Agriculture and Technical Instruction, with unionist and Parnellite Nationalist representation);[47] and (acting on its recommendations in a 1896 report), the founding of the Department of Agriculture and Technical Instruction (1899). To this list must be added ill-fated efforts to address issues of fiscal imbalance and wider financial relations in the wake of a Royal Commission (established under the Rosebery government, but which reported in 1896), and a number of land bills, culminating in the famous act of 1903.[48]

Not all historians subscribe to such a neat packaging of constructive unionism; nor should we accept the place of tourism within it as central. In many respects Crossley's quixotic campaign, even when it was supported by leading figures such as Redmond, Lord Houghton, and Lord Mayo, appeared to proceed parallel to, rather than in concert with, the great modernising programmes of the day, and seldom attracted attention beyond the ritual platitudinous endorsements of Dublin Castle. At the political level, Crossley's fervent hope that tourism might stifle the growing chorus for Home Rule signalled his political orientation, and suggests to the modern historian congruence with the precepts of constructive unionism. But Andrew Gailey has asked if constructive unionism was a coherent programme designed to stifle nationalism.[49] Alvin Jackson has shown that cleavages within unionism were amplified by specific policies and notes that the array of interests which constituted political unionism—a fragmented and disparate coalition of Irish unionists, British conservatives, and Liberal unionists—became coherent during moments of perceived crisis. They coalesced mainly in opposition to the first two Home Rule bills. Unionism's proponents included people who harboured expansive ambitions for social reconstruction through state sponsorship, and others who favoured much more modest plans. These divisions were exemplified by the controversy engendered by Lord Dunraven's Irish Reform Association devolution proposals in 1905. Moreover, the wider context of Irish and British politics within which chief secretaries pursued various Irish policies differed markedly. Gailey stresses that the Balfour brothers occupied the office during different periods in the life of both unionism and nationalism.[50]

The tourist-development movement had roots in the 1880s, but appeared to grow in the mid-1890s—when many of these cornerstones of constructive unionism were developed—and it won the conspicuous patronage of both Balfours, as well as a broad section of Irish political opinion. Yet it undoubtedly was no great motivator of broader political consensus. F.W. Crossley's professed motivations of social harmony and political union, expressed in tones of vague sentimentalism, can obscure the fact that his periodical, the *Irish Tourist*, served as a vehicle for promoting projects in which he and Tourist Development (Ireland), Ltd. had a direct pecuniary interest. Indeed, the national movement often has the appearance of being somewhat marginal, dominated by a few eccentric, if enthusiastic, personalities, firmly within Crossley's orbit, with the notional support of the Castle and Dublin elite. Nor indeed was tourist development universally welcomed by locals or prominent Irishmen who assailed the "Saxon's" footprint—or, more specifically, the baleful influence of the cockney excursionist.

"WHAT IS IT TO ME?": NATIONAL DEBATES OVER TOURISM IN LATE-VICTORIAN AND EDWARDIAN IRELAND

Many efforts to improve the tourist infrastructure of the country, from light-railway development to private hotel investment, won praise from leading newspapers and guide-books in the 1890s. In 1910 the *Manchester Guardian* declared that the big hotels in Killarney and Glengarriff compared favourably with any in Europe, and reported that the local tourist development association had turned its attentions to road improvement, especially with the growing interest in motoring holidays.[51] This was part of a wider local effort to respond to new modes of touring and new tastes. Along with Irish expatriates from America, Britons were a desirable tourist market, given the island's proximity and affluence. Yet their preference for the continent over the sister isle frustrated Irish tourist-development advocates. The *Irish Times* praised *The Times* of London for noting the improvements in the sector, and also remarked in 1900 that travellers who usually ventured abroad were now unwilling to "quit the confines of the United Kingdom, fearing that at present they cannot rely upon the customary courtesy of the Continent".[52] "Anti-British" feeling, stoked by the Boer War, was a factor. It combined with a more favourable attitude towards Ireland on the part of people in England, following what the *Irish Times* judged to be a highly successful Royal Tour in Ireland by the Queen in the spring, and also the gallantry of Irish soldiers in the field in South Africa. Better hotels and communications, lower costs, and improved promotion of the island offered further inducements to travel there.

But Irish tourism also engendered anxieties centred on its corrosive cultural impacts. The railways, beneficiaries from the tourist's purse, were sometimes cast as rapacious profiteers. Recently knighted Sir Horace Plunkett (who, by this point, had alienated large sections of both unionist and nationalist opinion) acknowledged several points of contention in a speech at an Ireland Club Dinner in 1904. Amongst them were concerns that railways and hotel proprietors were profiting handsomely from the trade, and an allegation that:

> [A]round those tourist resorts there was a wholesale demoralisation of the peasantry, who were believed during the brief tourist season to gain enough by means not too dignified to enable them to live in idleness during the remainder of the year; and lastly, there was the charge that the tourist traffic had a tendency to Anglicise Ireland, and so to counteract the other things which many earnest and patriotic Irishmen were trying to exercise upon the minds of our unhappy people.[53]

Plunkett saw little merit in criticism of the railway firms as unpatriotic. And in response to claims that tourism was undermining the efforts of such groups as the Gaelic League, "which are trying to restore to Ireland the national life which the country has not enjoyed for many centuries", Plunkett called upon the meeting to sympathise not only with the "feelings and aspirations of the Irish people", but extend them to English tourists, legislators, and businessmen, so that they might communicate to them how "not as a matter of abstract reason, but of practical experience . . . they were laying down the basis of a most useful kind of industrial and commercial development for their country".

In addition to concerns that centred on the profiteering of business interests, some commentators expressed deep unease about both the broad spectrum of tourists who now visited Ireland, and the ways in which the tourism sector might seek to meet their crass demands. Indeed, several critics feared that mass tourism and its attendant crass and despoiling features might degrade Ireland's cultural treasures. Sometimes the English tourist served as proxy for the country more generally. In 1904, the *Irish Tourist* denounced such rhetoric when it castigated the "Hooligans of the Irish gutter press" for "having raised their inane heads from their native slush, babble re Irish Ireland".[54] Claiming that this gutter press delighted in pillorying the English tourist, it shot back:

> The Hooligans won't have foreigners coming to the island which had the honour of being selected for their place of birth. Of course, like all rules, this has an exception. Though the foreign Englishman, the foreign Scotsman, and the foreigner from the Isle of Man are accursed, the sleek Italian tourist is welcomed; yea, Irish Ireland prostrates itself before him in its encircling mudwash.[55]

Castigating such hypocrisy, the periodical asserted that "[w]e have sent Reelers to the St. Louis Exhibition and real native bandsmen in Irish Ireland warpaint; also ancient umbrella of St. O'Connell [*sic*], found in Bog of Allen", yet at the same time cursed the "foreign Englishman" "in the 'holy name of Irish Ireland'". It denounced such incendiary rhetoric: "In the presence of such slavish twaddle, the average, intelligent Irishman must feel ashamed unless he is saved by a sense of humour."[56]

The trade organ launched a robust response to these attacks by critics of British tourism, even as some commentators expressed concern about ways in which mass tourism, and especially travellers drawn from widening social backgrounds and in ever-larger numbers, threatened the fragile treasures of Irish Antiquity. Casting themselves as patriotic defenders of the nation's treasures, their rhetorical foil was a figure often associated with the pollluting regime of the Bank Holiday and Cook's tours, and with the blinkered sensibilities of the tourist hordes: the cockney tourist. The cockney tourist was enlisted as a discursive contrast for proponents of the Gaelic Revival, such as George William Russell (writing as "Æ"), who deplored the ravages of mass tourism that attended the cockney's arrival on Ireland's shores.[57] R.A.S. Macalister, an archaeologist active in excavations in the Near East and later a distinguished Professor of Celtic Archaeology at University College Dublin, offered such a stinging critique in "The Debit Account of the Tourist Movement" in *The New Ireland Review*.[58] For argument's sake, he accepted that tourism might bring money to Ireland and help to remedy the estrangement between "the English and Irish races". "The question before us, however," he wrote, "is not the extent to which this movement will cure these troubles, but whether it will not be accompanied by sacrifices so considerable as to detract from all benefits that may flow from it."[59] Macalister's chief concern was the effect of mass tourism and the "species" of tourist who might be encouraged to visit Ireland as it opened up to a wider spectrum of travellers. In contrast, he expressed some satisfaction that "[h]itherto Ireland has been tolerably fortunate in the species of tourist which has sought her shores."[60] Macalister speculated on impacts that mass tourism might wreak when cockney met Gael, beginning with the despoilment of the peasantry, and in particular the "pauperism and shameless beggary" which accompanied tourism and diminished "[o]ne of the finest traits of the unspoiled Irish peasant": independence.[61] With more than a hint of the anti-materialism that informed the cultural revival, and in particular its conflation of Gaelic purity, autarky, and peasant folkways, he lamented that in the Aran Islands a noble and independent peasant culture had been diminished as it became tethered to the dictates of mass tourism. Here, too, the question of tourism condensed a wider political discourse on the preservation of Gaeldom deeply influenced by the Celtic Twilight.

As for the sites of antiquity which lay at the heart of his vision of the nation's treasures, Macalister warned that tourism would sully Ireland's glories. Perhaps with an eye to the calumnies which had befallen Killarney under the reign of Kate Kearney's "granddaughter", he imagined with horror the day when "St. Brendan's oratory is gone, and its place is occupied by a gaudy drinking booth, filled with a boisterous cockney crowd with handfuls of shamrocks crushed (in ridicule) into the ribbons of their hats; some of them bawling the latest garbage of the London music-halls".[62] The "desecration" wrought by the mountain railway might follow,[63] then perhaps the razing of a remote, unspoilt village in the interest of tourism, and its replacement, through the offices of the tourist agent, with "a stucco nightmare of lodging-house atrocities which he would call 'Sea-View Esplanade'", complemented with "artificial 'attractions'". "[T]he precincts of the ruins—now in the picturesque confusion of reverent neglect—would be smoothed and turfed, and a skittle alley, or 'Aunt Sally,' or something equally intellectual would be adapted to the nave of the ancient church, an old woman with an apple-stall, of course, being established in one corner" (here a native figure, cynically tapping the tourist's curiosity, appeared).[64] To this eminent scholar and Celticist, tourism imperilled the nation's soul. Its monuments would be disfigured, and the Irish language endangered— all for the sake of meeting the uncultivated tourist's insatiable thirst for vulgar diversions. "[M]ust *everything* good and beautiful perish before the rampant commercialism of the day? Look at England, where this process is going on rapidly, and ask, are we to imitate her example in this?"[65] Macalister insisted proponents of tourist development "must see to it that the Irish National character is not corrupted, that the self-respect of the peasant is safeguarded, that poverty is not sunk to pauperism".[66] And he asserted that the landscape of the nation should be preserved against the encroachment of popular tourism, whose corrosive effects were so visible in England:

> They must see to it that the beauty of the country is not ruined with big wheel and high tower vulgarities, or advertisement placard and

mountain railway eyesores. They must see to it that the forts and tombs of our ancient kings, the shrines of our ancient saints, the humble, beautiful monuments of our ancient Christian men and women are preserved from decoration. They must see to it that our quiet sea-side towns and villages are not made hideous with lodging-house terraces, bathing-boxes, nigger minstrel and barrel-organ vagabonds, and all the other accompaniments of popular sea-side resorts. They must see to it that our National language and traditions are fostered and kept from contamination or injury. They must see to it that Erin of the saints degenerates not into a mere cockney-run; a magnified Wembley Park or Hampstead Heath.[67]

In reconciling the guardianship of national treasures with their tasteful appreciation, Macalister endorsed a more tasteful form of travel undertaken by the cultivated visitor whose feet trod gently, even reverentially, over Irish soil. He cautioned against the ruinous impact of mass tourism on the Irish landscape, enlisting the cockney as his discursive foil. Nationalists such as Robert Lynd and William Bulfin also voiced a measure of despair at certain species of English tourists, and professed a strong desire to protect Ireland from their desecrations.[68] They shared a belief that a new species of tourist now upset the balance between prosperity and destruction. The context of their anxiety was the expanding social base and growing flows of tourists into Ireland. Walter J. Farquharson, writing in *The New Ireland Review* in 1896, asserted that hitherto the Emerald Isle had met acquaintance with only two of the three classes of English tourist: the "gentleman tourist, the man of refinement and education", for whom Macalister writing only a few years later evinced such affection, and the "workingman visitor", whose limited means restricted travel to the seaboard cities. Farquharson joined the tourist-development bodies in issuing a welcome to the third type, the *bourgeois* tourist, who, "[i]f he can conquer the fear that he will be shot by Moonlighters, or mutilated by gorilla-faced natives, and can be morally certain of a well-cooked substantial dinner and a comfortable bed", would show the value to Ireland of his "chief merit": "his money".[69] The *bourgeois* tourist, however quixotic and perplexing in comportment, was welcome in a country grappling to define the value of a developing sector, while weighing its social and cultural consequences.

If R.A.S. Macalister, in his unbridled, classist assault on cockney sensibilities, feared that the untutored tourist would wash over Ireland, desecrating national treasures, there were still other voices of opposition to the tourist-development movement which interwove antipathy towards both the tourist movement and the Union within the fabric of hard-line republicanism in fin-de-siècle Ireland. The Parnellite nationalist newspaper *United Ireland* railed in 1897 against proposals for a royal residence in Ireland—an issue under long discussion that had been raised in connection with the Duke and Duchess of York's recent visit to Ireland.[70] It lumped tourist development together with other Westminster-sponsored schemes for agricultural and industrial improvement, and dismissed as fanciful the notion that "a good Tourist Development scheme would be the dawn of a new era of prosperity for the country."[71] "These various specifics, and the zeal and confidence with which they are prescribed by the various quacks responsible for their publicity," it contended, "might each and all promote the well-being of the country if applied through the agency of a native legislature, the very institution for which each of them is held up to public admiration as an unfailing substitute." The objection—that tourism was an extension of the British state's efforts to tighten its grip over the island and deny it a "native" legislature—reflected Parnellites' concerns that tourist development represented an externally directed effort to smother Home Rule after two failed attempts at Westminster. But it constituted one strand of critical opinion on tourism—sharing that stance with R.A.S. Macalister, whose antiquarian position was nourished by altogether different concerns. What united them, rhetorically, was a dismissal of the capacity of the tourist to properly know Ireland under current conditions—a denial of the potential for the epistemological project of the modern tour to properly nourish the Irish economy or preserve its fragile culture.

CONCLUSION

The profound ambivalence expressed in debates over tourist development, and particularly its ambiguous relationship to diverse constructions of "patriotism", both British and Irish, was reflected in L.M. McCraith's piece "Does Ireland Want Tourists?", published in *The New Ireland Review* in August 1908. Considering a decade of efforts at improvement, Ireland's historic reputation as inhospitable touring-ground, and Norway's and Switzerland's successful embrace of the tourist, McCraith remarked that touring in Ireland remained costly, yet "St. George's Channel crossed, the Irish 'atmosphere' begins to take curious and transforming effect upon the average Britisher" who hitherto "probably, cared little for Ireland".[72]

As to whether Ireland wanted tourists, McCraith captured the ambivalence that attended that question succinctly: "Probably those who say 'no,' and those who say 'yes' belie their words equally."[73] Despite efforts to remedy long-standing complaints—through the improvement of hotels, the ubiquity of the German waiter (a signifier of professional hospitality), the provision of baths and electricity, and the banishing of brogue "on lips of guests, or host, or servants"—McCraith remarked that high tourist expenditures were "of very little direct benefit to the country".[74] "If you talk to a Connemara or a Kerry peasant about tourist development and its local benefits," McCraith contended, "he will answer you with the question—'What is it to me?'"[75] The railway hotels were "nourished by exotic produce" ("Even butter and eggs are imported"), while "[l]ocal car-drivers, guides, and boatmen occasionally benefit substantially, although intermittently, but very frequently cars and boats are in the hands of the hotel proprietor, or the company, with practical eyes to their own profits first, and a desire for the absolute monopoly over tourists' expenditure."[76] Those who ventured off the beaten track in search of "Irish Ireland" found some truth in the time-honoured caricature of poor-quality Irish hostelry—"a big, half-empty house, unfamiliar with paper and paint".[77] So, in answer to the question posed in the title of the piece, McCraith answered that "[t]he answer lies closer than might be supposed to the national welfare." The imperative for Irish men and women was to reclaim the mantle of hospitality in Ireland from its cosmopolitan moorings, and demonstrate the fallacy that only a German waiter and railway hotel could offer a comfortable welcome to the visitor. For, "[i]f dreams are to become realities, it is not to be by exotic effort, or outside interference, but by solid hard work, and by native initiative."[78] After all, McCraith exhorted: "There is more wanted than Capital. One of the things wanted is Character. There is another thing also. It has a grand old name, which, in Ireland, has fallen on evil days in the past, but, in the present, falls upon new ears with a new sound. It is Patriotism."

F.W. Crossley issued a public rejoinder in a subsequent issue, insisting that McCraith grossly distorted touring conditions, magnifying the anxieties that attended travel (with Crossley alleging that "[f]or many years certain sections of the English Press have delighted in slandering this country by exaggerated descriptions of its lawlessness, etc., and the British public in general have come to regard Ireland as a sort of uncivilised and impossible region"[79]). To Crossley, McCraith's unpatriotic denunciation of tourist amenities on the island endorsed such ill-founded views and undermined decades of work to place the sector on firm footings. As this exchange suggests, the merits and disadvantages of tourism figured within wider debates of the island's political status, the position of its peasantry, and its potential for economic and social development. Consequently it assumed many meanings and forms: a post-Famine "Irish tour" in a gesture of friendship towards the benighted sister isle; travel by Irish men and women themselves, forsaking their propensity for vacationing abroad; efforts to arrest or limit the sector's growth and thereby preserve Irish culture from desecrations wrought by cockneyfied tourism; proud refurbishment of the nation's infrastructure to burnish the island's reputation as a hospitable country. Debates over tourist development crystallised in Killarney, which was the historic centre of the trade and the focus for disputes over tourism and its impact on Irish culture. It became a testing-ground for ideologies for tourist development, a battleground over access to land and authority, and a locus for diverse performances of Irish travel, many of which centred on tropes of disappointment, despair, and denunciations of mercenary contrivances and crass commercialisation that reached their apotheosis at the craftily staged site known as Kate Kearney's Cottage.

3 The Colourful Cast of Characters

Fresh from a visit to the Cork Exhibition, Rebecca McEvoy, an ostrich-feather dresser, and a friend, Julia Glenville, purchased tickets from Henry Gaze and Sons' office in Cork to do the Lakes of Killarney in July 1902.[1] Later, they claimed that they had advised the clerk, Arthur Callender, that they had never ridden ponies before, and he asked if they would like ponies through the Gap, for a separate charge (Callender later disputed this account, claiming never to have dealt with the women personally). Reaching Killarney, McEvoy and Glenville joined a party of excursionists and set off in a waggonnette to the Gap. When the party arrived at French's Cottage—a customary alighting point—they disembarked, and the well-known local guide Jeremiah O'Connell took charge of the tour. The pony guides led them forward and left them at a site called Saint Patrick's Cottage, vowing to meet up with them after taking a shortcut by foot. But within a short time, Glenville discovered McEvoy on the ground, bleeding from the mouth, initially unable to speak. When she was able to utter her first words, McEvoy asked an attendant who raced to the scene why she had been left alone with the pony.

The case was heard in 1902 before the Court of King's Bench in Dublin. McEvoy had taken action against Henry Gaze and Sons. The case for the defence rested on Messrs Gaze receiving only 6d. of the 2s. 6d. charge for the ponies. It disputed the women's claim that the Cork office clerk had offered assurances that the party would be accompanied the whole way. Instead, their representative asserted that "the cause of the accident was the lady's nervousness and her want of familiarity with animals."[2] Indeed, in defending his claim that the ponymen had full control over the animals, the guide Jeremiah O'Connell contended, to laughter in the court, that the ponies knew the route so well that they 'could nearly point out the scenery'. Nonetheless, the jury found in favour of the plaintiff, awarding McEvoy damages of £300.[3]

Even in light of these events, and despite the encouragement of Thomas Cook and Son, ponymen refused to take out insurance against liability, and declined the company's offer of an advance to pay for proper saddles and equipment. Frustrated with their inaction, Cook then instigated a programmatic effort to displace the ponymen. In 1903 the company proposed to substitute cars for ponies, provoking the opposition of Lord Kenmare, who protested that such a change would destroy the ride through the Gap, "one of the attractive features of Killarney".[4] The prominent local landlord, who stood on the precipice of insolvency from the 1880s, found such debates instrumental in building solidarities with local workers in the trade (and would later proclaim himself a defender of locals and their traditional conveyances when electric gondolas were mooted for Killarney's lakes). Under a headline entitled "Cooking the Gap", the *Killarney Echo* asserted that accidents while tourists rode through the Gap were "very few and far between" and commended Kenmare for his "very spirited protest" against plans to displace "the old and time-honoured custom of employing saddle ponies for the use of tourists".[5] Thomas Cook and Son's persistent efforts to consolidate authority over the trade met with stiff resistance, and even violence. In May 1907, for instance, a tourist claimed that shots were fired at a car hired through the firm while it made its way through the Gap.[6] The party had hired ponies at the Lakes to proceed through the Gap, but their car progressed ahead of them, carrying their coats and accompanied by policemen. When the ponies reached Gap Cottage, the party heard a volley of gunfire: "It appears that Cook's have let this tour to a contractor," the tourist related, "and the pony-owners resent the cars going through the Gap. One of them told me that there are three hundred people depending on the pony traffic. I hear that a car was stopped last Sunday week by trees and rocks being put on the road." The disputes expanded in the first decade of the twentieth century to encompass licensing and the regulation of boatmen's and carmen's charges—as the local tourist association and institutions of local government collaborated to redress perceptions that tourists were promiscuously fleeced.

A tour of Killarney brought together tourists such as Rebecca McEvoy and Julia Glenville and an array of local characters. Not all of their encounters ended in acrimony or litigation, yet alone gunfire. Indeed, many turned on ironic performances of hospitality proffered by "the enemy", as Clement W. Scott, a prominent London-born theatre critic and writer, christened the wily locals. Before stage-managed enactments of "aboriginality" became fashionable features of twentieth-century tourism promotion in diverse theatres, and despite the efforts of commercial actors and local and national associations to regulate the tourist's encounter with the Killarney peasantry, locals exercised profound influence over the contours of the Killarney tour. They honed performances and rituals to signify peasant hospitality—whether a taste of the mountain dew, or a fanciful tale embedded within an elaborate elocutionary performance, inevitably followed by a request for loose change. They understood that travellers recognised elements of the "stage" Irishman and -woman in their enactments, and arrived in Killarney familiar with Kate Kearney's legend. In fact, peasant character roles derived in part from cultural stereotypes that were performed by

Killarney natives through what Spurgeon W. Thompson has described as a "double consciousness—one that is created by being obliged to relate, to answer continually to a vast body of mass-produced representations".[7] These Irish types were deeply embedded in Anglophone popular culture— most notably the comic Irishman of the Victorian stage—a poor, superstitious, exuberant, and blundering character bestowed with verbal talents with which he charmed others, to pecuniary advantage.[8] Killarney "folk" also tapped what Edward Lengal has identified as a set of discourses in the emerging post-Famine tourist industry that interwove narratives of the Irish "race" with discussions of their hospitality and *habitus*.[9] Excursionists professed shock at the temerity of locals, who engaged in caricatural performances and lampooned the local regime of toll-gates with their own regimes of exchange. Irony pervaded all dimensions of these encounters, as tourists feigned shock at such audacity, while locals professed to be extending no more than native hospitality to visitors in the peasant realm.[10] As this blatant kitsch intensified, the writers, poets, and painters of the Gaelic Revival looked westwards, to Connacht, and also west of Killarney to other parts of Co. Kerry, in search of an Irish peasantry uncorrupted by tourism, for an autarkic Gaeldom sliding into history. As we have seen, these self-appointed guardians of the remnants of Celtic Antiquity cast an uneasy glance at accelerating, polluting tourism and feared coster-monger horrors might spread beyond Killarney.

"ONLY RAIN IS TO BE HAD FOR NOTHING": PERFORMING TOURIST EXCHANGES AT KILLARNEY

An important trope in excursionist narratives was that Killarney was a bustling, even chaotic, tourist centre in which the solitary traveller dissolved into a crowd shepherded from one "lion" to another along a regulation route by colourful locals. This standardised, commodified experience repudiated narratives which dramatised the emptiness of the rural landscape, and suggested that locals tightened their grips on the tourist's purse, dictated what some travellers professed to be outlandish terms, and resisted efforts to encroach upon their realm. Killarney was described as a place teeming with people whose livelihoods were not rooted in the soil, but in the modern tourist economy.[11] No longer depicted as a solitary encounter with an eclectic geography of the picturesque and the sublime, "doing" Killarney denoted a series of intense and inevitable misadventures in which the native fiendishly ensnared the excursionist in an unscrupulous regime of exchange.

If Killarney's denizens attracted the opprobrium of many travellers professing to attempt, in vain, to reproduce Romantic travel conventions, this was, as we have seen, not an entirely new feature of Killarney travel accounts, though it was firmly entrenched in post-Famine narratives. It did, however, reflect the travellers' keen observations on the district's seemingly inexhaustible supply of beggars. In 1846, Killarney was cited in *Slater's Commercial Directory* as one of only two places in the county (along with Tralee, the county town and a major port and market) showing signs of prosperity, due to its staple industry: tourism.[12] (Visiting Co. Kerry in November 1845, Thomas Campbell Foster described widespread privation, and, writing of the peninsular districts of the county that lay west of Killarney, contended that the isolated position of its peasantry made the "peculiarities of individuals" ever-more striking).[13] Killarney men and women were not alone in tapping the tourist's purse: William H.A. Williams has noted the number of writers who bemoaned the exactions of beggars and pedlars, and the number of guides who offered services;[14] every holy well had its superintendent, every old abbey its caretaker, and every tourist district boasted locals eager to explicate fantastical lore. At Glendalough, Co. Wicklow, along the popular tourist places in Co. Clare, and at the Giant's Causeway, the hue and cry of beggars and hucksters were decried as stains upon places of natural beauty and historic import. In his account of travels to the Giant's Causeway in the 1830s, the Scottish-born writer Leitch Ritchie described such a scene:

> The regular charge of the guides I understood to be five shillings, and that of the boatmen, twelve shillings and sixpence; but besides these there are a variety of incidental items which render the Causeway rather an expensive exhibition. One man fires the pistol which produces the echo prescribed by the books; another professes to keep the path to the cave clear for your honour's feet; and a smoke-dried carline gives you to drink of the Giant's Well, a spring of pure water which oozes up between two of the pillars, and which, on tasting, you find to have been miraculously converted *in transitu* by the old witch into whisky. Lastly, more than a dozen men and boys follow you through the whole adventure, in spite of your expostulations, to offer boxes of mineralogical specimens.[15]

Killarney's denizens bore a marked resemblance to such counterparts. As Thomas Campbell Foster wrote, "There is the same eager pouncing on a stranger as a prize whom is fair game to pluck; the same excess of civility; and not a whit the less sense of extortionate exaction."[16] This parallel informal tourist economy was nourished by tourists feigning to escape the "regulation route" and locals who tapped their prurience and sense of adventure.

Killarney town came to define the district in a way that urban centres did in few other tourist destinations. Writers routinely dismissed it as ugly, with some noting as an exception the magnificent neo-Gothic Roman Catholic cathedral designed by Augustus Welby Pugin (a majestic marker of the Kenmare family's faith and munificence). Still, *Murray's* bemoaned that "its inhabitants chiefly consist of boat-men, guides, car-drivers, and the general hangers-on of a favourite tourist resort."[17] C.S. Ward, author of a *Thorough Guide* volume, dismissed the town as "dull" and "uninteresting", but remarked that tourists could find "any forgotten impedimenta of travel" there, and joined *Murray's* in lamenting that hitherto authorities had taken little interest in abating the ceaseless begging. Of the ubiquitous "professional beggars", Ward contended: "In self-defence the visitor is almost compelled to encourage these clamorous but by no means needy intruders."[18] Killarney's small industrial base also focussed on supplying tourists with souvenirs: by the mid-nineteenth century, the town boasted many arbutus-wood manufactories, described in the mid-1840s as the *"sole trade of this town"*.[19] Otherwise, as John U. Higinbotham, in a travelogue of a journey from New York through Europe declared, "there is very little industry here except that of cajoling the wide-eyed sightseer."[20]

The intensity of such cajoling was coincident with the tourist season in Killarney, which lasted for a few short months, reaching its height in July and August. The inflow created a short but lucrative opportunity for locals to profit from the huge seasonal influx of visitors. Interlaced agrarian, institutional, and demographic regimes also supported livelihood strategies that focussed on the tourist's purse. The tourism sector was underpinned by a varied and much-lauded topography and by codes of landscape aesthetics that ensconced it in popular imagination long before the railway penetrated Killarney and travel writers began to recount their breathless efforts to flee local hordes. But the sector's growth was also supported by demographic and institutional regimes that drew comment. Co. Kerry experienced a transition to lower marriage and birth rates, coinciding with landlords' efforts to curb subletting and subdivision of holdings, before the 1840s.[21] Kieran Foley notes that by 1841 its population density was the lowest in the province of Munster—but also that the county's topography of mountain and bog, and subletting and subdivision, may have rendered its population more vulnerable during the subsequent subsistence crisis.[22] Indeed, the county's relatively low rates of emigration and low-quality arable land contributed to more dramatic Famine era privation than aggregate printed census data suggest, especially in remote districts with high degrees of existing poverty. When the Famine struck in 1845, Killarney's Poor Law guardians (who superintended an institution opened in 1845) acted expeditiously. Killarney's poor law regime was calibrated to peculiarities of local experience. The town became the base for a central relief committee, which co-ordinated the local response to the crisis.[23] It raised subscriptions, including substantial donations from local landlords, purchased and distributed foodstuffs, and initiated modest work programmes that preceded the central government's wider efforts.[24] Sir Robert Peel's Tories moved to establish a framework for relief modelled in part on their response to previous subsistence crises, comprising a relief commission with local committees and a public-works programme. When Lord John Russell's Whig ministry replaced Peel's government in June 1846, strategies changed. Peel's relief commission apparatus was dismantled and replaced with a new system of food relief and work programmes. But from 1847 to 1852 the Poor Law, financed by local rates, became the primary framework for relief, under a re-established relief commission and reconstituted local committees. It provided outdoor support to the disabled (broadly defined), those who suffered from severe sickness or serious accident, and poor widows with two or more legitimate children.[25]

Relief in Knockane parish (in which the Gap of Dunloe was situated) was administered through the apparatus of two unions: Tralee and Killarney, with the majority of its townlands in the Killarney union. The powerful Herbert and Kenmare families backed its relief efforts. In a signal of the autonomy of such local institutions, the unions' practices departed markedly from the Russell ministry's regime, notably its insistence on setting market rates for the sale of provisions, which the local committee condemned.[26] In 1847 the government empowered it to address the full extent of the Famine, bridged between winter and summer by soup kitchen relief. It was soon clear that the Killarney workhouse could not accommodate the growing numbers of inmates, even as guardians scrambled to add auxiliary buildings and extend outdoor relief.[27] The extension of outdoor relief through the Killarney workhouse ended in August 1849; at that point, Killarney had the greatest resources of any union in Ireland, the least-pressing distress, and therefore the lowest expenditures in relation to property valuation.[28] Foley's analysis of the Killarney workhouse reveals that in the years 1848–49 and 1849–50, it housed the lowest proportion of adult males, and the highest proportion of "under 15s" in the county.[29] This profile of the inmates reflected to some extent the supply of labour to the most unstable elements of the tourism sector—the young women in particular whose performances would vex and entertain many observers—but also clearly signals their precariousness in these years of distress, when fewer recreational tourists visited the district.

As both Foley and James S. Donnelly note, Co. Kerry's experience in the post-Famine era is striking. Amidst widespread social upheaval in many parts of Ireland, this dairying county's distribution of landholdings persisted, stubbornly resisting consolidation. Its small and powerful landlord class demonstrated equal resilience, as their peers were being swept away in many parts of the country.[30] Moreover, farther down the social spectrum, the demographic regime showed few signs of the transition to higher ages of marriage, and to lower rates of marriage that began to prevail elsewhere. As for migration, between 1861 and 1891, the Killarney poor law union experienced comparatively low levels of population loss in the context of the county overall. Though many young damsels who affected to court tourists professed to be unwed, perhaps more than a few were married and had children, as many tourists discovered to their surprise. There is no doubt that the tourism sector provided opportunities for seasonal work interlaced with agrarian activity, supplying casual and remunerative labour, especially in the summer. Thomas Campbell Foster remarked that tourism produced bold efforts to cajole visitors out of loose change.[31] When Nassau Senior toured Killarney in 1852, he commented on the wretchedness of the town to the local landlord Mr Herbert. Herbert contended that the people exhibited no more misery than those of any agricultural town in the south of Ireland, and that "[t]he half-starved and quarter-clothed loungers about the streets are attracted thither from the neighbouring country by the hope of casual employment from visitors."[32]

If Herbert saw these people as migrants to the town attempting to exploit its historic functions as a tourism centre, hawkers who approached tourists in Killarney and its surrounding sites also attracted the opprobrium of many travel writers, ranking with the rain as one of the two great nuisances of the district, in T.O. Russell's opinion.[33] Many warned that the streets of the town teemed with mendicants, lending it an uninviting, and even menacing, air.[34] Equally vexatious were the "professional beggars"[35] and hangers-on found around the rural district. The Gap of Dunloe was cited as the place where such features were most visible and most audible. As James M. Hoyt, whose impressions of three months of travel with his son, a Baptist minister in Brooklyn, were vividly recounted in the pages of *Glances on the Wing at Foreign Lands* (printed for a wider circle of family and friends at their request), declared:

> I omitted, in the account of the excursion yesterday through Gap Dunloe [*sic*], all mention of the throngs of beggars—men, women and children—which at every hamlet, turn of the road, and stopping place, streamed out and ran after us, some asking for money directly, some offering mountain dew (whisky,) goat's milk, and knick-knacks, for sale. I never imagined such pertinacity. I filled my pockets when leaving the hotel, with all the small silver and copper I could get, and long before returning, I had run dry.[36]

Overwhelmed by the thunderous noise and the impertinence of hucksters, Clement W. Scott despaired of the bedlam that attended his tour. Indeed, during his tour through "Colleen Bawn Land", Scott had been assaulted by bands of boisterous hawkers at every turn. He lamented the extent to which it had undermined his desire to appraise Killarney's scenery in solitude:

> There surely are some people in the world who in such scenery as this like to be quiet for a little, to think for themselves, and to be left alone. But this is exactly the thing that is not permitted. From morning till night you are bullied for money, or worried with pointless stories, framed merely for the purpose of talk. You are hardly clear of the hotel-gates before the girls with the baskets are at you, pouring out a distressing catalogue of the trumpery contents of their basket—girls fleet of foot, who refuse to be shaken off, and absolutely shut their ears, when the verdict of "No"

is pronounced. I suppose it never strikes these strange girls that no one, ignorant of the interior of Bedlam, would be disposed to start on a day's outing, laden with paper-cutters, deers' feet, work-boxes, and needle-books. They are without reason and unreasonable. [37]

"But", he remarked archly, "think not that at the entrance of the famous Gap of Dunloe, and at this early hour of the morning, you have shaken off the enemy." Here, Scott and many other writers agreed, the assault on the tourists' senses, and their pocket-books, reached new heights. These textual codifications of the Killarney excursion—as a surreal journey through a district whose bucolic landscapes were stalked by rapacious locals—were firmly entrenched by the 1860s. Their protestations to the contrary, it was clear to any purportedly bewildered tourist who set out to do Killarney that the journey would involve, in addition to payments to travel agents and hoteliers, myriad transactions with locals that hinged on cultural performances and distinctive regimes of value.

The loosely scripted, widely prefigured exchanges between excursionists and local guides, ponymen, carmen, buglers, and hawkers of heather, trinkets, and mountain dew became as essential to doing Killarney as beholding the scenery. Advice in guide-books on pecuniary matters, and especially counsel on how to navigate the local culture of exchange and the choreography of local encounters, occupied as much print as guidance on routes to take and sights to see. The day began with tourists ensuring that they had a heavy load of pocket-change. A humorous 1844 piece penned by Charles Lever, written to satirise those tourists who wished to know "How to See Killarney in One Day", enumerated the sums a tourist would disburse, producing a costing for the commodified experience of the place: eight shillings would satisfy the guide, but up to 15 would win his highest approval (of the guides the author commented that "[e]ach resembles the other exactly—has the same voice, look, gesture, and manner—the same powers of description—the same lies and legends").[38] The same was true of the boatmen, who also required two dinners, one "paid for in the bill", and the second at landing. As for the signature Gap libation, goat's-milk was one shilling per glass (often with a request for sixpence more), with goat's-milk and poitín "for the ladies" rising from two shillings in the valleys to three or four on Mangerton and the Reeks—popular tourist sites. Ferns and heather cost a shilling a sprig; the "names of gentleman's seats, mountains, islands, churches, and school-houses" were "usually paid for at sixpence each; but the informant will always be 'satisfied with a shilling'".[39] What element of the day escaped such crass commercialisation? "[O]nly rain is to be had for nothing," Lever lamented.[40]

The rituals of these encounters appeared chaotic to many observers, but in fact they were embedded within regimes of exchange which commodified peasant culture for tourist consumption, enveloped it in performance, and assigned to it a (disputed) value as a cultural material.[41] Take a typical transaction, over the cost of a trinket or souvenir, or perhaps a service such as bringing forth the echoes of the Lakes by bugling. The natives of Killarney might propose a charge at which the tourist would express initial disbelief. But the tourist would also come with pocket-change in hand, prepared for such demands. The transaction would in due course be settled—and not always to the parties' mutual satisfaction, with the tourist narrating exasperation at the rigmarole, and relief in having at last acquired the good or service. This is how Rev. G.N. Wright, author of an 1822 guide to Killarney, described the negotiations, comparing them unfavourably with the Lake District:

> The first thing to be resolved upon, on arriving at the inn, is the route that is to be adopted for the following day. If it be the Gap of Dunloe, horses are to be provided, which are to be had here on much more rea- sonable terms than in Westmoreland; but if the intention be to visit the Lake, the cockswain who steers the boat, the bugle-man, gunner, &c., are to be sent for, and directed to be in readiness. And here certainly the most disgraceful circumstance connected with a visit to the Lakes of Killarney is discovered: the hire of a boat is a very extravagant sum in the first instance, but this the cockswain, or boatmen, cannot inter- fere with, the boats being the property of Lord Kenmare, from one of whose stewards they are procured; but, in addition, the boatmen and cockswain (five persons at least) are to be paid two shillings each for their labour, a bottle of whiskey a man, with dinner for the entire party, including a bugle-man and fisherman. How different from the modest charges of Derwent or Windermere![42]

This account foreshadowed features of the Gap tour in the post-Famine period, when tourists made the same comparisons with the Lake District, and found the English touring region less demanding on their purses, while at other Irish sites they remarked on similar efforts to loosen the tourist's purse-strings.

Tourists to Killarney consumed a bewildering array of services, and par ticipated in an extensive tourism sector founded upon dual economies—one for locals and the other for tourists. Accounts of the Killarney tour were replete with descriptions of moments when offended travellers detected the imposts levied on them. Occasionally the service for which payment was demanded was invisible and perplexing—even infuriating—to the con- sumer. One excursionist encountered a man demanding payment at the end of the day of touring. The local man contended that he had been sur- reptitiously performing a service in diligently monitoring the touring party throughout the day, prepared to correct anything that might have gone awry. "It would be curious to collect a list of the services supposed to have a market value round Killarney," the author wrote, in a tone of bewilder- ment and exasperation.[43] Not all such comments were either stinging or playful. Sometimes these performances nourished scathing assessments of

Irish indolence. Others described them as expressions of underlying social problems to which Ireland's historic poverty, and even modern tourism, contributed. Margaret Tyner, writing in *The Ladies' Treasury*, depicted Killarney folk as representative of the Irish beggars whom she found throughout Ireland; she also described Killarney in the tourist season as the "capital of Beggardom, the El Dorado of the mendicant", and commented that "it is most amusing to see the extra Irish 'get up' which they put on specially for the benefit of unwary English and American travellers."[44]

The "fleecing" of the tourist attracted disapproval from writers and local leaders in the tourism sector alike. In 1852, a writer in *The Ladies' Repository* declared that these nuisances formed "a large discount, to be deducted from the pleasures of enjoying the fine scenery of the county Kerry", and (worryingly for tourism advocates in the immediate post-Famine period) contended that it bespoke "a state of the people of the land, to be mourned and lamented over".[45] In fact the ferocity of such commentaries was cause for concern amongst leaders of the tourist-development movement of the 1890s. Despite vigorous efforts, they were unable to stamp out a feature of the Gap and Killarney tourism which was widely derided in travel literature. Under the title "Case for Complaint", the *Kerry Sentinel* ran a leader on 9 September 1899, describing how a large number of tourists on the last excursion of the season had enjoyed fine weather, but were displeased by the charged levies by carmen for drives in the vicinity of the Lakes,[46] one of those charges being, in the newspaper's view, "extortionate". Locals' relentless pursuit of the spoils of tourism was especially aggressive, though it was neither unique to Killarney, nor to Ireland; in Scotland, tourists faced similar petty extortions, centred on charges and tips levied in Highland hotels.[47] But the *Kerry Sentinel* proclaimed in 1899 that "the Killarney car owners pursued a very foolish and short-sighted policy in availing of an opportunity such as that afforded by last Sunday's excursion, to fleece tourists."[48] Tourists would find little incentive to return to the Lakes on account of this behaviour. Apparent collusion to maintain a high price for tourist services frustrated them further. One correspondent to the *Irish Times* in 1895 suggested that hotels intervene and advise guests not to dispense any change to these beggars—who were agents of this subversion.[49] Indeed to exasperated tourists, the Killarney hotel, with its regime of established rates and organised excursions, offered a refuge from capricious exactions by the local populace. On some occasions, tourists took the matter into their own hands. An 1866 piece in *The Suburban Magazine* recounted how a touring party had used sticks to beat a crowd of mostly young boys off their car; the tourists had also playfully and parodoxically reversed roles in the established script, proposing a charge for "showing *them* [the locals] the scenery, with a request to give us something on account before commencing our description".[50] But, if the sums demanded of excursionists by Killarney locals were extortionate, the parallel system of prices for many common provisions in the town attracted even stronger criticism.

While visitors regularly availed themselves of tourist services and purchased signature items—souvenir arbutus trinkets, umbrellas, and other accoutrements of travel—on some occasions when they purchased other items from local shops, they became cognisant of apparent gaping differences in prices demanded of them and of locals. A writer noted in *The Scotsman* in 1850 that a friend who was in need of a "small article of dress" that could be purchased in Edinburgh for 15*d*. or 18*d*. was told it would cost 4*s*. in Killarney (though a nearby shop sold a similar article for 7*d*.). "And yet more startling differences were exhibited in the wilderness," the author wrote, as his party had found that locals were grateful for pennies "on the untoured side of the mountain", whereas "the same number of shillings would have been regarded with greedy contempt within the magic circle of the Killarney tour."[51] For most tourists who acquired provisions through their hotels in town, the disparity between markets for locals and those for tourists was inconspicuous. But pronounced variances in some prices attracted local attention, resulting in vain efforts at remediation. Roche's, a major hotel in the district, proposed in 1850 "to check the system of miscellaneous pillage" by establishing fixed charges for the various services available to tourists, but even these were judged to be high, though Roche "and his brethren will have to distribute a considerable amount of black mail around them".[52] Indeed, most efforts to regulate or displace these practices were frustrated by the deeply entrenched systems of customary behaviour and an informal economy that rested on value created within the context of a fleeting relationship between tourists—most of whom rushed to do Killarney—and locals, who profited from the tourists' haste and unfamiliarity with the district, as well as from the informal agreements amongst providers of tourist services which reduced competition during the short tourist season. The performances of exchange were suffused with ironic enactions of peasant hospitality, as well as protestations of shock by travel writers who nonetheless anticipated these extensively prefigured transactions, which were foregrounded in the circuitry of texts centred on the Gap tour. And despite their avowed antipathy, excursionists' narratives also recounted how they submitted to these performances—and paid, however unwillingly, the going price.

"THE INDIGENOUS CELEBRITIES IN HUMBLE LIFE": THE CAST OF KILLARNEY CHARACTERS

The principal popular guide-books produced in the decades after the Famine, *Murray's* and *Black's*, made few comments on the Irish peasantry *per se*. They focussed instead on ruins as emblems of an eclipsed indigenous culture,[53] though *Murray's* characterised the human presence in the Gap as a curiosity, noting solitary cottages as key markers of a human presence: "One singular feature of the Gap of Dunloe is the population that is scattered through it. Although at a distance appearing as though far removed from man's haunts, the eye soon detects little sad-coloured cabins with their plot of potato or rye ground perched here and there amongst the rocks and streams."[54] In some guide-books, however, Irish peasants were colourful subjects. M.D. Frazar, in the *Practical Guide to Great Britain and Ireland*, for instance, wrote that "[t]he people of the south are happy-go-lucky, cheerful folk, full of wit and fancy and superstition. They take life easily, and make it as joyful as possible."[55] The Gap was sparsely populated, though its denizens grew in number over the Famine decade: between 1841 and 1851 the population of the vast "Dunloe, Upper" townland, in which the Gap was situated, more than doubled to 214 inhabitants—still a very small population distributed over a large piece of land, generally in small cabins, engaged at least partly in agriculture as tenant-farmers, but profiting, if not from fertile land, then from the fertile imagination of the tourist.[56] But they were joined by legions more people who tapped lucrative, seasonal work in the informal tourism economy. Travellers commented on the ubiquity of guides, buglers, fiddlers, and mountain dew girls, and described the Gap as a site of raucous carnival, while locals insisted—with a wink of the eye—that their traditions were as timeless as the mists that enveloped the Kerry mountains.

Various devices valorised the writers' culture by highlighting the contrasting, negative qualities of the "host",[57] even if this was done in the context of a narrative of leisure travel, and with the "surprises" encountered at Killarney recounted with more than a touch of irony. Some writers, guide-books in hand, commented acidly on the patently choreographed encounters and contrived performances, drawing on a suite of received understandings of the Irish native.[58] Many narrated the natives' wiliness as an Irish trait, while others explored the nuanced contours of the intercultural encounter between tourist and native. The earl of Mayo, an ardent proponent of tourism, advised readers of the *Irish Tourist* in May 1898 that "Irishmen are not the least impressed by an overbearing manner, or a loud voice, and if this tone is adopted, it generally ends in the Irishman beginning to chaff, and eventually laugh at the traveller, more especially if there is a fuss, and a crowd collects."[59] The tourist might not find the comforts and amenities that were available in other lands, but, if seeking amusement, he "will find lots of the natives to laugh with him, and drink with him, if he is so inclined".[60]

All the same, writers admitted their weakness to persistent blandishments, and recounted their submission to the artful seduction of peasant elocution. Dr Henry M. Field, a distinguished American author and clergyman, perceived their exaggerated flattery as a lucrative native resource: "This quick wit of the Irish serves them better than their poverty in appealing for charity," he wrote, admitting to having, against the advice of the charitable societies, filled his pockets with pennies to distribute amongst "hordes of ragamuffins, as well as to old women, to hear their answers, which, though largely infused with Irish blarney, have a flavor of native wit".[61] On a tour through the Gap, Field playfully remarked that the women, having failed to persuade two theological professors in his party to part with change, turned instead to him:

> An old siren, coming up in a tender and confiding way, whispered to me, "You're the best looking of the lot; and it is a nice lady ye have ye, and a fine couple ye make." That was enough; she got her money. I felt a little elated with the distinguished and superior air which even beggars had discovered in my aspect and bearing, till on returning to the hotel, one of our professors coolly informed me that the same old witch had previously told him that "*he* was the darling of the party!" After that, who will ever believe a beggar's compliment again?[62]

Travel writers employed narrative conventions in rendering their verbal exchanges with natives in print. They included highly stylised representations of the Irish brogue, phonetically printed for the reader's amusement, and honorific-laden quotations attributed to natives which established the learnedness of the narrator. "Blarney", and its treatment in printed texts, was a nuanced means by which, through elocution, mixing wit, and strategic flattery, power relations between locals and excursionists were negotiated and expressed.[63] It would be a mistake to characterise these speech acts as embellished practices entirely designed for the tourist's consumption. Hiberno-English had distinctive grammatical and other elements with a long lineage. But much of the honorific-laden, beseeching tone of the speech act evoked the Killarney guides' embellishment, which apparently gave rise to the popular expression: "He lies like a Killarney carman."[64] Blarney, as a speech performance, was central to the social framing of the Gap tour. In travel writing, it was critical to the establishment of the authorial subject and his or her social and cultural distance from the Irish peasant; to the locals, it was part of the cultural arsenal deployed in an elaborate cultural performance.

As far as the languages of Killarney, the district's linguistic landscape was rich and complex. As late as 1911, the census of the Gap district shows that a large majority of the local population spoke both English and Irish: 78 percent of the population in the townland of Upper Dunloe. Yet core features of the narration of intercultural difference in the tourist encounter were the style and content of speech performances—the medium of which was a tongue, English, in which the locals were proficient. Travel writers who transliterated these verbal stylings represented peasant speech as being ridden with impenetrable syntax, codifying stereotypes surrounding the peasant temperament as vehement, exuberant, and emphatic.[65] As Luke Gibbons has noted, in the absence of any physical, racialised marker of inferiority, blarney became, for some commentators on the Irish, the most significant marker of their cultural "retardation".[66] But, as Gibbons also notes, there was scope for language to be deployed by the "Irish" figure against such narratives of dominance. Guides, carmen, hawkers, and others performed florid speech acts which entertained, bewildered, and confounded the tourist as they enveloped transactions of money for trinkets, mountain dew, and goat's-milk within an exotic speech code. In addition to this inflection, the content of the speech act revolved around exaggerated flattery, in which tourists detected an underlying pecuniary aim. Narrators professed weakness and recounted seduction and submission to its charms. Charles M. Taylor found his party the object of sedulous attention from women in the Gap who "deluge us with persuasive compliments".[67] He recounted the entreaties of one woman: "One old woman tells me that she has many daughters so beautiful that it would break the heart of St. Patrick himself to see them leave auld Ireland, but I am 'that fascinatin', that she will give me my choice of these fairies of the Gap."[68] Alluding to the thinly disguised motivation behind this verbal play, the Canadian traveller Canniff Haight, citing numerous examples of entreaties to him and his party, insisted that "[t]his is the place for persons to come who are fond of distinctive titles—they can get be-honored and be-lorded to their heart's content by a judicious outlay of sixpences."[69]

"FROM 'GINERATION TO GINERATION'": THE KILLARNEY GUIDE

Beyond such visible characters, engaged in profitable performances of native hospitality, the labour of legions of local tourism workers was obscured or elided in narratives of travel. Travel writers invariably privileged the entertaining caricature over the mundane labourer—the witty Irish carman and flirtatious mountain dew vendor over the railway clerk or hotel servant—thereby foregrounding quirky and quixotic figures in Killarney. Tellingly, the 1859 *Illustrated Handbook to Cork, the Lakes of Killarney and the South of Ireland* enumerated "the indigenous celebrities in humble life" who peopled narratives of travel in Killarney. It listed "the pipers; the chief of whom is Gandsey" and "the Mountain Dew Girls, who were wont to insist upon the tourist disposing of his small change in return for their whiskey and goat's milk".[70] They were joined by the "arbutus wood ornament sellers", who travelled about the Lakes and hotels, and, lastly, the "accomplished, shameless, irrepressible, professional beggars—all impostors"; the tourist was advised to resist the temptation to bestow alms on them, thereby injuring the "cause of true charity".[71] They constituted a colourful cast of characters who peopled the Killarney tourist landscape.

Kate Kearney's ribald "granddaughter", conducting the business of tourism from her profitable perch, was amongst many colourful characters in the Rabelesian enclave. The "granddaughter" was not alone in attracting comment for preternatural youth. Other seemingly age-defying characters invited tourists to encounter them as incarnations of famous stock-Irishmen and -women, including the "Colleen Bawn" and "Happy Jack", the local guide made famous in Samuel Carter and Maria Halls' celebrated account of Killarney. The mysterious power of Jack and other Killarney characters to defy age over generations was one ironic conceit used by writers to convey their understanding of the contrived nature of the tourist encounter. One visitor, upon meeting Jack many years after the Halls had encountered him, noted wryly that he "looked too youthful to be down in that now somewhat antiquated work".[72] This was not the only tourist site in Ireland where guides evinced such implausible longevity: at Glendalough, Co. Wicklow, where guides were also thick on the ground, and some became as famous as any natural element in the landscape, Joe Irwin enjoyed a similarly legendary stature.[73]

Amongst the guides found throughout Ireland, the local Killarney guide was depicted as an especially colourful and entertaining character. Indeed, guide-books abjured their own authority in favour of his own inimitable performance. If judiciously selected, the guide conveyed "knowledge" which no book could, in good faith, relay to the travellers.[74] By encouraging excursionists to carry guide-books with them, but also to seek local human guides to add a local flavour, guide-book editors struck a careful balance between underscoring the comical character of the guide's knowledge and their own authority in discerning how Killarney might be done without buffoonery and exaggeration. Yet, as a foil to such erudition, travellers delighted in recounting their wily guide's tales—stories as incredible as their uncanny youthfulness.

The quick-witted and artful Killarney guide was a central character in narratives of Killarney—and a representative male type. He was a master-practitioner of the elocutionary art of blarney, and many writers appraised his knowledge as patently incredible. When delivered in his trademark brogue, it was occasionally impenetrable. The author of "A Week in Ireland", published in the *Manchester Guardian* in 1852, had engaged a guide at his hotel, having refused the entreaties of one man who had claimed to be "'Mrs Hall's own Guide'".[75] Instead, the writer opted for a man with the "euphonious name of Kerry O'Leary". "[A]nd certainly," the author remarked, "he possesses in perfection that peculiar quality for which travellers have been so renowned, ever since the days of Baron Munchausen, Maundeville, and the renowned Ferdinand Mendez Pinto, that 'liar of the first magnitude'".[76] There were publications, perhaps most famously the antiquarian T. Crofton Croker's *Legends of the Lakes*, which codified the local colourful "sayings and doings" of the district.[77] But the guide brought them to life, and was the custodian of fantastical oral tradition which he conveyed in inimitable fashion. Many shared the views put forth by the guide-book writer John Bradbury:

> In describing the day's journey, I shall almost entirely avoid relating any of the fairy legends which attach to the various islands, lakes, &c., as the one infliction you will be favoured with from the guide will probably be sufficiently interesting—besides, it would be taking the

business of the guides, who relate them in the genuine brogue, and as handed down from "gineration to gineration," from the time of the great O'Don't-know-who himself, with an elastic authenticity, nicely adjusted by the observing eye of the guide to suit the requirements of the most credulous or sceptical.[78]

If Happy Jack was, like Kate Kearney's "granddaughter", a mysteriously immortal local figure, evidently engaged in a playful masquerade and appealing to the visitors' predisposition to encounter what Georges Zimmermann has labelled "living monuments",[79] other figures also appear to be less fictional. The *Illustrated Handbook to Cork, the Lakes of Killarney and the South of Ireland* commended the famous Spillane brothers to readers, though it noted that their services had become increasingly difficult to obtain.[80] Another guide, "O'Connell", appeared to be an actual person—a famous, roguish local guide, profiled in an 1896 issue of the *Pall Mall Gazette*. The author described him affectionately as a loquacious fellow—a bachelor with such charm as to bring a smile and blush to the cheeks of every "barefooted girl he meets on the road".[81] O'Connell interlaced his commentary with tales of playing the coronet for "Prince 'Eddie'" (the Prince of Wales), as part of a "delightful patter" which the "dull party of day trippers" saw as "part of a programme to be gone through", including an account of a visitor to the Devil's Punch Bowl who dove into the water, and came out several weeks later in Australia. The author asserted the comparatively advanced cultural and social sensibility of the touring party by insisting that even an English tourist of low social station could detect the ruse. "A coach-builder from Clapham," the author wrote, "thinks this is only a part of the scheme of lies which has surrounded him since he entered Ireland."[82] In 1899 a writer in the *Killarney Echo* profiled "Jeremiah O'Connell". O'Connell had apparently been in the band of the "Royal Inniskelling Fusiliers [*sic*]" for eight years until leaving the army in 1892, and, while playing the cornet solo in the company of friends on the Lower Lake, was noticed by a representative of Thomas Cook's firm. He subsequently entered their employment for three years, before moving to the firm's chief competitor, "Messrs Gaze and Sons, Limited", in whose employ he appeared in a court-room in the case that opened this chapter.[83]

In the context of the rise of the carnivalesque narrative, though, and the putative collapse of Romantic travel codes, guides such as O'Connell could also offer excursionists valuable services. One writer recounted how, prior to setting out that day, travellers had been enjoined to take with them a "ragged retainer—called, by a fine stroke of Irish humour, 'The Captain'", to, their landlady had suggested, keep other guides at the Gap "'from botherin'".[84] Using *Shaw's* guide-book, the tourists had amused themselves by recounting the "stock stories before he had time to get them out", though he trumped them with a story they had not heard concerning the origins of the Black Lough.[85] The Captain also served a useful purpose by drinking poitín that the tourists were offered (indeed the Captain drank nearly a quart of the whiskey by the end of the day).[86] Full of incredible stories recounted in a rich Irish brogue, he reinforced popular images and prejudices surrounding the male Irish peasant: loquacious, prone to exaggeration, fond of the bottle, but also with more than a hint of Lear's Fool to his manner. Writers, meanwhile, described him with magniloquence, evaluated his many legends with playful scepticism, and embraced him as a welcome companion on the tour.

Not all writers caricatured the Killarney folk as either artful or entertaining. Some extolled their wit and charm, and enjoined tourists not only to lend them patronage as actors in the tourist economy, but to regard them as men, women, and children imbued with noble qualities of acumen and intelligence. Beatrice Grimshaw, for instance,[87] contended that the excursion to Dunloe "can be managed quite satisfactorily without a guide, cycling, riding, or driving—but the traveller should certainly engage one, if only for the reason that it makes the guide so exceedingly happy; and the conferring of perfect bliss on a fellow-creature is surely worth the minor sufferings inflicted by the constant companionship of a key-bugle".[88] Extolling his qualities, Grimshaw declared that "[t]here never was such a happy fellow as this our joyous guide. He is young, he is stalwart and ruddy, and his fair moustache curls upwards with an endless smile."[89] Comparing him with a "boy with a perennially insatiable appetite for sweets", Grimshaw offered no sceptical appraisals of his motivations, insisting that "his work is continual holidaying" and that "[t]he 500th tour over the Gap is the same breathless delight to him as the first," while also writing that her guide had pointedly told her that he had recently been to London. Without rendering his words as ungrammatical—indeed depicting him as a worldly and learned figure—Grimshaw's guide offered a contrast to the caricatural purveyor of tall tales found in other accounts of travel in Killarney.

In addition to the verbal conceit of embellished elocution, locals also offered tourists other exotic auditory treats as part of the Killarney tour. Bugling, for instance, brought forth the famous echoes of the district, and interlaced the landscape, local practitioners, and sound to produce a supposedly singular auditory experience. To some commentators the bugler was an indispensable companion on the Gap tour, though to others there was enough "enjoyment to be derived from good scenery without resorting to these artificial methods of enhancing it".[90] William H.A. Williams has explored the performance of the Killarney echo in the vein of the Romantic-era tour; later, the bugle was often drowned out by the cacophony associated with the Gap carnival.[91] Bugles supplied one instrument to enliven the sensorial appreciation of Killarney. In 1852 a correspondent to the *Manchester Guardian* rhapsodised about the sounds heard reverberating in the Gap, producing the signature "echoes of Killarney" which heightened the excursionist's appreciation of the landscape's majesty.[92] The correspondent wrote of hearing echoes produced by "four various means", all involving the efforts of locals. The skilled sound of the bugle, the cannon, the guide's cry, and the fiddle, all producing a majestic echo, contrasted with the disordered noise of the assembled throng of touts, guides, and vendors at the Gap in a number of ways. They were services performed for tourists' entertainment or pleasure, and at their behest. Moreover, writers often judged the results to be *musical* in quality, and products of native skill. They provided a narrative counterpoint to the raucous carnival of the Killarney tour, which overwhelmed the senses and became a much-lamented central auditory conceit of the Gap tour.

Writers found few occasions to praise the strains of the bugle and the lyrical echoes of Killarney as their accounts narrated a landscape teeming with raucous and rollicking figures, and legions of guileless tourists. In such narratives of travel, carnivalesque features of the new Gap tour involved the dissolution of Romantic spectatorship, and allied mental and emotional engagement, as writers found themselves immersed in the carnivalesque.[93] Indeed, this colourful human tapestry led the writer Burton E. Stevenson to assert that "[t]he accompaniments of the ride are more diverting than the ride itself."[94] Some writers rendered this new experience as otherworldly and sensuously overwhelming. Indeed, the author of an 1862 description of the Gap of Dunloe asserted that nowhere were the importunities of Killarney's ubiquitous beggars more "overpowering as on the road to the Gap of Dunloe".[95] In this respect it was a place where many insalubrious features of Killarney were on show, and where the commercialisation of the landscape for tourism reached its apotheosis in a kind of themed space—where the principal "sights" were the people themselves. As John F. Sears has argued in his study of nineteenth-century Niagara Falls, these performances produced a "unifying spectacle", encompassing diverse attractions in a single site of consumption, and thereby resembling the public museum, the exposition, and the resort.[96] Certainly, as Stevenson contended, the district had achieved an iconic status amongst the country's tourist destinations: "Now Killarney is to Ireland what the Trossachs are to Scotland and Niagara Falls to America—in other words, its most famous show-place."[97] At the same time, the markers of the district were transformed, as the romantic idiom within which many accounts of Kate Kearney's life were rendered was eclipsed by narratives of the tourist's encounters with Kate's descendant at the Gap of Dunloe in which her audacity and outrageous efforts at subterfuge were recounted in tones of ironic surprise. At her cottage, one visitor encountered this "granddaughter": "[T]he bright glances, so dangerous in the grandmother, are, however, moderated from the eyes of her descendant, whose appearance is far from attractive, and whose 'mountain dew' of goat's-milk and whisky, strongly impregnated with peat smoke, is as unpalatable a beverage as I ever had the misfortune to taste."[98] And Kate Kearney's alleged "granddaughter" supplied a figure for travellers, in language interlaced with humour and opprobrium, to combine spectatorship with participation in the carnival, and to provide a narrative which entertained readers but still articulated the authors' reluctance to submit to "native" regimes.

"TALL, BOLD, AND GREEDY, WITH THE GAIT OF A MOUNTAINEER": THE IMPOSTER AT THE GAP

Amongst a cavalcade of larger-than-life characters, Kate Kearney was the Gap's pre-eminent denizen. Women competed to claim her mantle and win the profitable attention of tourists—and none more confidently or (in) famously than her self-styled "granddaughter". Anna Maria and Samuel Carter Hall advised tourists that they would encounter her as soon as they arrived at the Gap. She was the hostess of Kate Kearney's Cottage and a descendant of Owenson's Kate:

> Something more than a line, however, seems to be demanded by Kate Kearney—a name famous in song. The tourist will pass the dwelling of the grand-daughter of that Kate Kearney, who—we care not to say how many years ago—inspired the muse of Miss Owenson—Sydney, Lady Morgan:—
> "Oh! did ye ne'er hear of Kate Kearney?
> She lives by the Lake of Killarney."
> The grand-daughter—herself the mamma of a fine family, Irish in number and in growth—is not unworthy the high fame of her grand-dame. She is what in Ireland is called a "fine fla-hu-lagh woman,"—meaning that she has "blood and bone," but as for the "beauty"—we shall not be ungallant enough to question her legitimate right. The Tourist will find cakes and goat's-milk at her cottage, which neatness and order might very much improve. The cottage is close to the entrance to the Gap of Dunloe, so that he will be sure to see her: for he may be quite certain that she will be at hand with her "offerings."[99]

As with so many other descriptions of her, the Halls' "granddaughter" was a projection of rural Irish femininity, constructed in part through an "Othering" gaze. The above quotation, from an 1865 publication, expounded on the Halls' discussion 24 years earlier, when their account of the Gap remarked only that it was famous as a "haunt" for the woman made famous by song, and also that:

> For a century at least, there has always been a "Kate," and no doubt will be to the end of time. A remarkably old woman, a few years ago, inhabited one of the cabins in the Gap; and when she had numbered five score and six, she received the honourable and not unproductive distinction; this however was not, we presume, the Kate of whom the Poet says "There's mischief in every dimple."[100]

The Halls lamented that they did not have occasion to meet "the present 'Kate Kearney'" who, they were told, was "'up de mountain wid de goats'", leaving them only to imagine her as "a fine, stout, healthy lass, a worthy descendant of the Milesian giant".[101] For those excursionists who met this wily pretender to Kate's charms, the sentimentalised figure of Killarney lore was embodied by a disjarringly different figure. Occasionally sensationalised accounts of meeting Kate's granddaughter mixed irony and abhorrence at her physical transgressions of the romantic ideal of the mountain enchantress. Many Gap excursionists were, at least, vaguely familiar with Owenson's poem, often through short excerpts printed in their guide-books,[102] and through allusions to Kate Kearney in well-known travel writings by authors such as the Halls, who delineated her customs in colourful prose.

Tourists encountered Kate in the Gap through a proxy—her "granddaughter". Writers' caustic appraisals of this woman's implausible claims of consanguinity conveyed their cultural and intellectual authority, and they evidently revelled in the occasion to appraise her in flamboyant prose. The German poet, traveller, and writer Julius Rodenberg offered an extensive description of an encounter in which he interlaced playful scepticism with commentary on its overtly theatrical features. Having encountered an "old witch", "Sally of Dunloe", Rodenberg found himself at the approach to the Gap, where he encountered a more pleasing specimen:

> A charming creature with a deliciously fresh face, blue eyes, light hair, and naked feet, was walking up and down; but in spite of the soft hue of her hair and eyes, there was something strange and wild in her whole appearance. She brought the drivers and donkey boys outside something to eat and drink, and then re-entered the cabin.
>
> Thady, after laughing, assumed a rather serious face, and imparted to me the fact that this pretty creature's name was Kate, and she was the granddaughter of that wondrously beautiful Kate Kearney, to whom the song referred, which I must know. A very great Irish lady, who had been here once on a visit, and drunk milk at Kate Kearney's, wrote the song; her name was Lady Morgan, and she had been living for many years in England, and was perhaps dead. Kate Kearney, the grandmother, had also been long dead, but the song still lived which told of her beauty, and was daily sung round the lakes, every child knowing it by heart.[103]

Rodenberg was then entertained by a fiddler, accompanied by the horse boys in song, before being left alone with Thady to enter the cabin. There, they partook of Kearney's libation, and made these evaluations of the young girl's claims to descend from Kate Kearney, in which their superior intelligence was conveyed through humorous appraisals of such preposterous claims:

The bare-footed maiden of Dunloe brought us a glass of milk, into which she poured a few drops of "mountain dew," gave the driver something to eat, and left me to my reflections. Either the song or nature was in the wrong, or the dark beauty of the grandmother must have been converted strangely in the granddaughter into blue and blonde. A powerfully-built man, with a strong beard, walked past me to the door, and a child of about five years of age, was crawling about the floor.

"Well, Kate," I said, "how old are you?"

"Fifteen, sir," Kate answered.

"And this child here?"

"Is my sister."

"And the man at the door ?"

"Is my brother."

If Thady the driver ever laughed in his life, he did so now, when Kate went off to meet a car just arriving.

"Eh," he said, and laughed so loudly, that the horse outside began whinnying, "so long as I have known Kate, and that is getting on for twelve years, she has always been fifteen. Eh, this Kate doesn't grow any older; and her husband has been her husband for these seven years, and her child is six—eh, eh, the Kate!"[104]

Rodenberg observed efforts by Kearney's putative descendants to parlay their incredible genealogy into a lucrative trade, and linked his encounter to a wider appraisal of Irish peasants' acts of plunder. These themes recurred frequently in narratives of the Gap tour, with travellers affecting displeasure at the peasants' temerity, and expressing humour at their brazen efforts to extract money from them. Locals reappropriated images of the rural Irish in popular culture and deployed them to profitable ends as they performed as caricatural figures, as well as famous literary characters—not just before German and British travellers, but also before legions of Irish and other excursionists for whom the Killarney tour was the premier Irish tourist route.

Kate Kearney's presence in the Gap engendered curiosity, and gave locals considerable scope for embellishment, either by proclaiming themselves to be direct descendants or by performing as a coquettish mountain hostess more loosely modelled on her. In performing as Kate, women reached back to a long lineage of romantic legend and articulated it within the idiom of commercial tourism. Claiming improbable descent from the apocryphal beauty—a figure partly modelled on Owenson herself, and inspired by local lore—the "granddaughter" offered the eponymous cottage as tangible evidence of this lineage,[105] calculating that it would resonate with the touring public. Nonetheless, her claims aroused strong scepticism and led to assessments of the Gap tour that often depicted her masquerade as an emblem of grubby commercialisation. To writers wishing to place themselves above the fray of guileless tourist masses, and also desiring to produce an entertaining account of travel, this woman's behaviour offered an opportunity to expound on the Irish predilection to exaggerate and flatter for the tour-ist's shilling. Charles Mackay, touring the district immediately following the Famine, wrote in the *Illustrated London News* in 1849 that, before approaching the cottage, a "granddaughter" had already pressed mountain dew upon the party. "The relationship," he commented wryly, "which, as our very accurate and conscientious guide informed us, is real, and not pre-tended, is anything but unprofitable to her." At Kate Kearney's Cottage the party found "some new claimants upon our loose change", before entering the Spartan abode, furnished only with two chairs, and decorated with a picture of Saint Patrick.[106] Kate Kearney's Cottage became a site where the assault on the tourists' purses began in earnest. And guide-books, such as *Murray's Handbook*, assessed the "granddaughter's" claims to lineal descent with marked scepticism:

> When fairly within the entrance, the car pulls up at (8 ½ m.) *Kate Kear-ney's Cottage*, where dwells the representative of the famous beauty who reigned here early in this cent., and dispensed mountain dew, or potheen, to the tourists. Her cottage disappeared long ago, but her name clings to the spot and has been adopted by her successors; the relationship of the present holder of it to her is doubtful. She offers hospitality, of which the tourist is expected to partake; being the first instalment of successive troops of attendant Hebes, who press their attentions on him, which tend to destroy the charm of the solitary grandeur of the gap by their ceaseless gabble and importunities.[107]

Even if they chafed at the authority that she exercised over the encounter, tourists were not unwitting participants in these meetings; if so, they had ignored cautionary remarks and sceptical evaluations of her "granddaugh-ter's" authenticity in innumerable guide-books and travelogues. In a mis-chievous tone, writers noted wryly that the "granddaughter" had succeeded in establishing a very profitable trade on the site of her putative forebear's abode. C.S. Ward, in the *Thorough Guide*, identified the "granddaugh-ter" as the wife of Daniel Moriarty, proprietor of Kate Kearney's Cottage, where, the author cautioned readers, "'milk and whiskey' troubles are in full force!"[108]

Kate Kearney. No one now (1888) living remembers to have seen this person, who is reputed to have been strikingly beautiful, to have sold potheen to tourists, and to have died about the beginning of the pres-ent century. Her house, levelled long ago, was near the slate house, "Kate Kearney's cottage," where Daniel Moriarty now holds a spirit license, &c., and Mrs. D.M. has adopted "Kate Kearney" as a kind of trade-mark. Sometimes it is given out that she is the original, some-times a daughter or near relative, but her maiden name was Burke, and the relationship needs proving. Mrs. M., who in her day was not a bad-looking woman (she is now well aged), sells her own photographs as Kate's.[109] **[Bolded as in original]**

Ward recounted this disguise and portrayed it as Moriarty's attempt to establish proprietorship over Kearney's "trade-mark", tapping growing post-Famine tourist interest in the site as she laid claim to be a descendant of the "real" Kate herself. Evidently, narratives of the frustrated search was grounded in irony, as much as the "granddaughter's" performance of lineal descent. Being married to the local publican, with his holdings profitably placed at the start of the conventional Gap tour, the Mrs Moriarty identified by Ward in 1888 was well placed to make her claim both to Kate's mantle, and to the pocket-change of tourists.

Rather than level accusations of outright deception, travel writers used novel literary conceits to articulate scepticism. One trope in post-Famine tourist narratives was the "granddaughter's" jarring embodied contrast with the romantic image of her forebear. It was incontrovertible evidence of her ruse, and offered a pretext for literary grandiloquence as travellers sought to re-establish practices and discourses of Romantic travel. In evaluating the "granddaughter's" claims, travel writers asked if she resembled the bewitching forebear of legend and lore, and, through these contrasts, portrayed her "granddaughter" as a repugnant hag. The embodied encounter between tourist and "granddaughter" offered occasion to ironically narrate surprise, disappointment, and suspicion at her mercenary motives, and to lament the eclipse of Romantic travel, with its repertoire of mental practices and emotional modes of engagement grounded in the individual, unmediated apprehension of scenery. If the legendary Kate Kearney was a siren, described by one guide-book as a beauty with Spanish blood coursing through her veins,[110] her "granddaughter" was a decidedly unattractive specimen of Irish womanhood. Indeed, the contrasts led to a common, categorical conclusion: that the "granddaughter" was a bold peddler of tall tales, proffering mountain dew of equally questionable authenticity.

The "granddaughter's" body was inscribed with increasingly virulent commentary as writers exhausted descriptors for her vile countenance, denouncing her ruse and implicitly condemning the desecration of Killarney. Moreover, in condemning the artificiality and flagrant deception which permeated the Killarney tour, writers adopted an exaggerated narrative voice. E.K. Washington, in his published memoir of travels to Europe from the USA, described her mountain dew as "perfectly execrable" and the woman as "an ugly old Irish witch-faced hag—notwithstanding her ancestor was remarkable for her beauty".[111] His invocation of the hag as a denizen of Dunloe reflected a trope through which the Gap was cast, like the body of the woman herself, as a locus of the grotesque and a site of carnival. A piece written for the *Ulster Times* by "J.K." described the author's encounter with her at the "Dunloe Hotel"—the same ironic name given to the hovel by Thomas Carlyle some years later.[112]

In a similar vein, the Canadian traveller Canniff Haight depicted Kate's "granddaughter" as a witch when recounting his visit to Kate Kearney's Cottage. The woman whom he encountered in the flesh was a disappointing contrast to the figure of his mind's-eye. Haight remarked that "[o]ur dreams of the beautiful Kate were of brief duration, for we had scarcely got abreast of the cottage when there streamed out of it a dozen or more squalid wretches, who gave chase with shouts and swooped down upon us like so many starved eagles."[113] Expanding the predatory metaphor, he described how, upon disembarking from his jaunting-car at the entrance to the Gap, the assembled beggars "huddled and howled like a pack of wolves round me".[114] Bewailing the futility of his efforts to out-ride the mob, and regarding both his pony and guide as accomplices in this act of outright ambush, Haight wrote of a "hungry pack" descending on him, "howling and shrieking after me".[115]

Not all writers reproduced this predatory metaphor, or invoked heavily gendered imagery of the witch, though most suggested that she was preying on excursionists to some extent, and in so doing represented her as a specimen of the troublesome Killarney beggar, especially the old crone, who featured prominently in travel writing. Travellers commented on the extent to which she hounded them until they reluctantly gave in to her demands for money. Others focussed on her grotesque body, and contrasted it with the famously comely mountain damsel. A piece in *The Scotsman* in 1871, for instance, recounted a meeting with Kate Kearney's "granddaughter", a woman who "has as much of 'Meg Merrilies' in her as we saw in Ireland", being "tall, bold, and greedy, with the gait of a mountaineer"; when the party was at a safe distance from her, they remarked that as she strode up to their car to welcome them to the Gap, they felt that her spell was "as likely to be that of a witch as of a fairy".[116] S. Reynolds Hole declared that she was no exemplar of the dictum: "*O matre pulchrâ Filia pulchrior!*"[117] In addition to reinforcing the guide-book identification of her as Mrs Moriarty, this caustic commentary was embedded within a comical narrative in which the author constituted himself as a sceptical outsider cognisant of the wily "granddaughter's" ruse. In *Harper's New Monthly Magazine*, the American writer Junius Henri Browne's disparaging remarks were also laced with humour. This constituted an assertion of his intelligence, erudition, and authority over the artful peasant:

> Near by [*sic*] is a solitary hostelry kept by a putative grand-daughter of the apocryphal Kate Kearney. Kate is reputed to have been extremely lovely; but if she were lovely, if she ever existed, and if the young woman I saw was her daughter's daughter, the young woman is a most striking illustration of the theory that beauty is not hereditary.[118]

The body of the "granddaughter" thus exposed the deception—and became the conceit through which, ultimately, the writer's authority over the audacious, rapacious woman was established through the printed word—with comical effect. The narrative focus on the physicality of the encounter between tourist and hostess, and her own features and bearing, underscored her importance in constituting the carnival theme. Not only did her countenance transgress the romantic images of Kate, but, in her vulgarity and extortion, she embodied a violation of ideals of feminine hospitality.[119] In this respect, narratives of encounters with Kate were expositions on gender, ruminations on the "granddaughter's" artful but unconvincing ruse, and grandiloquent expressions of authorial distance from her, the wider Gap carnival, and the culture of deception which it engendered.

Departing from this caustic and often ironic tone, some travel writers depicted the "granddaughter" as more pitiable than sinister. A writer in *Eliza Cook's Journal* offered this evocative description of Kate, whose plight reflected lamentable *conditions* in rural Ireland:

> Near the entrance to the Gap, is the house of the famous "Kate Kearney," whose descendant still occupies the premises, now a shebeen, or public-house. A black-faced, black-haired, and black-eyed girl, was holding up the door-cheek as we drove up. "Surely that can't be the darling Kate," said my uncle. "No, your honour, that's Kate's grand-daughter!" said the driver. Certainly, the beauty seemed not to have descended in a right line. Kate's daughter, the mother of the black girl, approached the car with the favourite beverage of "mountain dew,"—whiskey and goat's-milk. She was a stalwart, dark-eyed woman,—strong-boned,—somewhat of a gipsy in the cast of her features, and she may have been beautiful in her youth,—for they say that, like the women of many southern countries, Celtic beauty does not last so well as Saxon. But in Ireland, the poor feeding and the horrible discomfort in which the peasantry live, may account for the rapid falling off in the looks of the women, after they have passed the age of twenty or twenty-five.[120]

Such sympathetic renderings of the "granddaughter" were few. Most writers portrayed her impersonation as tiresome. Hinting at how the carnivalesque atmosphere was making the Gap a place of prurient pilgrimage, a correspondent of the *Freeman's Journal* offered this withering appraisal of Kate in his account of a visit to Killarney by members of the British Medical Association: "Why should not the nation pension off 'Kate Kearney'? I am afraid the poor old girl's wrinkled face and bad whiskey and dirty cabin are no helps to the romance of the place."[121] Most other appraisals openly scoffed at her purported lineage. Writers described surprise, even astonishment, accompanied by disappointment, in acerbic tones as they distanced themselves from the Irish "Other", as well as from any tourists who might fall for the woman's ruse. After all, they had no difficulty in detecting the deceptions of the woman whom one writer dismissed as "an old fraud impudently calling herself 'Kate Kearney'".[122]

THE "ROADSIDE *POSADA*": THE COTTAGE IN THE LANDSCAPE

If the body of Kate's "granddaughter" offered a focus for grandiloquent narration, her dwelling—styled Kate Kearney's Cottage—was ambiguously positioned in narratives of the Irish landscape and its inhabitants. The geography of the built landscape was mapped out in travel accounts which described not only half-ruins such as Muckross Abbey, but also a number of bucolic cottages which were associated with the landscapes of the picturesque, and, by extension, the genteel hospitality of the Romantic-era tour. Travel writing charted paths that encompassed Lady Kenmare's Cottage (also known as Glena Cottage), where Victoria had enjoyed her grand repast, and Dinis (or "Dinish") Cottage, which also served as a refreshment stop.[123] They supplied a focus for idylls that extolled the district's picturesque charms.[124] These pretty, thatched buildings were popularised in watercolour and in print, and became architectural expressions of aristocratic patronage. Depictions of them as elements of an "improved landscape" featured in pre-Famine rustic painting—which was revived as part of a set of wider political discourses in the early-twentieth century—as a vernacular building in which potent constructions of the family, industry, and Irish rurality were sited.[125] The most famous local cottage attracted a far more ambivalent response than either the pretty refreshment stops or the peasant cottages of the West that were implanted in the imaginary as icons of rural culture and society. Kate Kearney's Cottage was located at the approach to the Gap of Dunloe, on the left of the River Loe, which issued from the Gap. It was situated on the site where the original Kate Kearney's modest hut was said to have once stood, and on land owned by a relatively small Mahony estate. While the pre-eminent Scottish writer Thomas Carlyle had deplored the squalid state of the hovel where he had imbibed a "greasy abomination",[126] travel writers in the second-half of the nineteenth century offered diverse appraisals of the site. Some seemed to suggest that perhaps more than one cottage may have laid claim to the name. In 1851, one author wrote: "We peeped into Kate Kearney's cottage. Its floor was of clay, its walls were bare, and its furnishing of the scantiest. But it was of stone, so that it was far above the average of Irish peasants' houses. Pigs roamed about the doors, and hens chuckled amongst the rafters overhead, so that doubtless this descendant of Kate is a thriving woman, doing well in the world."[127] The remarkably different assessments offered in these two accounts (Carlyle's written only two years before the other), may be explained by the apparent recent construction of the cottage: in 1859, the *Illustrated Handbook to Cork, the Lakes of Killarney and the South of Ireland* described it as "a roadside *posada*" that has "recently been erected",[128] suggesting a different building from the dingy hovel which Thomas Carlyle had visited in the previous decade. In 1841, Samuel Carter and Maria Hall had remarked on two cottages mid-way through the Gap—one of which evoked foreign places: "a sort of hostelrie [*sic*], that reminded us of the little foreign mountain inns. A long narrow room neatly white-washed, and adorned with a few prints, shelters a very clean deal table, upon which whiskey, goat's-milk, and brown bread, is placed for the refreshment of travellers who choose to partake thereof."[129] Beyond it they discovered the home of the hostelry's proprietors, which was a "wretched dwelling" where "the woman" was making a linen shirt for her husband, and they found the piggins for milk "exquisitely clean".[130] The contrast between the clean building catering to the tourist and the dingy native abode was gradually effaced in tourist accounts, so that by the 1860s the pretensions of "Kate Kearney's Cottage" to be both the ancestral dwelling-place of Kate herself and an expansive refreshment stop were conflated in the tourist imagination. Indeed, by the end of the nineteenth century, the cottage was a bustling commercial centre, where tourists hired ponies, imbibed whiskey, purchased umbrellas and arbutus souvenirs, and memorialised their presence by having their photographs taken with a woman who passed herself off as the real Kate or her granddaughter.[131]

In its transformation from signifier of rural privation to a celebrated site of production and sociality, the iconic building was appropriated by more than its eponymous landlady to serve as a showcase for Irish hospitality. It was also elevated as a national dwelling-place. In May 1893, ahead of the World's Columbian Exposition in Chicago, the countess of Aberdeen, an ardent promoter of Irish industries and the wife of the former (and future) Lord Lieutenant of Ireland, explicitly cited it as the model for a building which lay at the heart of the "great attraction" of the "Irish Village" she was organising as part of Ireland's presence there: a dairy, complete with milkmaids and Kerry cows.[132] It stood at the centre of a romanticised, bucolic site where work and hospitality were also heavily feminised, and where the village and the nation were intertwined in an idealised narrative of rurality. A writer in the *Clare Journal* praised the Village, a place peopled by young women, some in cottages displaying the arts of textile production, and others at the dairy, where "three lusty, rosy-cheeked, handsome girls are churning milk into butter, so sweet and delicious that one's mouth fairly waters for it, and selling buttermilk that tastes like nectar."[133] Here the cottage was implicated in the commodification of an idealised rural landscape, and was used to market the manufactures that Aberdeen tirelessly promoted as emblems of Ireland's distinctive path towards industrialisation.[134] The parade of cheery milkmaids who attended Aberdeen's Village display attested to an idealised and heavily gendered representation of peasant work, space, and hospitality. It was an ideologically freighted performance of domesticity and nationality. The popular construction of Kate Kearney's Cottage became an exercise in which specific, putatively national qualities were inscribed in her abode.[135] As for the building many thousands of miles away which purported to serve as Lady Aberdeen's inspiration, Thomas Carlyle's commentary sometimes echoed in later assessments of the cottage—in his 1899 travelogue, for instance, the American traveller

Charles M. Taylor described Kate Kearney's Cottage as a place "so dirty, and the handmaids in charge so untidy" that his party did not avail itself of the proffered goat's-milk.[136] But it was more firmly established in popular imagination as a centre of travel performances by native and guest—in a district whose bucolic features were diluted by grubby commercialisation, and by the grotesque bearing and temerity of the cottage's hostess.

As we have seen, the artful ways in which local actors joined Kate's "granddaughter" in extracting the pocket-change of travellers at the cottage and beyond was a prominent theme in travel narratives. The tourist's arrival at Kate Kearney's Cottage heralded a particular intensification of such efforts. Many writers bemoaned the collusion of locals who shepherded tourists there—and despoiled the sublime landscape. The Canadian traveller Canniff Haight, styling himself a descendant of loyalist stock on a tour of his "home land",[137] contended that his driver mischievously reversed his jaunting-car at Kate Kearney's Cottage, against Haight's expressed wishes, as an assembled throng swooped down on him.[138] "The rascal Jerry," Haight wrote, "was no doubt in league with the crew, for although we ordered him repeatedly to drive on faster, he professed that something was wrong with his horse, and he 'wouldn't budge aff a walk.'"[139] In his *Three Weeks in the British Isles*, which recounted his rapid tour (at least one reviewer claimed that an account of earlier peregrinations in Europe had occasionally been marred by hasty observations[140]), John U. Higinbotham commented that his touring party alighted there in drenching rain, and waited half-an-hour before setting out on horseback in lighter rain. Of the cottage, he wrote that although it is "always referred to impressively", it was "simply a roadside souvenir store and bar-room combined".[141] He went on to echo the remarks of others who stopped there, and who observed a tacit collusion amongst locals:

> Just why the excursion is broken at Kate Kearney's cottage is not apparent, unless, like the benevolent cannibal and the missionary, the idea is to make the tourist reach as many natives as possible. It would perhaps be more exact to say: Let as many natives as possible reach the tourist.[142]

Indeed, of all the key stages of the Killarney tour, the Gap of Dunloe was narrated as the apotheosis of this disorderly and disgraceful behaviour—a marker of local actors' collective control over the tourist encounter. The cottage marked the entrance to a raucous realm. It was a site of loud, competing, and audacious bids for custom that were underpinned by a nuanced choreography. One tourist, writing in *The Scotsman*, declared the Gap to be the "'noisiest place I ever was in in my life'".[143] Its custodian had privileged access to excursionists, her cottage serving as a gateway to a world of distinctive sounds, sights, tastes, and social relations which produced jarring contrasts with the buxom milkmaids and bucolic images of Aberdeen's Irish Village.

The anthropology of tourism offers insight into how Kate Kearney's Cottage was endowed with symbolic importance through repeated performances of social and commercial exchange on the tourist route. Killarney was not a devotional site, unlike wells and "holy" places which attracted pilgrims in Ireland—even if those wells were closely watched by locals keen to loosen the pilgrim's purse. If the wider literature on pilgrimage is criticised for being "place-based", at the expense of themes of mobility and motion,[144] adapting the idea of tourism as a secular pilgrimage to explore the cottage as a "transition" point in the Killarney tour illuminates intersections of mobility and sociality in producing peculiar tourist sensibilities, routes, and places. The extensive literature on the "secular pilgrimage" is useful here,[145] even if debates persist over the distinctions between the modern pilgrim and the tourist, and phenomenological differences between the two categories.[146] Victor Turner and Edith L.B. Turner's model of the ritual process begins with an initial "separation" from routines of everyday life;[147] a subsequent entrance into a state of "liminality" in which the structures of the everyday are suspended, challenged, or even inverted; a state of "communitas" in which new relationships are forged, premised on a common identity developed outside the structures of everyday life; and then a return to that everyday condition. Specific points along this pathway are collectively understood to demarcate the beginning and end of new codes of social conduct, new forms of bodily engagement with space, new sensibilities, and new forms of commercial and cultural exchange. It is instructive, in adopting this lens, to recall Thomas W. Silloway and Lee L. Powers's reluctant submission to the "granddaughter's" insistence that they imbibe her horrid concoction—transgressing their professed "abstinence" principles.

In popular imagination, the cottage was the point at which the Gap tour began—and particularly where excursionists submitted to regimes of indigenous mobility and sociality. Over generations, Kate Kearney's "granddaughter" greeted touring parties as they arrived at the Gap. Tellingly, a writer in the *Manchester Guardian* in 1852 described her cottage as a "sort of poetic toll-bar, where tourists usually stop a few moments to pay their homage to the 'genius loci' in the shape of the veritable granddaughter of the Kate immortalised by Miss Owenson (Lady Morgan)".[148] Beyond the cottage, amid the cacophonous clamour of Killarney's guides, ponymen, and trinket-vendors, some writers narrated a repudiation of the beaten path, local hangers-on, and guileless tourists by employing the conceits of pedestrianism and "flight" from the hordes.

"THE SOLITARY PEDESTRIAN STILL THINKS HE HAD THE BEST OF IT": MOVING THROUGH THE GAP

How were writers to escape this commotion, and simultaneously narrate their authority as arbiters of tasteful travel? To writers anxious to stake

such credentials, position themselves beyond both the grasps of predatory locals and the company of Cook's excursionists, narrative strategies
involved corporeal disengagement—signalled by an embrace of pedestrianism. Gender inflected performances of the tour and contours of social
interactions with Killarney's natives. Guides, for instance, were described
as eager to convince male travellers of the necessity of procuring the services of "'a pony for the lady, yer honour'".[149] In contrast, walking, rather
than riding, through the Gap was performed as an especially manly means
of apprehending scenery, as well as a way of undermining the conventions
and codes associated with immersion in its carnival atmosphere. Dispens-
ing with guides allowed some travellers to align themselves with precepts of
Romantic travel.[150] This was partly achieved through travellers physically
separating themselves from the crowds of jostling excursionists—veering
away from the bridle-path and the strictures of collective choreography, as
they attempted to uncouple themselves from both fellow excursionists and
locals.[151] James N. Matthews, in a travelogue that comprised in good part
a series of editorial correspondence to the *Buffalo Commercial Advertiser*,
narrated the effort of one tourist to detach himself from the crowd and
apprehend the scenery as a "solitary pedestrian":

> Such a crowd of urgent half-beggars gathered about us at this point, all
> insisting upon our buying something—lace, bog-wood ornaments, or
> other trumpery—that we were glad to break away and mount horses for
> the passage through the Gap, as the carriage could proceed no further.
> All did mount horses, I say, but one dismounted again, very quickly, for
> he soon discovered that he could not ride a horse with ease or safety. It
> was quite a little cavalcade that rode gaily through the Gap of Dunloe
> that morning, but the solitary pedestrian still thinks he had the best of
> it, for his were much the best opportunities to note the singular scenery
> of that four miles of narrow mountain defile.[152]

Similarly, pedestrianism was described in ways that stressed the *type* of
pedestrian activity and practices associated with it—notably conveying
its degree of purposefulness, and its improvisational qualities. Narratives invoked "rambling", "tramping", and "walking" to denote distinctive ways of engaging the landscape on foot, implying independence from
the beaten track. It often conveyed a less deliberate, more leisurely and
meandering movement that afforded observations of, and participation
in, Irish culture—and contrasted with mass movement by rail and coach,
and "shepherding" by guides along well-established routes. In this respect,
pedestrianism encoded the Romantic desire to apprehend the scenery in
privileged solitude, while telegraphing social distance from participants
in the Gap hurly-burly.[153] Yet a humorous trope in such narratives was
the inevitable failure of such efforts as scrambling pedestrians fell into the
clutches of Gap natives who overtook them in hot pursuit of lucre.

CONCLUSION

Few writers claimed success in recovering a landscape unmediated by guides and unadulterated by tourist hordes. At the Gap of Dunloe, the Killarney tour dissolved into the Bakhtinian carnivalesque: a place of openly transgressive behaviour where the potential existed for boundaries to be withdrawn and social hierarchies subverted.[154] While many writers affected outright disdain for the antics of locals, others related with comical exaggeration, and with humour, how boisterous crowds of locals intermingled with legions of excursionists, with cannon fire and bugles echoing through the valley, and how mountain damsels pressed their attentions on male tourists, who meekly protested as nubile peasants coaxed them to imbibe their mountain dew. A detailed description of a Gap tour penned by Westoth Ide in *London Society* asserted that the throngs of people who pressed their attentions upon excursionists despoiled the solitary grandeur of the Gap. Ide despaired of assaults on the tourist's pocket-book in an account of how sublime solitude had yielded to the thunderous hoofs of ponies and the loud cries of beggars:

> The view before us was totally unlike anything we had seen. Instead of the bright, green foliage, the mountains rose grand and rugged, with their bare outlines clearly defined against the cloudless sky. There was no sign of vegetation not yet of human habitation, but a solemn stillness reigned, and instinctively we felt that we were in the very presence of nature's God . . .
>
> Surely no sermon uttered nor line penned could impress one with the power and majesty of a Creator as did this awe-inspiring sight. And then, like the noise of distant thunder, came echoes resounding through the hills, and from peak to peak we heard the sound of a far-away bugle. At that moment the feeling uppermost in one's heart was an intense desire to be alone—to stand in the midst of the awful stillness and imagine we really were far from the haunts of men, but one of those interruptions which come so often in life, and by their suddenness tend to mar our plans, was upon us. Instantly we were in the midst of a group of girls who, with their bare feet, pretty smiling faces and unique costumes, were forcing upon us goats' milk. We were told to expect the "black army regiment," but these bright faces and picturesque costumes seemed to have nothing of darkness about them, as with their pretty Irish brogue they told us of their home in the valley where food and work was scarce and then spoke with pleasure of going to America, where they heard both were to be had in abundance. It has been said that all the Irish have at some time or other kissed the "Blarney Stone."[155]

By the mid-Victorian period, this cast of Killarney characters was so firmly implanted in the tourist imagination, and their behaviour so vividly foreshadowed by guide-books and travelogues, that no tourist could plausibly claim to be unprepared for their performances and exactions. Few tourists arrived without the requisite pocket-change or, implicitly, without an understanding that any pretence to solitary travel was a charade. While the West was cast as the home of the undiluted, autarkic Gael, Killarney served as its foil: a centre of popular, polluting, populist tourism where peasant culture yielded to extensive commercialisation, and where hopes of encountering an unspoilt culture amid the mountain fastnesses and glistening lakes offered a foil for the comic rendering of the carnivalesque. It was a place where travellers professing bewilderment with pervasive deceptions on one hand, and on the other hand, loquacious locals and the mysterious matriarch of the Gap, were both spinning tales as tall as Mangerton Mountain.

Plates

Plate 1   Gap of Dunloe tourists on ponies. National Library of Ireland STP 1328. Courtesy of the National Library of Ireland.

Plate 2   Postcard image of Kate Kearney, stamped 1904.

Plate 3   Mountain dew girls.
Source: Lucy Langdon Williams and Emma V. McLoughlin, A Too Short Vacation (Philadelphia: J.B. Lippincott Company, 1892): 35.

Plate 4   Pony-boy and tourist at Killarney.
Source: "The Victim" [pseud.], "Killarney's Lakes and Dells", The Idler Magazine. An Illustrated Monthly, 6 (August 1894 to January 1895): 25.

Plate 5 Mountain dew girls.
Source: "The Victim" [pseud.], "Killarney's Lakes and Dells", The Idler Magazine. An Illustrated Monthly, 6 (August 1894 to January 1895): 26.

Plate 6 Barrister on horseback with mountain dew girl.
Source: "The Victim" [pseud.], "Killarney's Lakes and Dells", The Idler Magazine. An Illustrated Monthly, 6 (August 1894 to January 1895): 27.

Plate 7   Mary Hartnett.

Plate 8   Bridge Sweeney.

Plate 9   Mary Sullivan.

Plate 10   Joanna Keefe.

Plates 7–13 Gap of Dunloe, Full-length Portraits of Mary Hartnett, Bridge Sweeney, Mary Sullivan, Joanna Keefe, Mary O'Grady, Norah O'Connell, Mary Burke (Formerly numbered as 1, 3, 5, 6, 8, 9, 10 in a series entitled Gap Girls), Killarney, Kerry, n.d. c. 1860–1870.

National Library of Ireland, STP 2851, 2852, 2853, 2854, 2855, 2856, 2857. Courtesy of the National Library of Ireland.

Plate 11 Mary O'Grady.

Plate 12 Norah O'Connell.

Plate 13 Mary Burke.

Plate 14 A Mountain Dew Girl: Killarney.
Photograph by Henry Peach Robinson © National Media Museum / Science & Society Picture Library.

Plate 15 A Mountain Dew Girl, from the Gap of Dunloe, Killarney, Ireland.
Photograph by Henry Peach Robinson. *Source:* H.P. Robinson, The Elements of a Pictorial Photograph (Bradford & London: Percy Lund & Co, 1896), p. 99.

4 Hospitality, Charity, Carnival, and Courtship

Writing in the *Western Mail* in 1899 under a *nom-de-plume*, "Idris" extolled the Killarney's mountain dew girl's charms, which even her ragged clothes could not disguise:

> As I write these words the vision rises before me of a bonny girl near the Gap of Dunloe. Poor lass, her clothes were scanty, her head and feet were bare. But she had a face of beauty of which a titled dame might well have envied, and her manners had a simple grace that was exquisite. True, the poor girl was selling a "dhrop" of "potheen"—contraband it must be confessed; but if she resembled the vast proportion of her sisters she was pure and sweet as the air round her mountain cot, and to pity her seemed almost an impertinence.'[1]

If irony pervaded many light-hearted renderings of the leisure tour of Killarney, and of purportedly unanticipated encounters with loquacious jarvies, feisty hucksters, and Kate Kearney's indomitable "granddaughter", a trip to Ireland's tourist Mecca also produced ambivalent assessments of tourism. Some disavowed ludic motivations and found in this rural realm, however marred by the ravages of tourism, hints of dignity. Many also detected the polluting influence, however inadvertent, of tourism. While codes and conventions of the Killarney were now entrenched firmly within the carnivalesque, "Idris's" image of a noble, benighted figure suggests how, to some writers, the Killarney mountains supplied a backdrop to narrate, in print, photography, and painting, the position of rural women. Could they still embody the purity of Irish culture—of the Irish race, and family, in contradistinction to the ribald woman at Kate Kearney's Cottage? In Killarney, this question centred on one figure—the mountain dew girl—and writers, photographers, and postcard picture painters answered it in varied and ambiguous ways.

In contrast with professions of disbelief and disdain that greeted the district's most famous daughter, some writers reached for the vocabulary of the picturesque as they recounted the persistence of the Killarney peasantry. As famine stalked the land, Sybil Sylvester offered this evocative description of Irish rural life in a piece published in 1846:

The Irish people can only be appreciated at home, amid the mountain fastnesses of their own poetic country; where the quiet lake and the gushing rock-fountain sparkle in the sunbeam; where the shady dell and flower-scented solitude are eloquent of the true fairy-land; where the hills, in whose purple sides the eagles have built their nests for centuries, pillow their heads in golden light; or don their coronet of clouds; where every stone, every path, every desolate ruin, is haunted with some old legend of the glorious past. These are the spots upon which to study the Irish character and admire the romance, the life, the generous freshness of thought, and the striking heart-warmth of a people that suffering does not seem to dispirit, penury render selfish; nor privation rob of some of the noblest traits of our common nature.[2]

Not all writers echoed Sylvester's language extolling this enchanted "fairy land", but many enjoined travellers to venture forth to Killarney. Even in this hive of tourist activity, they insisted that there was much of old Ireland to be found. Especially for travellers eschewing the recreational mode of travel and disavowing ludic motivations, the seriously minded, quasi-investigative idiom offered an elegant way to interlace patriotic and philanthropic duty, and also to narrate the cultural landscape in sentimental, often elegiac, tones. In fact, the epistemological exercise of "understanding" the condition of Ireland forswore recreational motivation and was bound with a documentary mode of travel writing—one that often evoked contemporary narratives of social investigation of life on the "margins" of industrial Britain. Accounts of meeting comely pretenders to Kate's mantle became expositions on rural femininity, tourism, and rural culture as travellers adopted a variety of positions: that of the social investigator, portraying the mountain dew girl in a tragic mode; and that of the playful excursionist, fleetingly engaging the youthful seductress in encounters freighted with mildly erotic associations.[3]

"PURE AND SWEET AS THE AIR ROUND THE MOUNTAIN COT"? POVERTY, TOURISM, AND NARRATIVES OF THE MOUNTAIN DEW GIRL

To many recreational excursionists, encounters with Irish female peasants turned playfully and ironically on the offer of authentic native hospitality in ways that recollect performances at Kate Kearney's Cottage. They offered extensive scope to narrate relations of social and cultural authority in photography and in print. Passing into the Gap of Dunloe offered visitors an intensified sense of the unfamiliar—and sometimes a heightened sense of playfulness, where the pretext of entering a peasant realm was licence for fleeting transgressions of taste and respectability. They ranged from the willing exchange of money for a supposedly illicit drink to flirtatious

banter between male tourists and the mountain belles. Mountain dew vendors were not exclusive to Killarney—in Connemara, at the Giant's Causeway, and in Glendalough, Co. Wicklow, travellers encountered "colleens"
who made claims on their change in exchange for the famous concoction.[4]
But at Killarney the cast of characters was especially famous and the tourism scripts long established. Still, not all local figures were appraised in the
same vein. A formidable woman exacted compensation at Kate Kearney's
Cottage. In contrast, writers portrayed the mountain dew girls as coquettish, even cloying figures who cleverly tricked them out of change. Their
designs were enabled by the topography of the district: travellers claimed
that they had been "penned in" by the rocky defile, with no prospect for
escape, while their "assailants" pounced out from behind rocks. The inevitable encounter with them involved heavy bartering. One correspondent
to *The Scotsman* recounted how poitín sellers approached his party while
on a tour of Killarney. They took a drink from the girls and were told it
would cost 4s. The girls, after voluble protest, settled for half that amount.[5]
Mountain dew girls often leavened the transaction with flirtatious banter
delivered in heavy Irish brogue, in exchanges that won both praise and
withering comment. In fact, writers were as varied in their assessments of
the taste of the famous mountain dew as they were of the wider encounter.
An 1859 guide-book pronounced that "however disinclined we may be for
this inspiring beverage on the outset of the journey, after riding through
the Pass for a few miles we become not insensible to its merits".[6] Another
guide-book published in 1846 described Killarney "girls and boys carrying
goats' milk and poteen, a horrid mixture; which, if you wish to be well for
the rest of the day, you will not touch".[7] As for its vendors, a writer in the
Dublin University Magazine suggested that the girls were merely mendicants, not unlike the other locals who hounded tourists in the district:

> We had gathered by the way, in this desolate region, as many com-
> panions as a recruiting-sergeant on a market day; for, to the standing
> reproach of this region, idlers abound. There is some pretence of traf-
> fic, it is true, with many, like the eternal sawdust pincushions, luci-
> fer matches, tagged laces, and Turkey rhubarb of Cheapside; for they
> offer you milk, whisky, and later on in the season sundry wild berries,
> besides their services as guides; but disguised mendicancy is the main
> reliance of most.[8]

Many observers lamented such deplorable outgrowths of mass tourism and
also believed that a "pretence of traffic" only thinly disguised beggary. At
the core of their appraisals were pessimistic views on the relationship of
modern tourism to rural society. They echoed in fin-de-siècle debates over
tourism, purity, and pollution in the era of the Celtic Twilight that preoccu-
pied R.A.S. Macalister: was tourism an agent of the preservation or debase-
ment of peasant culture? In contrast to Kate Kearney's "granddaughter",

mountain dew girls attracted as much sympathy as scorn. Writing in 1899 in the periodical *Wings* (successor to *The British Women's Temperance Journal*), for instance, Helen L.S. Roberts bemoaned the lamentable consequence of tourism:

> The guide books warn one against drinking from those bottles which the sweet-faced girls have no license to sell from. It seems such a pity, such a terrible, crying pity, that it is *worth while* for those girls to waste hours that might be filled with useful, renumerative [*sic*] work, in this illegal trade. Who is to blame? It seems as if everybody is, more or less, in fault. The tourist first of all who creates the demand, the girl who stoops illegally to sell it, the policeman who sits on a rock round the corner, and has a fine eye for a distant landscape, and is as oblivious to mundane affairs as "that good saint." [*sic*] young Saint Kevin, who "little knew, what that wily sex could do." All are to blame, and all need much inward enlightenment.[9]

To Roberts, tourism impelled the mountain dew girl to lose her pure, feminine innocence. Her labour bore no resemblance to "honest work" in fields, with family and above all in that pre-eminently feminine rural domestic space: the cottage. If the comedic tone of the travelogue provided amusement for readers of proliferating fire-side weeklies and monthlies, Christian periodicals provided a forum for travel writers to expound on this analysis of the mountain dew girls' condition. A writer in *The Baptist Magazine* in 1872 expressed a familiar mixture of pity and denigration with which many self-identified Protestants came to view locals' superstition and beggary:

> As an example of the ignorance which abounds in these beautiful regions, I may mention that one day, just after we had left a mountain-pass in the south, a girl, apparently twelve or thirteen years old, came out of a wretched cabin, holding in each hand a bottle, which contained mountain-dew and goat's milk. From answers which she gave to our questions, we found that she had never been at school, knew not a letter in the alphabet, could not tell who was the Saviour of men, nor the names of the first man and woman. Mr. N. ____ repeated the hymn beginning, "Jesus who lived above the sky," and asked her to say it after him, which she did; but her young heart coveted money rather than instruction. Like the daughters of the horseleech, her cry was, "Give, give!" She wanted £4 of the £8 which was required to take her to America; would the gentlemen give her a trifle, or buy her mountain-dew? "And what is mountain-dew?"—"It's the rale poteen." "Who makes it?"—"Kate Kearney, yer honour." Kate Kearney is one of those weird, half real, half mythical characters, around whose name has gathered much that is romantic. If such a person ever lived, it is certain that she never dies. In the legends of that region she is the chief

figure. A white hut in a deep glen is pointed out as Kate's cottage. Her voice yet wakes the mountain echoes, and her apparition glides along the pass in the clear still moonlight.[10]

Concerns over the ignorant and impoverished condition of rural children exercised female evangelicals in particular, for whom mountain dew girls embodied a rural version of the urban street "Arabs". These street children, cast as industrialism's under-class, became a focus for energetic voluntary action in the Victorian period. Assessments of the rural mountain dew girls' conditions evoked similar sentiments and were coupled to remarkably ambivalent evaluations of mass tourism and its impact on rural society, especially through tourists' promiscuous and indiscriminate (if well-intentioned) alms-giving. It perpetuated dependency, discouraged emigration, and made the mountain dew girl an ephemeral (and unvirtuous) bride of the tourist, rather than a model of rural domesticity.

As much as the mountain dew girl was grounded in the landscape of Killarney, counterparts abounded elsewhere, and attracted similar, ambivalent responses: but at Killarney, where the tourism sector was so developed, they attracted especially extensive commentary. Describing Killarney, the Canadian traveller Margaret Dixon McDougall, a woman of Irish Protestant stock writing as "Norah" in the *Montreal Witness*, mixed exasperation with the importunities of the buglers, hawkers, and guides, with pity for the precariousness of their position:

> One impudent woman followed us for quite a way to sell us her photograph, as the photograph of Eily O'Connor, murdered here by her lover many years ago—murdered not at the gap but in the lake. There was a large party of us and these followers, horse, foot and artillery, I may say were a persistent nuisance all the way. The ponies, crowds of them, followed us to the entrance of the Gap, where they disappeared, but the women and girls never faltered for the five miles. The reiterated and re-reiterated offer of goat's milk and poteen became exasperating; the bodyguard of these pertinacious women that could not be shaken off was most annoying. The tourists are to the inhabitants of Killarney what a wreck used to be to the coast people of Cornwall, a God-send.[11]

In exploring McDougall's travel writings, the historian Cecilia Morgan has shown that, far from reiterating social commentaries that cast the Catholic Irish as degenerate, McDougall developed a highly nuanced appraisal of rural social conditions, especially relating to the land question, in Ireland.[12] Perhaps ironically, many of McDougall's most frustrated appraisals of the Irish people were reserved for those in the service of the tourist at Killarney—reflecting the extent to which she shared the view that the commercial tourism somehow generated, or at least amplified, deeper social and cultural problems in Ireland.

How might this "problem" of rampant and ill-disguised beggary be resolved? One answer was to be found in restraint and good judgement—on the tourists' part. Commentators, professing wisdom and philanthropic motivations, counselled well-intentioned tourists not to part with their pocket-change. Such generosity cultivated a culture of dependence. [13] In comparison with the universally negative or at most playfully exasperated appraisal of Kate's "granddaughter", mountain dew girls engendered much more ambivalent assessments. Their pursuit of a sixpence or shilling, for instance, presented acute moral dangers to the women themselves: one author lamented that "so many promising young persons should be compelled to earn a trifle in so precarious a manner, and one so unsuited to their sex".[14] By framing this tourist exchange as active in creating the Gap of Dunloe and other areas as polluted and sexualised space, writers implicitly distanced their own travel practices from those of mass tourism. They depicted these women as emblems of the ravages of tourism, their hucksterism a sad contrast to the purer domestic roles of mother and bride. If the eminent British author Dinah Maria Mulock Craik was sceptical of the girls' professed poverty, she critiqued their estrangement from regimes of respectable domesticity, to which she also exhorted them to return:

> An intelligent American at the *table d'hôte*—many Americans take Killarney *en route* from Queenstown—warned us of the nuisance of beggars. And, sure enough, as soon as we reached Kate Kearney's cottage—that lovely young woman "who lived by the banks of Killarney" has much to answer for!—they bore down upon us in shoals, offering stockings, milk, "potheen," and then entreating shillings and sixpences with the most shameless persistency; for they were not ragged beggars, but very respectably clad. It was easy to believe the American's story, that yesterday, when he said he had not got a sixpence, they offered to change his half-sovereign!
>
> Determined to be rid of them, I tried first moral suasion, which signally failed, then a volley of rapid French, which so amazed them that they retired for the moment; then to a woman, who had run after the ponies for about half a mile, an indignant reproach, "I am Irish, and you make me ashamed of my country. What would my husband say to me if I went gadding about like this, instead of doing my work indoors? Go home, and do *your* work."[15]

To Craik, tourism deflected these women from domestic duties, and inculcated artfulfulness. Indeed, like Kate Kearney's "granddaughter" and age-defying Killarney guides, the troupe of mountain damsels sometimes openly masqueraded as Eily O'Connor, the long-dead "Colleen Bawn".[16] With these practices in mind, some writers saw the charade not as an amusement, or even a mere irritant, but an audacious act of duplicity.

Casting a wide rhetorical net over Ireland peasantry, Margaret Tyner, in an 1885 issue of *The Ladies' Treasury*, issued a withering critique of beggary, which she identified as a national trait.[17] "First and foremost" in a class of peculiarly Irish "professionals", she declared, using the term facetiously, was the beggar.[18] Using the metaphor of parasites (and indeed explicitly referring to the Killarney beggars in the tourist season as swarming "like midges"[19]), Tyner decried the Irish vagabonds who made a living off the generosity of country-folk throughout Ireland. But beggars could be found everywhere, amongst all sexes and ages. All shared an outrageous belief that they were not "under the slightest obligation of gratitude for any charity bestowed on them".[20] Tyner wrote of women who took to "professional begging, or 'travelling'", including ubiquitous "old crones" who made a living by acting as pilgrims to holy sites on behalf of others. She also castigated the "professional fool, that is, some half-witted person, who is generally more of a knave than a fool, and who studiously cultivates his or her eccentricities to attract notice and extort money",[21] the "pedlar", the obnoxious "'Gombeen Mon'",[22] and the female "egg huckster". In contrast with Tyner's disparaging caricatures, Susan Gavan Duffy, writing in *The Irish Monthly*, attacked the short-handing of the "typical Irishman" as a "half-starved Connemara peasant" and the caricaturing of blundering, awkwardness, thriftlessness, or "some piece of downright stupidity" as "Irish". Could not such characteristics be seen as outgrowths of systemic inequality and disadvantages under which Ireland suffered? From this perspective, the mountain dew girl was an emblem of profound, and not immutable, inequality. "If six baby John Bulls, six infant Sandies, and six little Patricks, were taken by chance from London, Edinburgh, and Dublin, carried off to France or Germany, educated alike, and given the same start in life," she wrote, "does anyone seriously believe that the last-named boys would not bear themselves as bravely, and achieve the same meed of success as either of the former?"[23] There were many others who joined Duffy in extolling the nobility of the Irish peasantry, and even some who looked to Killarney, where its position seemed perilous. Especially as the Celtic Revival took root, they invested the Western peasantry with political and cultural importance as the bearer of the Irish nation's traditions, as an enduring emblem of its virtues, and as an embodiment of its resistance to modernity, Anglicisation, and subjugation. Indeed some writers used them, their customs, and Irish rural culture as a foil for the ravages of British industrialisation; they also extolled the comparative sophistication of Irish Antiquity.[24]

Inspired by images of tenacious rural people, sympathetic writers described the Killarney mountain dew girl clinging to the paltry alms of the tourist as a way to forestall emigration, and implicitly framed tourist exchanges as motivated in equal measure by philanthropy and patriotism. Here the performance of peasant hospitality was not artful or devious, but imbued with desperation. The famous novelist Mary Elizabeth Braddon, for instance, the English-born daughter of a Cornish father and Irish mother, invited readers to consider, in her account of "the smiling Irish maidens" who "trot barefoot beside the tourist's pony", the condition of the local population in the winter months, "cut off from all communication with the world beyond that awful vale, walled in by all those mountains, forgotten of all mankind—think of them in the bleak winter, and grudge not the shilling which rewards their genial smiles and preferred [*sic*] goat's milk or potheen, and do not even refuse to purchase the photographic semblance of the young woman who informs you that she is the Colleen Bawn".[25] Another writer commented on the persistence of these girls, "some of whom were pretty": "Their perseverance is commendable, as they were poorly clad and barefoot, yet, despite our repeated refusals, they followed us four miles . . . But let them not be despised. It is their only means of making a living, and of getting to America, which name is as sweet to their ears as Heaven."[26] These writers expressed palpable empathy for the women—and linked their circumstances to the wider condition of the Irish peasant. Their appraisals may also be read as expressing concern for upholding female "sexual purity"[27] by endorsing the women's activities as legitimate in light of their limited livelihood strategies.

Other writers, however, were acutely anxious about the sexual dimension of their tourist performances. They appeared to be freighted with erotic tensions and transgressed gendered notions of propriety, as girls and women ensnared tourists—especially men—within their web of seduction and deceit. Writers positioned themselves and the peasant women within discourses of "rescue" which were central to many female-led philanthropic exercises in Ireland. They evoked other, less ambiguous "public" (and "fallen") girls, especially in urban centres such as Dublin, where an elaborate institutional and voluntary apparatus was erected to minister to these figures.[28] In rural Ireland, these efforts drew on fewer resources and faced what appeared to be the insurmountable problem of a dispersed population and disruption to state and voluntary surveillance. There was no one street or area where the problem was concentrated—and which could consequently be contained and "cleansed". Instead, these women and girls inhabited a vast rural district and appeared in narratives as peripatetic figures, participating in mock-guerrilla assaults upon the unsuspecting tourist. In the absence of an extensive and organised rural philanthropic network, the workhouse was the primary institution—and the poor law the dominant regime—through which their poverty was addressed. As we have seen, commentators nervously debated the meaning of charity in tourism, questioned its conflation with the disbursement of sixpence to the various characters whom tourists encountered, cautioned the unwitting and well-intentioned excursionists against nourishing dependence, and attempted to establish parameters for respectable interactions with locals. Discussions of the mountain dew girls reflected conflicting assessments of tourism and rural femininity, and anxieties over the girls' susceptibility to exploitation, as well as over their own cunning, which was sometimes cast as deception—and even as betrayal.

"MANY THINGS INTERESTING, INSTRUCTIVE, AND AMUSING, AND SO FAR REMOVED FROM THE ORDINARY PLEASURES AND SIGHTS TO BE MET WITH ELSEWHERE": POITÍN AND THE COMMODIFICATION OF PEASANT CULTURE

A central conceit of the encounter with both Kate Kearney's "descendant" and the ubiquitous mountain dew girl was exchange of money for the concoction of whiskey and goat's-milk. This performance reproduced Kate's famous hospitality, and was thus infused with romantic and slightly dangerous associations: the provenance of the drink was, after all, a mystery. A writer in the *Aberdeen Journal* slyly commented in 1882 that tourists to the Gap would assuredly be "regaled with a cup of goat's milk not entirely innocent of cinder, and, if you happen to be in luck, presented to you by the fair hands of the real Kate Kearney, of whom there is an unlimited supply in the district".[29] Irony abounded in this account of peasant hospitality. In the context of what Andrew Shryock has characterised as the mass "mediation" of tourism, such hospitality lost its co-ordinates in the private social relations of the domestic sphere and offered a discursive veneer for transactions within tourism.[30] Indeed, throughout Killarney, the offer of "illicit" mountain dew took place on highly public stages, though the discourse of hospitality notionally elided women's labour, foregrounding their role as hostesses.

The allegedly illegal character of mountain dew, in particular, heightened tourists' sense of having entered a licentious peasant world.[31] British theatre critic Clement W. Scott contrasted the signature Gap beverage offered to him at Kate Kearney's Cottage with the heavy repast he had enjoyed earlier that day at the venerable Victoria Hotel: "Fancy goat's milk and whisky while you are digesting the Victoria breakfast, eggs, 'squish,' bitter ale, and all!"[32] In this respect, the consumption of the Gap libation was constructed, albeit mildly, as a risk—food that was unfamiliar and unexplored, "experiential" rather than "functional". As Erik Cohen and Nir Avieli have noted, eating (and drinking) involves the incorporation "of stuff from the environment". While sight can be controlled by looking away, the ingestion of food and drink cannot be undone, heightening the importance of what they have termed "the novel" and "the unaccustomed" in relation to bodily risk.[33] The mountain-dew concoction was consumed as part of a sensual and symbolic pantomime that evoked a degree of risk in accepting a peasant beverage from insalubrious hands. The heightened sense of risk was dramatised in travel writing, as writers positioned themselves as intrepid figures foraying into the unknown.

The mountain dew girls represented their poitín as the product of surreptitious manufacture in peasant dwelling-spaces which few tourists breached. Their goats, tourists were told, had made the milk; their cottage stills had produced the whisky. This leant an aura of exoticism and mild danger to the concoction, binding identity and space production to ingestion of the beverage as a cultural product.[34] Of course, travellers had other occasions to ingest "native" food and drink while journeying through the Gap. Charles D. Poston, for instance, commented on the "good and bracing" poitín served to him at Kate Kearney's Cottage, followed by dinner "in a real Irish cottage" arranged by his guide, Happy Jack. Commenting on his meal of mutton, turnips, and potatoes, Poston remarked that the food, accompanied by "a few mugs of ale drunk by a warm peat fire, made us comfortable", and exclaimed that "[t]he potatoes in Ireland are better than anywhere else, and the skins burst open, too generous to hold the nutritious food within."[35] To others, the ingestion of peasant drink became a conceit through which, without crossing the threshold of the cabin door as Poston had done, the tourist was bodily incorporated within the peasant home and culture.[36] For Poston, commensality, as well as the ingestion of food that was not only a rural staple but a signifier of rural Ireland's tumultuous and tragic recent history, conferred the *imprimatur* of cultural authenticity. Taste, and to a much less-documented extent, smell, were activated in the imaginative framing, and indeed the physical consumption, of the concoction. Yet the excursionists' evaluation of the beverage was often unfavourable, displaying a flamboyant connoisseurship to contrast with the untutored palate of the native (one traveller described the taste of the concoction offered to tourists at Kate Kearney's Cottage as "an odious and headache-engendering mixture"[37]). Elsewhere in the district, tourists could enjoy more familiar and palatable fare, if on a less lavish scale than Queen Victoria had in 1861—most notably at Lord Brandon's Cottage, where excursionists met the boat that then ferried them through the Lakes, and also at the cottage on Dinish Island.[38] These rustic cottages were mere refreshment stops, where tourists enjoyed hotel food and drink in a sanitised, custom-built environment. Potentially more enticing, because they offered tourists an entrée into the peasant realm, were "native" repasts and libations, including the Gap's signature beverage.

Travel writers framed their consumption of the unlicensed drink in ways that implicitly linked Irish culture to others that operated beyond the writ of law. The *Irish Tourist* in 1897 published a piece entitled "Potheen" written by "Nunquam non Paratus", accompanied by a photograph purporting to show two peasants "making potheen".[39] The author began by remarking that "[w]hen making holiday in Ireland the traveller finds many things interesting, instructive, and amusing, and so far removed from the ordinary pleasures and sights to be met with elsewhere, that he can afterwards look back upon his holiday with the keenest delight." "One thing," the author remarked, "peculiar to Ireland is undoubtedly the illicit distillation which is even yet carried on to a great extent." In seeking to supply the Irish people's infamous and unquenchable thirst for "'the bottle'", the peasantry had raised this manufacture to "a fine art, and especially so as so many connisseurs [*sic*] have contributed to its praise". The writer vividly described the process of distillation witnessed "a short time ago" in the "mother bed of this industry"—Co. Donegal. Under the careful watch of guides and others who were ever vigilant of detection, the author praised the cleanliness of the process and remarked that his guide, Brocket Hughey, "[t]all, muscular, and lithe", was "the most perfect specimen of manhood I had ever seen".[40] Another piece, published in 1899 in *Chambers's Journal*, described "Poteen-Hunting in the Wild West of Ireland", where the "loneliness and remoteness of the spots chosen for making it, almost inaccessible through the mountains and bogs save to those who know something about the country", added to its allure.[41] The writer, accompanying the constabulary by night in search of illicit distillers, pursued them as they took flight from the law. Their quarry made every effort at evasion, and then accepted their apprehension with "sportsman-like spirit".[42] If the manufacture and commerce of illicit whiskey had the air of a hunt about it, especially in the remote West, this sport also featured in the Gap tourist performance, where it often assumed a playful character, especially when its purveyors were narrated as nubile women who, in a reversal of roles, gave "chase" to tourists.

The gendering of feminine mountain *hospitality* was as marked as the masculine *manufacture* of poitín. The narrative of illicit peasant production in Ireland also referenced a wider political economy of peasant spirit commerce which found parallels in regions of the Scottish Highlands, and also in the Appalachian mountain districts of America (where the mountaineer "moonshiners" achieved an iconic status). All were depicted as places where pre-modern cultural and economic forms survived in the practices of "contemporary ancestors", and where discourses of illicit spirit distillation were part of wider narratives of primitive civilisation and the halting extension of metropolitan legal regimes—embodied by the iconic excise-man.[43] Debates surrounding the problem of illicit distilling in Ireland were part of an outgrowth of intensified efforts to define legal distillation through the imposition of excise taxes.[44] Poitín was incorporated within retail markets and was not clearly produced exclusively for domestic consumption.[45] Although there were remarkable divergences in manufacture and commerce between the Scottish Highlands, Appalachia, and Western Ireland—in the extent of production and incorporation within "modern" markets; systems of distribution; sexual divisions of labour; and indeed the character of the spirits themselves—they were all implicated in wider discourses endowing mountain peasantries with qualities of primitiveness. As mountain dew girls withdrew poitín from their cloaks in a furtive fashion, entreating custom in rich Irish brogue, they heightened the illicit and unfamiliar elements of the tourist encounter. And if the "real" Kate Kearney was an elusive figure, the extended search for her was a playful conceit around which their tour was implicitly structured. Encounters with mountain dew girls as travellers "penetrated" the Gap engendered diverse evaluations.[46] Some tourists narrated the playful guerrilla-vendor practices with withering criticism, while others confessed a playful openness to their artful seduction.

"THE VERY GREAT GRACE AND BEAUTY OF THEIR FORMS AND FEATURES": EROTICISM, GENDER, AND TOURIST PERFORMANCES AT THE GAP

Investigative narratives, many framed by the discourse of Protestant mis-
sionisation, encoded deep anxieties about the sexuality of the mountain
dew girl, and tapped long-standing concerns about the destructive features
of mass tourism, the fragility of Irish femininity, and the precariousness of
rural culture. Other writers professed less concern for contributing to the
girl's moral descent, and instead suggested that the mountain dew girl was
artful and seductive in equal measures, in ways that Kate Kearney's supposed
"granddaughter" could not achieve. The ludic master-narrative of travel
offered an image of comely colleens that reproduced romantic accounts of
Kate, and added a degree of sexual *frisson* in episodes which described dal-
liances between the mountain dew girls and male tourists who fell briefly
under their spell. Travel writers described being hemmed in by "assailants"
(these young girls already engaged in the trangressive act of stalking their
"prey"), excursionists affecting flight from the pressing female hordes, and
women suggestively withdrawing their bottles and glasses from behind
their petticoats and gesturing to them as "offerings". Many writers proclaimed exasperation with the episode, while some admitted to submitting
to the seduction, and bemoaned their ultimate betrayal. The relationship
between eroticism, voyeurism, and tourism has long interested scholars of
tourism and sex-based "pleasure-seeking"—and the Gap of Dunloe offered
a setting for such practices and encounters.[47] Through narratives of the
mountain dew girls' brazen designs on them, writers sometimes embraced
the Gap as a liminoid zone for mock-unlicensed encounters and the women
as agents of corruption.

A special correspondent for the *Freeman's Journal* in 1879 playfully
recounted a meeting between the visiting "John Bull, M.D."—presumably
a stereotyped representative member of a party of excursionists from the
British Medical Association—and a "buxom, barefooted gypsy [*sic*]",
described as one of the "true sunburnt sons and daughters of the mountains, with the honest eyes and the liquid Kerry brogue", declaring them
to be a "delightful race".[48] The narrator often had two foils—one was the
mountain dew girl, and the other was Kate Kearney's "granddaughter".[49]
And contrasts between the "granddaughter" and the mountain dew girl
were often stark. Whereas one writer described the "granddaughter"
as "a degenerate specimen of that stock" proffering "a hideous beverage compounded of questionable goat's milk and unquestionably bad
whiskey", the "troop of mountain damsels" encountered later in the Gap
were "chiefly remarkable for the shortness of their petticoats, the extreme
brownness of the naked limbs thereby disclosed, their persistent solicita-
tions for you to buy something from them, and the very great grace and
beauty of their forms and features".[50] If dress, as an object laden with

symbolic meaning, is constructive of the national community,[51] the considerable attention devoted to discussing the mountain dew girls' movement, accoutrements, and clothing (inevitably including the "traditional" peasant shawl) supplies a rich source for exploring how they were represented as more authentic representatives of the Irish race than the hideous, brazen denizen of Kate Kearney's Cottage. Travellers also depicted them as both socially and bodily different from the tourist and fellow travellers, especially when they focussed on the physiques and gestures of the women, and the lack of bodily covering which often revealed their hair, feet, and sun-darkened limbs.

In such accounts, the writer's self-presentation vacillated between that of bemused observer and unwitting participants in mock-courtship. Many affected mild disapproval while all the while entertaining the mountain dew girls' teasing banter. Female travellers, in contrast, whether in tones of charitable sympathy or of condemnation, narrated categorical distance from both male excursionists and local women, and occasionally voiced opprobrium at the comportment of both. In this respect, the encounter generated broadly, but not exclusively, masculine and feminine narratives of the tourist encounter. Many male tourists readily entertained a liminoid experience, during which unfamiliar geographical and social boundaries intersected and they suspended the norms of everyday life.[52] Markers of social and cultural difference, as well as those of sex, may have intensified the allure of the male tourist's meeting with bare-footed women, who contrasted with female members of touring parties, and indeed the clothing, bearing, dialect, and behaviour of "respectable" women "at home". The Canadian traveller Canniff Haight, in his 1895 travelogue, described how "[o]ut from behind rocks and bushes start Irish girls, who step lightly into the path and tempt you with 'goat's milk and mountain-dew'."[53] He noted their attractiveness:

[N]ot bad-looking girls, some of them—and with all the arts and wiles of their sex they besiege you at one of your most vulnerable points. To a man who must confess a weakness for the feminine portion of creation the situation was desperate. A single taste from each would have upset us, so there was no other way but to decline with thanks. "An' sure yer honour must be fatagued intirely afther climin' the Gap an' 'ud like a drap o' mountain dew to moisten yer mouth wid." "Give the gintlemin a drap wid a taste o' goat's milk, Peggy: sure an' he'll nivir begrudge a sixpence for a taste in the Gap o' Dunloe." "Oh, thin, an' sure her honour 'ud niver have a poor lone Irish girl come runin' down the mountain wid me goat's milk fresh from the goats up yonder, an' the rale mountain dew longin' to pass yer lips. Didn't we see the gintlemin a–comin', Biddy." "An' sure yer honour would niver have it to say to yer beautiful lady, that's longin' for yer comin', God bless her, that he wint thro' the Gap o' Dunloe widout one sup, or widout drinkin' her health, an' me holdin' it in me hand all this while, all for the sake o' sixpence."[54]

The brogue in which Haight rendered the women's entreaties constituted a familiar device for conveying social and cultural distance. It marked efforts to stake the writer's learned identity in relation to the exotic peasants, whose speech he rendered in highly stylised ways conveying non-conventional syntax and diction. But the episode was also one of playful seduction by women whom he admitted finding pleasing, and who drew him within their orbit.

Mountain dew girls could be found at other places in Ireland. At the Giant's Causeway in Co. Antrim, William Whittaker Barry, in addition to finding the "Giant's Well" superintended by an old man who supplied glasses of well water to the traveller, remarked on the "pretty young woman, with flaxen hair and a red petticoat, who takes up her position there [at the Causeway] to sell fossils and photographs".[55] Barry remarked that a small volume could be written by visitors "containing their impressions of this young woman", and contended that her popularity amongst male tourists would be found to be in inverse proportion to that amongst females. At Killarney, Barry described a fleeting encounter with a mountain dew vendor at Dinish Island, where, veering on foot from the common paths, he found himself proceeding over bog and morass, and through dense thickets.[56] At O'Sullivan's Cascade he was thirsty for a taste of "goats' milk and whisky while wandering through these wilds! How welcome! But the mountain dew girls never penetrate into these pathless solitudes. No guide bores the traveller here!"[57] He engaged the services of a young boy, Daniel Moriarty, at the Gap but, owing to the lateness of the hour, did not encounter Kate's "granddaughter" (whom he was told by a gentleman at the Lake Hotel was "'dry as dust'"). Moriarty led him through the darkness into the Gap, where they found refreshments of mountain dew and goat's-milk. Barry found it "most refreshing and strengthening".[58] Leaving the Gap, he encountered successive sellers of mountain dew. And on his ascent of Mangerton, Barry met several girls at the car stop at the base of the mountain. His illuminating account of the meeting is more than mildly suggestive of a fleeting romantic encounter. Indeed, Barry playfully rendered it as a brief "love affair" in which he was unwittingly duped by a mountain nymph:

> They were on this occasion about six in number, including two sisters to my mind the prettiest, one eighteen and the younger one sixteen. So each of us had at least one belle to accompany up the mountain. Had choice directed I should have selected the eldest of the two sisters as being the prettier, but chance gave me as companion the younger. She, however, proved so faithful that I began to feel quite in love with her; for carrying a knapsack, and being fatigued with my hard day's work yesterday, I was obliged at the steeper part of the ascent fairly to lag behind and to sit down once or twice to rest. But this young girl instead of running on to her companions remained to keep me company, and

refreshed by her with a glass of mountain dew, I after awhile rejoined my companions. Our conversation was free, but for the most part innocent enough, though one or two of my fellow-travellers were indulging in some *double entendres* which in the case of virtuous girls is a practice highly reprehensible; though my own question to the elder of the two sisters, whether she had had many opportunities of changing her condition, passed perhaps the proper bounds of decorum.[59]

Barry wrote of his growing affection for the genial "belle" who accompanied him, but her unfaithfulness and ulterior, mercenary motives were progressively laid bare, to his increasing despair. First, they were signalled by the charge she levied for the enjoyment of her fleeting, if "faithful" company. Then Barry discovered, and described in a tone of ironic outrage, how she surreptitiously attempted to exact more of his money—the "belle" with whom he had been "quite in love" now little more than an "impudent young hussy" who had outfoxed him:

> Then my fair young companion reminds me of the pledge to take some more mountain dew at the Devil's Punch Bowl. I state my interpretation of what I meant. It won't do, she says she only came up so far on my account. As if indeed she would have left her sister and companions, and gone back alone from the middle of the mountain. However, a promise is a promise, but I have nothing less than a sovereign. She will get change. So I partake of some more mountain dew. Then from among her companions she obtains the change, for the most part in small coins. For form's sake I count. There is a sixpence short. I call the young girl's attention to the circumstance. With such a number of coins the slightest explanation would be satisfactory, but she says I had put the sixpence into my other hand. This I felt sure was not the case, so I count again. Still there is a sixpence short. Then the young girl looks caught and guilty, and looking down is silent. Oh! what a contrast with the young widow of the Claddagh! I give the girl sixpence for the further supply of mountain dew, but I am not thus easily to escape from the hands of this impudent young hussy. She further demands threepence for giving change, though it had been done exclusively for her own benefit, on the ground that this charge is customary. As if in this wild spot money could have been changed often enough for any custom to become established in the matter. Nay, more, has any traveller been fool enough ever to change a sovereign here before? I doubt it. However, the young girl looked so flushed and pretty at my stern determination to resist such an unheard of, though small imposition, and my friends and her companions had gone on up the mountain side, leaving me alone engaged in this ridiculous dispute with a mere child, that at length I gave in and handed her a threepenny-bit on the express understanding that we parted friends.[60]

The mountain dew girl's engaging banter flavoured a meeting in which Barry portrayed himself as a sincere victim of the peasant girl's artful seduction—and an unwitting victim of her betrayal. Barry narrated this realisation of bald pecuniary intentions as a recovery of a social distance and position of spectatorship—both of which had been lost in the physical and emotional engagement with the mountain dew girl as he and his colleagues indulged in behaviours impossible with "virtuous girls". Yet the fleeting, pseudo-romantic encounter supplied a transgressive moment in which Barry narrated participation in a brief courtship with an anonymous Irish peasant girl. He reproduced voyeuristic narratives of immersion in the seamy world of the Victorian urban under-class—so-called "slumming"—in which middle-class men, under a variety of pretexts and with many motivations, exposed themselves to the moral dangers against which they had been cautioned since boyhood, while vacillating between prurient interest and professed observation of the world of the poor.[61] Indeed, the mountain dew girl in this account is cast as an artful seductress, with Barry characterising himself as being shocked by the unfolding encounter, while abjuring any sexual motivation or class privilege of his own. It offers a window onto playful authorial self-presentation: could these men really have expected that flirtatious banter and professions of interest on the part of young girls did not have a primary, mercenary motivation? Sometimes travellers bemoaned such deception in highly comical ways. The reports of the 46th annual meeting of the Cambrian Archaeological Association, held in Kerry in August 1891, for instance, illustrate the extent to which the weighty business of touring the district's ruins was contrasted with the fun and irreverence occasioned by an encounter with mountain dew girls:

> Some of the syrens who try to tempt the unwary by offers of mountain dew are decidedly pretty, and fully understand the art of dropping the eyelids and then suddenly unmasking a battery of beautiful eyes upon the victim. If this can be successfully resisted, a softly-modulated wheedling "Ah, do, sorr!" generally completes the conquest. It is amusing to observe the conventionality of the stage-laugh which is put on as a matter of business as each successive tourist passes by.[62]

The author's explicit reference to a "stage laugh" hints at an awareness of the overtly performative character of the exchange, which began with the approach of the girl, her offer of mountain dew in a verbal play that was teasing and peppered with compliments and honorifics, and then, after its consumption, the inevitable negotiations over the gratuity. Writers almost invariably confessed to having parted with more money than they felt was due, owing to the successful efforts of the beguiling girls to win them over. Indeed, many writers confessed to abandoning resistance in the face of their playful seduction. One writer wrote of the mountain dew girls that "[s]till one cannot fall out with them, they look so good-natured, and, in a free country, have a right to push an honest trade."[63] E.K. Washington also wrote approvingly of some of the mountain dew girls whom he met in his tour of the Gap, while remarking on their brazen attempts at subterfuge. He commented that "[t]hese were really pleasant, graceful, pretty Irish girls, who re-enforced their 'mountain-dew' with smiles, wit, and perseveringly following us for miles, till we drank the 'dew,' though with a *wry* face, probably because it was made of rye."[64]

There was no homogeneous "masculine" scripting of these encounters. Some male excursionists professed shock at their temerity, immodesty, and overt sexuality; still, narratives of the encounters also suggest how both performance and account were broadly inflected by gender. The American writer Charles M. Taylor, for instance, in *The British Isles through an Opera Glass*, noted a striking distinction between the attention paid to male and female members of his party of excursionists: "Now and then the ladies stop their horses to give us a breathing spell. When they turn to look for us they find us the centre of a group of young girls, who merrily try to sell us something to eat or drink."[65] At Kate Kearney's Cottage, Burton E. Stevenson noted that while the women in his party retired to the open fire at one end of the room, the men "paused before the bar for a taste of potheen".[66] Women established a calculated aloofness from the puckish mountain dew vendors and became spectators, rather than participants, in the exchanges, acting out a script of respectable disengagement that reinforced their class and gendered identities. Modes of transport also reinforced this gendered distance and relative purity: women were frequently described as making their way through the Gap on horse-back, thereby removing themselves physically from (indeed literally placing themselves "above") interactions with the peasant girls. This calculation emphasised their spectatorship as the space became increasingly sexualised. This social and physical distance was further reinforced by narratives in which they voiced explicit disapproval, pity, or a mixture of the two sentiments. By emphasising their spectatorship, they established a narrative of corporeal disengagement from the mildly erotic carnival, contrasting themselves with the poor, boisterous peasant girls, as well as with male excursionists who entertained the girls' attention.[67] The French writer Marie-Anne de Bovet also remarked on how the women of the Gap "pay particular attention to the men, whom they pursue with gross flatteries", although she declared that "[t]his Pass of Dunloe would be very lovely if we could only be alone with Nature."[68] In this respect, the Gap tour presented the female author-traveller with a stage and script to perform class identities in contradistinction to "natives" encountered by the touring party—and gendered identities in contrast with the "playful" male traveller. The American traveller Grace Carew Sheldon illustrated this strategy when she commented that as her party left Kate Kearney's Cottage and the nearby inlaid-wood shops and manufactories and proceeded through the Gap: "It was comparatively an easy matter for us to get rid of the persistent natives," she wrote, "but several good-looking men were besieged by Bridgets, Marys, and Ellens, who carried socks under one arm, and a bottle of milk and mountain-dew under the other."[69] These encounters had the potential to either consolidate, or even fleetingly violate, the identity of the subject in relation to behaviours "at home", and to promote diverse narratives and social positions of spectatorship and participation; so doing, they engendered complex performances of self and others deep in the recesses of the Gap.

"FROM THEIR OWN KODAK": POSTCARDS, PHOTOGRAPHS, AND THE MOUNTAIN DEW GIRL

Visual culture played an especially important role in disseminating images of the mountain dew girl and implanting her in popular imagination as an iconic Killarney figure. It also referenced wider tropes of composition and disguise expounded by many who put pen to paper and recounted their Killarney tours. In picture-postcards [Plate 2], the poitín Kate elevated in her hands became a signifier of mountain hospitality, proffered by the exemplar of a buxom Irish peasant. This artist-designed, non-photographic image had referents in Owenson's beguiling figure, but stripped her of bewitching referents to produce a sanitised "hostess", Kate now a genial emblem of modern tourist commerce. In fact, deprived of her iconic vessels of goat's-milk and whiskey, this shawled, ruby-cheeked girl closely resembled other renderings of the generic Irish colleen. Wider national rural imagery furnished material for producing colourful images of Killarney figures, affirming Orvar Löfgren's contention that "[t]he cultural grammar of developing a national folk culture also becomes the model for promoting local or regional heritages for touristic purposes."[70]

Photographs also nourished the Victorian tourist imagination and provided a means of vicariously engaging the famed Killarney landscape. Even so, viewing scenery at first hand, and by extension participating more fully in the place, was held to be far superior to the glimpses of Killarney afforded by the two-dimensional images which circulated in the post or through exhibitions. "Either by camera and pen, or by actual acquaintance," *Cook's Traveller's Gazette* advised readers in 1910, "the old Weir Bridge, Muckross Abbey, the Gap of Dunloe, Torc Cascade and the rest of the places in Killarney and its neighbourhood have become familiar as household words."[71] However, the writer asserted—as one might expect of the author of a piece appearing in a Thomas Cook and Son publication—that "only the actual spectator" could truly appreciate the beauties of Killarney scenery. Such spectatorship increasingly implicated technologies and practices of photography—the addition of a new apparatus, the camera, to be carried from site to site; the identification of appropriate vantage points; the reproduction of famous vistas; and the assemblage of images in albums which reproduced the tourist's journey. The advent of amateur photography, especially from the 1860s, gave rise to a particularly powerful visual image of Kate Kearney—and, in the case of Kate's "grand-daughter", provided a new, lucrative opportunity to tap tourists' insatiable interest by posing as her forebear.

Professional photography in mid- to late-Victorian Ireland was famously associated with William Lawrence, whose business disseminated images around the world (the *Irish Tourist*, for instance, was lavishly illustrated with Lawrence's photographs). Many images effaced the human element in Killarney and reproduced the picturesque imagery of earlier texts: in the 1860s, for instance, Frederick Holland Mares promoted images of a misty and unpeopled Killarney landscape—part of a wider aesthetic which he developed with other photographic subjects, too.[72] Mares's cabinet and stereo negatives were subsequently acquired by Lawrence, whose celebrated photographer, Robert French, travelled throughout the country, producing iconic images that were disseminated in the Eblana stereoscopic views "Gems of Irish Scenery". Louis Anthony, a rival photographer, established himself at Killarney, and made Kate's Cottage the site at which he solicited patronage from excursionists.[73] Meeting parties of tourists again as they alighted from the tour at Ross Castle, he then made his way to the studio where he processed the orders and despatched them to the various hotels and guest-houses. By 1908 he employed seven photographers, generating one of the key souvenirs of a tourist's trip to the Gap.

Amateur photography constituted an important performance in its own right, with specific stages, actors, codes, and materials associated with the Gap. Cameras became essential accoutrements in the kit of many late-Victorian and Edwardian travellers to Killarney, as they became more portable and affordable devices which enabled the travellers themselves to emulate the image-making of professionals.[74] Lucy Langdon Williams and Emma V. McLoughlin, Americans whose travels through Europe were issued in 1892 as *A Too Short Vacation*, exemplified the Kodak-toting tourist in Killarney. At the outset of their travels, it was agreed that one of the women would be charged with the camera, to "receive impressions" and "get at the truth".[75] This idea of image "reception" underscores how they understood photography as a documentary act, rather than one that was actively constructive. Amongst the 48 photographs "from their own Kodak" that illustrated the women's book was one of three bare-headed mountain dew girls, grim and dark, looking at the camera lens [Plate 3]. Williams and McLoughlin described a troupe of "girls and women, bare-legged and curly-headed, holding two bottles", with a tumbler "under the inevitable shawl".[76] This image evoked conventions of photographic realism which privileged relatively still images of the subject. Another traveller's photographs, which accompanied his travelogue of a trip to Dunloe, illustrated a tour in the company of tourist "types"—"the Lady" and "the Barrister". The photographs include several of the "natives", including one whose caption described a "NICE BOY" who regaled the Lady with

"WONDERFUL LEGENDS ABOUT THE LAKES, WHICH PERHAPS SHE MIGHT HAVE BELIEVED IF SHE HAD NOT BEEN ON HORSE-BACK" [Plate 4].[77] Several others depict mountain dew girls—one showing them running on the side of the road, captioned: "AND THEY RAN, AND THEY RAN AFTER US, WITH THE UTMOST GOOD NATURE, JOYOUSLY RECOMMENDING THE MERITS OF THE INTOXICAT-ING FLUID THEY HAD IN A BOTTLE. BUT, ALAS, WE WERE A TEMPERANCE TROOP" [Plate 5].[78] In this image, the mountain dew girls were in active pursuit of tourists. The more formally posed image of a single mountain dew vendor, common in postcard and professional images, offered a contrasting popular representation. A second photograph in the account showed the Barrister on horseback, with the caption that "IT AMUSED THE GIRLS VERY MUCH TO SEE HIM ON HORSE-BACK. THEY COMPLIMENTED HIM HIGHLY, WHILE I TOOK HIS PHOTOGRAPH" [Figure 6].[79] Here, the visual framing of the girls' mock-dalliances and temptations to the self-described "temperance troop" reproduced episodes of the recreational tour found in myriad printed texts.

"SO NEAR THE REAL THING": PICTORIAL PHOTOGRAPHY AND THE MOUNTAIN DEW GIRL

Few writers attributed precise names to the mountain dew vendors whom they met (unlike the district's famous, if improbably long-lived guides); writing of his *Walking Tour Round England in 1865*, William Whittaker Barry identified several of the girls: "Bridget O'Sullivan, called the dark-eyed Bridget", and Mary Hartnett, called the "Queen of the Gap".[80] Seven images of "Gap Girls" [Plates 7, 8, 9, 10, 11, 12, 13], each of whom is separately posed against a similar outdoor backdrop, which were taken in the period 1860–70, depict sullen peasant women who are attired in traditional dress, holding their trademark bottles. In contrast with the more famous rustic photographs, these images were grounded in the representational strategies of photographic realism, which foreswore excessive manipulation or overt intervention in the composition of the photographic subject, preferably captured *in situ* (though they were evidently part of a wider ideological project, often aimed at dramatising poverty).[81] The context of these photographs' creation is unclear—but a wider body of contemporary photography includes joyless images of the urban poor, staring blankly at the camera lens. Images of mountain dew girls, bottles in hand or partly tucked under a shawl (though still visible) reflect familiar conventions in late-Victorian realism.[82] The representation of their "labour" here was symbolically organised around those materials, which, like the matchstick girls of urban London and other representative figures of industrial exploitation, infused sullenness and dirtiness with the image of their labour and reproduced the sunken-eyed hopelessness of grinding poverty.

In contrast with postcard images of Killarney's hostess, narratives of mountain dew girls as playful, would-be suitors in active pursuit of men, or photos of grim and dishevelled figures embodying rural immiseration, the most famous photographic image of the mountain dew girl placed her, beaming and bottles in hand, squarely within a rustic aesthetic which evoked the romantic, cherubic Kate Kearney of lore. Alongside the turf-cutters, turf-sellers, pony-men, fish sellers, wool-spinners, and market girls popularised in late-Victorian rural images of Ireland, she became part of a romantic ethnographic photographic project organised around labouring rural types.[83] It had important links to wider artistic and aesthetic movements which took as subjects representative rural figures from England, Scotland, and elsewhere and assembled them in a transnational photographic project. The incorporation of the mountain dew girl within this representational repertoire was signalled in part by ways in which she was labelled, using the generic moniker adopted in most printed texts which identified her by fusing a gender marker with the name of her signature drink.

The mountain dew girl became implicated in a deeply contentious project centred on the composition of representative types. The eminent Victorian photographer Henry Peach Robinson used a photograph of a mountain dew girl to expound on his photographic practices in an 1896 book *The Elements of a Pictorial Photograph*. Robinson also produced the famous photograph exhibited in 1864, entitled "A Mountain Dew Girl: Killarney", which was the first to be published illustrating W.B. Woodbury's experimental patent photo-relief process [Plate 14].[84] It was widely circulated through exhibition halls, including Paris in 1867, and featured prominently in the photographic press. The image was included, for instance, in a publication of several of Robinson's photos, displaying the new Dallmeyer lens, entitled "Portraits and Pictures"—a collection of 16-inch by 12-inch pictures accompanied by commentary which the *Photographic News* described as being confined "to a walk he has made especially his own, the depicting of illustrations of character in rural life". The periodical hailed them as "some of the finest pictures which have ever graced our art", including "a 'Market Girl,' with her basket, a handsome, good-humoured English peasant girl, in rustic attire", and "a 'Mountain Dew Girl, Killarney,' with her wood vessel, and her roguish bright eyes, ready to dispense 'mountain dew' to the tourist on his way to the Lakes, which are seen in the background behind her".[85] It praised Robinson's "most admirable composition and pictorial balance; the delicate modelling, the perfect gradation of tones". But the explicit "composition" of the image reflected a highly controversial approach to photography.

Robinson propounded an aesthetic theory grounded in the picturesque,[86] of which his image of the mountain dew girl was an exemplar. His embrace of, and innovations in, "pictorial photography" were subjects of intense debate amongst fellow practitioners.[87] Divisions between them ultimately resulted in a secession led by Robinson and like-minded "pictorialists" from the Photographic Society of Great Britain in 1891–92 (the seceders later established as "The Linked Ring Brotherhood").[88] To him, a good photographer deployed, like the good artist, skills of composition to produce "a perfect pictorial whole".[89] In contrast, his critics argued that photography's aim was "factual" recording, without such active intervention. This formed the fault-line between photographers who subscribed to the ideas of "realism", "truthfulness", and positivism, and those who embraced the photograph as a medium of representation—and what Jennifer Lewis-Green has called "metaphysical romanticism".[90] Robinson's approach was linked to wider discussions of the role of models and the construction of imagery to dramatise poverty—practices famously and controversially associated with the prominent Victorian social reformer Thomas Barnardo. Barnardo's depictions of urban street youth, often using the device of starkly contrasting images, nourished charges of manipulation and deception.[91] Robinson's rural imagery, in contrast to these urban scenes, was firmly grounded in a rustic aesthetic. He employed similar techniques of photographic intervention—but to markedly different ends.

To Robinson, to O.G. Rejlander, and to other like-minded practitioners, the photographic craft was more than a mere mimetic exercise; it was an artistic endeavour. Questions of contrivance and fiction that centred on the mountain dew girl—and Kate Kearney—in printed travel narratives (were they imposters? How impoverished were they really?) echoed in debates surrounding such embroideries in pictorial photography—but in this case the mountain drew girl was a creature of the photographer's manipulations, not an artful spinner of her own tall tales. Take, for instance, models—critical collaborators in Robinson's compositional practices. Robinson rued the day that he had openly discussed his selection of trained models; until that point, he was "envied the 'luck' that always seemed to supply me with the right figures just precisely when I wanted them".[92] However the effect for which he had been lauded was achieved not by luck, but rather by "a combination of intelligence and strict adherence to the *appearance* of nature in the models, and common sense and some knowledge of art, as well as power to invent a subject, in the photographer".[93] Nature, as Robinson judged it, could not compete with the "naturalness" and purity produced by deliberate, meticulous composition. In this, photography was akin to other forms of pictorial composition: a means of representing nature, not merely reproducing it. The judicious adornment of their bodies was critical to this exercise. Indeed, Robinson described purchasing clothes from "a girl in a lonely country lane" as a way of securing an appropriately "picturesque dress".[94] Peasant wear had to be meticulously assembled, as it became part of what M.R. Solomon has described as the "systematic encryption, transmission, and interpretation of social meaning".[95] Robinson's studio models were clothed in the traditional shawl, which was instantly recognisable as a signifier of a specific national, rural, and gendered identity.[96] The result was a hearty and hale rustic figure; rather than *being* authentic, the body beneath the costume had to *convey* authenticity.

Insofar as any of Killarney's mountain dew vendors were implicated in this photographic enterprise, it was largely by supplying a type that Robinson then elaborated in the studio, using a range of techniques, including casting a model for the part. In embracing the model, for instance, Robinson questioned the capacity of rural people to telegraph their own naturalness to the camera and beyond: "I seldom find the 'real thing' to quite answer my purpose," he lamented.[97] Indeed Robinson asserted that "[t]he aboriginal is seldom sufficiently intelligent to be of use, especially if you have 'intention' in your work." At the same time, he acknowledged that such practices were highly controversial: "I am quite conscious that I am laying myself open to the charge of masquerading," Robinson wrote,[98] acknowledging that his models "may be called to some extent artificial, but they are so near the real thing as to be taken for it by the real natives, just as the trout does not seem to know the difference between the natural and the artificial fly."[99] Robinson insisted that obedient and intelligent models could achieve a superior result than a peasant, who lacked the intelligence or acumen to represent nature to the camera. If Robinson warned that "[t]he worst models are theatrical people,"[100] so "[t]he lower classes are often picturesque, but too often too stupid to understand what is required."[101] This commentary formed part of a wider exposition on skilful "pictorial" composition. Skill was demanded of the model as her character joined a pantheon of rural types.

Outside the studio, which offered a favourable environment for such nature-making, intrusive features of modernity also had to be effaced in this pictorial project. Telegraph and telephone wires, and agricultural machinery undermined efforts to capture the picturesque in nature. The "gleaner", "the smock-frock and sun-bonnet", and other elements of a picturesque scene had all but disappeared from rural life, rendering pictorial composition all the more necessary.[102] Commenting specifically on the model for his undated photograph "Mountain Dew Girl, from the Gap of Dunloe, Killarney, Ireland" [Plate 15], Robinson asserted that "[a]ll that is visible is genuine nature, except the face and hands, which in unadulterated nature were quite too repulsive, except for impressionist painters of music-hall scenes and coster horrors."[103] Here, the hands of the "genuine" mountain dew girl were so disruptive to Robinson's careful composition of rustic femininity that they demanded replacement by those of a model. The particular "problem" posed by hands evokes the work of Arthur Munby, whose diary entries expressed a long fascination with representations of working-class women and with contrasts between their labour and that of the people they served.[104] This idea of the mountain dew girl's insalubrious, polluting qualities occasionally nourished assessments of her character, and certainly informed appraisals of the drink which she offered. The American traveller Burton E. Stevenson advised tourists to take the drink at Kate Kearney's

Cottage, for instance, rather than at other points in the Gap where it was on offer, as "here one gets a clean glass to drink it out of."[105] In this vein, Robinson's construction of the idealised image required him to substitute the "repulsive" hands of a mountain dew girl with those of a model, and thereby retain the overall effect of the composition, effacing the "dirty" and transgressive features of the body associated with rural work. His sanitised image then joined a corpus of rustic images in which the tensions between the idealised female body and the arduousness of her work were resolved by the addition of specific accoutrements to signify her labour,[106] rather than depicting her in the act of labour itself. Indeed, the item which most identified this figure as a vendor of Killarney's famous beverage was the cup that she held conspicuously under her arm. It was the iconic signifier of Gap hospitality, as excursionists, their imaginations nourished by this imagery, encountered an iconic national subject deep in the Gap of Dunloe. Elements of the visual corpus displayed in exhibitions and circulated on postcards prefigured narratives of playful, if somewhat predatory, hordes, while others recalled the solitary, romantic cherub; and still more called to mind the evocative descriptions of the rural pauper whose condition was bemoaned by travellers through the district.

CONCLUSION

The mountain dew girl was ambiguously situated within Irish rural iconography. She was enlisted in multiple narratives of travel that often competed with that of the Killarney carnival. Sometimes she evoked, however faintly, the Gap's famous matriarch. But, more often, she offered, in presentation and in demeanour, sharp contrasts with the proprietress of Kate Kearney's Cottage, whose pecuniary motives were naked. Widely associated with the Gap of Dunloe but evoking myriad other women and girls who plied their trade elsewhere in Killarney and Ireland, the mountain dew girl was nonetheless an iconic, and contentious, national figure, variously corrupting and vulnerable to corruption, recruited in narratives of rusticism, romanticism, and the ravages of tourist commerce. Cameras, the printed word, and postcard images produced narratives in which she supplied not only a curious libation, but also a freighted representation of rural Ireland and femininity.

5 Tourism, Landscape, and Nation

In 1891, members of the Royal Society of Antiquaries visited Killarney House, the home of Lord Kenmare. They set off to visit Ross Castle, where the trustees of the Muckross Estate granted them unfettered access to the demesne, then proceeded to the Torc Waterfall and the Abbey of Muckross, and Ross Island, on Lord Kenmare's demesne. Boats conveyed them to the island of Innisfallen, and then Muckross Demesne, belonging to the Herberts.[1] The next day they visited Aghadoe, famous for its ruins, and the nearby Ogham Cave of Dunloe (a local site of great archaeological interest). The party proceeded to Dunloe Castle, the residence of Dr George and Mrs Stoker, where members enjoyed a sumptuous luncheon before journeying half a mile to the entrance to the Gap of Dunloe, through which they passed before boarding boats for a tour of the Upper Lake, seeing the Old Weir Bridge, and then returning back to their hotels. These travellers enjoyed privileged access to Ross Castle and were fêted by local landlords on an excursion that reproduced performances associated with a genteel Romantic tour. It eschewed elements of the "regulation route", evading the disorderliness of the Gap carnival, the grip of the ubiquitous hucksters, and the flatteries of the mountain dew girls. Certainly no member of this tour seems to have returned home to pen a comedic account of "doing" the Gap, with its tropes of misadventure and exasperation. Most excursionists, however, were not afforded the same unfettered access to Muckross Demesne, and very few received an invitation to lunch at Dunloe Castle. Nor, as it happens, were other parties of antiquarian travellers so privileged.

The reports of the 46th annual meeting of the Cambrian Archaeological Association, held in Kerry in August 1891, offers a study in contrasts. Having undertaken an extensive tour of archaeological sites at Killarney, encompassing Aghadoe Cathedral and Castle, Dunloe Cave, and Dunloe Castle, the scholarly touring party was conveyed to the Gap. Their archaeological tour over, the party suspended serious business, and "members gave themselves up unreservedly to the enjoyment of the splendid mountain scenery of the Gap of Dunloe". A new narrative of the space opened in which scholarly inquiry yielded to frivolity and the crass materialism of the Killarney tour, including encounters with comely and flirtatious mountain dew girls. Leaving their carriages, as well as their antiquarian focus behind, the party made its way through the Gap. Yet despite the explicitly leisurely purpose of this excursion, "[t]he only draw-back to the thorough enjoyment of the beauties of nature," the report of their excursion recorded, "was the incessant pestering of beggars to which all tourists are subjected. The firing off of small cannons to pro-duce an echo and the everlasting demands for baksheesh quite destroy the solitude and silence so essential for the due appreciation of the wilder aspects of nature."[2] Giving "themselves up unreservedly" to the scenery did not imply total submission to the Gap cavalcade. As for solitariness and seclusion, no pretence could be offered to find a moment alone—not only because tourists usually arrived as a party, but also because of the clamorous crowd that surrounded them throughout the excursion. Unlike travellers on the Royal Society of Antiquaries tour, most excursionists' movements were limited to public spaces where they were sure to encoun-ter the familiar cast of Killarney characters, while access to many sites and routes of long-standing interest to the antiquarian and tourist alike were regulated by the landlord's toll-gate. It served as a visible reminder of their power in Killarney—and of their interest, like that of myriad local figures, in tapping the purse of the tourist.

This study is premised on an understanding of "landscape" as a pro-duction—one that is far more malleable and changing than primeval mountains and deep passes that were forged over millennia at Killarney. Discourses and embodied practices exercise constructive power over land-scapes, constituting them and endowing terrain such as the Gap of Dunloe with social and cultural meanings that changed over time, from the sublime landscape of the Romantic tour to the boisterous realm of Kate Kearney's cavalcade. Landscapes must be approached as ideological products, and as "texts" that are subjects of cultural contestation.[3] Applying the piercing insights of new cultural geography, with its interest in the "spatial turn",[4] tourist landscapes may be explored as discursive productions, grounded in material forms: as symbolic as well as material resources.[5] As we have seen, places such as the Gap and the tourism narratives that it signified were bound up with wider ideological programmes and contests in Ireland. More widely, the enclosure of land, the development of the Palladian garden, and the elevation of the English Gothic as a national landscape aesthetic offer examples of how historians have explored and explained the roles of ideol-ogy and material intervention in producing specific landscapes.[6] In Ireland, the politico-cultural elevation of the West as a pure peasant landscape—a national heartland that resisted Anglicisation, materialism, and adulter-ation (and indeed supplied foils for these qualities)—was central to this process of signification. To some tourists, such as members of the Royal Society of Antiquaries and Cambrian Archaeological Society parties, Kil-larney offered curious ruins and ancient sites that supplied evidence of a culture that was of increasing contemporary political interest. In an era when William Butler Yeats and others were promoting folklore as a vehicle to explore the history and identity of the Irish nation, the peasantry was seen as a carrier of distinctively Irish cultural values. As the writer J.M. Synge and the painters Alexander Williams and Paul Henry turned westwards for literary and artistic inspiration, Douglas Hyde and other Gaelic revivalists searched its verdant terrain to supply sites for their visions of a unified national culture. The expansion of mass tourism, which left few places beyond the sector's reach, had implications for their politico-cultural projects. To the writer William Bulfin, the cultural valorisation of the West as a pure, rural, and authentically Irish topos was allied with unease over tourism, and the wider question of proprietorship.[7] Cycling through Ireland, Bulfin found occasion to intertwine narratives of both anxieties: no sooner had he challenged a landowner and his prohibition against trespassing on Lough Derg than he despaired in "ancient Killaloe", now "becoming fashionable, and the tourist who fishes and plays golf, and drinks Scotch whiskey, is now an unlovely feature of the landscape".[8] At the same time, Gaelic Leaguers were insisting that the tourism supplied a means by which the Irish people could come to know and understand the touchstones of their culture and identity. No place was more central to these ethnographic, linguistic, and contemporary political programmes than the West, which patriotic Irishmen, women, and children were encouraged to tour. The Gaelic League sought to locate a site of primeval cultural origins in places such as the Aran Islands. Rather then shield them from view, Gaelic Leaguers believed that tours there could inculcate in precepts of nationhood by bringing Irish tourists closer to the pure origins of the nation itself (notwithstanding the high concentration of Anglo-Irish Protestants in the League and its projects). Encouraging the circulation of travellers with such intentions, and particularly the organisation of tours to promote language learning, the League also aimed to discourage the migration of rural people *away* from these areas, which were seen as a showcase for the peasant *habitus*. This Utopian project, promoting a heavily mediated experience of the Gaeltacht, was coupled, as Ríona Nic Congáil argues, with an elision of the district's material conditions of poverty.[9]

As William Bulfin discovered, and as the Gaelic League's sponsorship of tours through Gaeldom revealed, who was admitted, and who was excluded, physically and symbolically, from such landscapes—at Killarney and elsewhere—were central to their production and reproduction in Ireland. In Killarney, debates surrounding the land and tourism also revealed wider anxieties over whether travellers could enjoy it on their own terms, though not as a national "heartland" linked to an enduring primordial culture. At the turn of the century, a new culprit emerged in the drama of the traveller's frustrated efforts. The yoke of landlords, and a landscape marked by their tolls, supplied a rhetorical focus for those who denounced impediments to the Killarney tour, and it was rhetorically mobilised to denounce the choking and anachronistic power of the landed estates.

Even ardent Irish unionists claimed Killarney as their own, and hoped to share it in fraternal amity with British visitors. However, the landlord's toll-gate impeded (rather than regulated) visitors' movement, far more visibly and formally than local hucksters and hawkers, whom many writers shrugged off as mere annoyances, and who often proved instrumental in accounts designed to entertain, to engender pity and concern, and to stake out the traveller's *bona fides*. The toll-gate was a less subtle signifier of the landscape belonging to others than the famous "poetic toll-bar" carefully superintended by the fearsome proprietress of Kate Kearney's Cottage. Indeed, it was often depicted as a more alien and pernicious obstruction. The progressive weakening of the local estates by the end of the nineteenth century led advocates of public ownership to argue that Killarney could become a national place unencumbered by the narrow interests and exclusionary ethos of the landed classes. Increasingly, excursionists, as well as groups such as the National Trust, argued not only that these gates disrupted the Killarney excursion, but that the landlords' grip marred nature, which belonged not only to an ambiguously defined nation, but also to a touring public that hailed from all quarters of the United Kingdom and the globe.

Strong tensions persisted between duelling master-narratives of Killarney, starkly described by the *Parliamentary Gazetteer* in 1846: one grounded in Romantic-era landscape aesthetics, enduring in such monikers as "Heaven's Reflex" and "The Irish Lake District", and another grounded in the carnivalesque.[10] In the context of commercial tourism promotion, Romantic aesthetics were reinvigorated as railway companies and touring firms elided the carnivalesque elements of travel embodied in Killarney's hucksters, and instead praised the varied scenery and antiquarian associations of the district, from its lush foliage to the abbeys at Aghadoe, Innisfallen, and Muckross, "smoking not now with incense, or musical with the sonorous chant of monks and mitred abbots, but breathing in their decay a divine peace that lies upon the heart of the worldly wayfarer like magic balm".[11]

Thomas Cook and Son's 1895 guide-book to the "Emerald Isle", lavishly illustrated with photographs by Robert Welch, William Lawrence, and Guy & Co. of Cork, advised readers that "[e]very tourist, traveller, or visitor who leaves Ireland without seeing the world-famous lakes, bays, and arbutus-covered mountains of Killarney, the charming and ever-varying loveliness of its scenery, has much to regret."[12] Defying the travel writer's penchant for propounding on the scene-stealing antics of mischievous locals, the guide-book rhapsodised about "that wild, lonely, magnificent defile, lying between the Reeks and the Toomies, four miles long, in which the lofty mountains, apparently rent assunder [*sic*] by some strange convulsion of Nature, overhang the pathway, fearfully casting their gloomy shadows on the murmuring stream below", and extolled the "picturesque romantic loveliness of Glena Bay".[13] No mention was made of artful mountain dew girls, or of Kate Kearney's impudent "granddaughter". A Killarney, Cork,

Glengarriff, and South of Ireland Tourist Association promotional publication, illustrated by Lawrence's photographs, buttressed this bucolic narrative, interweaving an account of the "enchanting" district with practical advice on charges, entertainments, and suggested itineraries.[14] There was an especially important, mutually reinforcing interplay between narratives of unspoilt scenery in early-twentieth-century film, and those in the railway guide-book.[15] In the Great Southern and Western Railway's guide-book *The Sunny Side of Ireland*, John O'Mahony rhapsodised about the gloomy Gap of Dunloe, cleverly conflating the muscly pony-boys and their beasts, and narrating them not as disruptions to, but embodiments of, the dream-like landscape:

> Wonderful creatures they are, these horses and riders. The peasant boys are for all the world the modern prototypes of those "rake-helly horse boys" of Queen Elizabeth's reign, who filled so many pages of the State papers. Sinew and muscle knit their loose limbs together, and, in their eyes, mild and calm as those of the quiet cattle in the field, but like the surface of their native lakes, covering unfathomed depths, they conceal souls swept by deep thoughts, and minds clouded by many memories.[16]

As a sub-genre of the guide-book, these railway and touring-company publications constructed touring districts along the path of their commercial sponsors, referencing narratives which evoked the popular scenic souvenir albums of panoramic views using photographs by firms such as William Lawrence's.[17] Their photographic renderings of the Gap of Dunloe, and those in stereoscopic and other media, portrayed it as a wild, awe-inspiring landscape, stripped of Robinson's rustic vendors of mountain dew, but often incorporating the figure of the boatman cast against a broader picturesque composition of the land and lakes. This bucolic imagery was reproduced in early Irish cinema, as Killarney was recast through the affordances of moving pictures and viewers were transported vicariously on the Killarney tour. Such technologised performances of travel adopted a panoramic perspective and, intertwining steam and cinematography, reproduced picturesque and sublime imagery.

Early cinematic productions which charted movement through the district included the Warwick Trading Company's *A Trip through the Gap of Dunloe*, part of its "With the Bioscope through Ireland" series filmed at the turn of the twentieth century, and the Kalem Film Manufacturing Company's *The Colleen Bawn* (1911). Luke Gibbons has argued that the juxtaposition of scenery and story in the latter film is so uneven as to produce a narrative in which the story of the Colleen Bawn is "overridden" by the natural landscape.[18] In fact the Colleen Bawn supplied a tale amenable to cinematic emplotment, untouched by the overt nationalism that marked many contemporary works associated with the Celtic Twilight. In this respect, early cinema reproduced and circulated romantically infused images and narratives of landscape in which people, including those on screen and those viewing the film, were dwarfed and even obscured by the grandeur of its topography.[19] Several of the earliest documentary films, such as *Life on the Great Southern and Western Railway* (1904) and *London to Killarney* (1907)—the latter made by the British filmmaker Arthur Melbourne-Cooper—popularised tourist routes and allowed audiences to experience vicarious movement through routes without leaving their seats.[20] In both documentary and fictionalised cinemagraphic travelogues,[21] then, scenery did not serve as a backdrop to action, but was actively produced through film as an iconic landscape. Indeed, film invited viewers to participate in virtual movement through places in which Romantic landscape aesthetics framed the journey and complemented narratives in pages of the *Irish Tourist*, which used the hearty flora of the Gap of Dunloe to illustrate its sublimity:

> A few shrubs and trees, and some masses of dark ivy and luxuriant heather, have fixed their roots amid the crevices of the rocks, perpetuate here their frugal and precarious existence, and lend colour and picturesqueness to the prevailing desolation. The narrow rapid stream of the Lee winds and roars through the glen, intensifying this desolate but sublime character of the scene.[22]

In the context of this imagery, the private toll-gate imposed jarring imaginative limits—more so than the intrusions of the Killarney cavalcade—and also undermined an emerging rhetoric of public space unsullied by the exclusivist and exclusionist politics that pervaded other landscapes. It signalled the disruption of movement and the restrictions placed on a "national" economic and cultural resource.

Historically, landlords' authority over their private land was demarcated in a variety of ways, from the hosting of private stag-hunts that asserted their exclusive authority over land to the assessment of rents. But the toll-gate was the most visible and obtrusive marker of private terrain—an obstruction which impeded the fluid performance of travel as much as telegraph wires intruded on Henry Peach Robinson's carefully constructed rustic imagery. The toll-gate was an historic feature of the district whose status was sanctioned by law. A writer in the *Ulster Times* remarked that while the late Lord Brandon had erected a sign declaring "NO THOROUGHFARE" on the iron gate which was part of the stone wall regulating access to the Upper Lake from the Gap, and had enforced that prohibition (even against Sir Walter Scott), the proprietor who had succeeded him, a Mr Hutchinson, ended the proscription and now allowed access by tourists to boats moored on the lake.[23] There were many subsequent protests by lesser-known visitors to Killarney that the tourist's movement was undermined by the caprices of the landlord and an unwarranted regime of tolls.

"FOR THE NATION"? TOLLS, THRESHOLDS,
AND THE KILLARNEY TOUR

If, from the 1850s on, Irish landed estates were subjected to intense scrutiny and criticism, Killarney's landlords did not escape such invective, though they were heavily implicated in the development of local economic activity from forestry to agriculture, and historically supported the tourism sector's growth.[24] As we have seen, tourism allowed Lord Kenmare to build solidarities with local tourism actors as his riches ebbed, telegraphing his authority through conspicuous patronage while promoting the development of the town. In an effort to spur industrial development, for instance, he promoted ornamental souvenir "Killarney ware". In an era in which Irish industrial development was often seen as a means of achieving greater prosperity, such small-scale hand manufacture tapped the vein of antipathy towards mass manufacture exemplified by John Ruskin and others.[25] The goal was to exploit growing interest in the wares, which even in the 1890s were said to be primarily of continental manufacture,[26] and make the industry genuinely "indigenous"—contrasting in workmanship and quality with the cheap trinkets peddled by local hucksters, mountain dew girls, and a "granddaughter" at Kate Kearney's eponymous cottage. But as we have also seen, the tourist-development programme was suffused with politics, and bound up with contests over land, authority, and the political status of Ireland. In 1902 *The Times* reported that the United Irish League had, in the previous year, applied pressure so that the local Board of Guardians refused to make a request to the Kerry County Council for grant-in-aid to support Lady Castlerosse's Killarney wood-carving industry. It would have entitled it to £600 from the Department of Agriculture. The action of the Board of Guardians, decried by *The Times*, was apparently made on the grounds that her father-in-law, Lord Kenmare, had been involved in the eviction of tenants "some years ago".[27] Lingering resentment of the proprietor—though a staunch Catholic, Kenmare was a strong opponent of Home Rule and was deeply resented for his estate's evictions in the 1870s and 1880s—animated local politics and often drew the tourism sector into wider debates, at both the local and national levels. And if, as we have seen, writers reserved their most grandiloquent prose to caricature local guides, beggars, and mountain dew girls, many directed bolder and even more bombastic language at landlords in denouncing the system of tolls that signified their power.

The Herbert estate, which tourists briefly crossed after leaving the Gap, drew harsh criticism for levying one shilling upon tourists to cross the last few hundred yards of the tour before they reached the shores of the Upper Lake. The traveller John U. Higinbotham commented acidly that having braved the human cavalcade at the Gap, including women who grew belligerent if ignored, and then having been told at the end of the excursion by the owner of their touring horses that he would add a sixpence to the agreed charge owing to the discomfort of the journey, he now encountered "the last straw"—a toll which constituted "the only case that we recall in all of our travels where extortion is practiced or sanctioned by the nobility".[28] (By contrast, Clement W. Scott was happy to dispense with tuppence to be admitted to this refuge from "more girls with more ornaments and more hags with more milk" that hounded him through the Gap).[29] We have seen ways in which Kate Kearney's Cottage demarcated new regimes of sociality, mobility, and exchange as people reached and then passed beyond it. Its liminal space afforded scope for travellers to dispense with abstinence principles, and even engage in mock-courtships as they entered a peasant realm.[30] On emerging from the Gap, Lord Brandon's Gate boldly declared the end of this regime of values and performances, and signified the pecuniary interest and authority of the landlord. That realm was devoid of the playful scripting, bartering, and ludic features associated with the realm of Kate Kearney and the mountain dew girl. In late-Victorian and Edwardian Ireland, land formed the focal point of intense political debate and social foment, resulting in a series of Land Acts beginning in 1881 that offered greater security to tenants, and inched towards support for outright land purchase of holdings, with state financial support. The symbolic and political importance of these performances was heightened and embedded within their wider enactions of resistance to landlord power.

In fact, the local estates' parlous positions engendered hopes that Killarney might be conserved as national property—a project which took the form of initiatives to promote it as an equivalent iconographic landscape to the Scottish Highlands, Welsh mountains, and Swiss Alps. If tourist and native alike could wander unfettered through these other districts, why should the Irish—and legions of visitors, too—be deprived of similar opportunities to enjoy their land? This question were allied to another query: how could this singular landscape be mobilised as a productive resource and, at the same time, be conserved as recreational ground? The effort to remove encumbrances to movement through Killarney embraced tourism in ways that contemporaneous efforts to enshrine the West in the Irish national imaginary as a place of autarky, purity, and the repository of a Gaelic soul did not. Indeed, proponents of efforts to make Killarney both an inclusive "national", as well as leading tourist, landscape under common ownership implicitly offered it as an alternative to the West, and not coincidentally included many prominent unionists in their ranks. They sought—unsuccessfully—to enlist the state in these efforts. And they emphasised not indigenous culture as a resource in tourist development, but rather made nature itself the subject of commoditisation—framed as an economic "asset" demanding protection from those who would steward it carelessly in the service of private interests.

ENDING "THE GREAT RULE OF ENGLISH
EXCLUSIVENESS"? PROPRIETORSHIP,
CONSERVATION, AND TOURISM AT KILLARNEY

Voluble protests over the landed interest's dominance over Irish soil centred
on two families who became the focus of excursionists' ire. The Kenmare
and Herbert Estates claimed full ownership of the Killarney Lakes. The
only public rights to its banks were at Ross Castle, where visitors could
embark and disembark craft. Elsewhere, at long-established toll-gates, some
excursionists reported surreptitious efforts by locals to subvert the exclusive
authority of the landlord and extract more than the established charge, as
two regimes of exchange, and cultures of transaction, intermingled: one the
dynamic bartering practices associated with the peasant regimes of value
and exchange and imposed by Kate Kearney's "granddaughter" and the
many colourful figures who surrounded her, and the other a system of fixed
tolls levied by estates. The author of "A Run to and through Paddy's Land",
serialised in the *Glasgow Daily Herald*, for instance, described "an old
woman" who opened the gate for the party of excursionists at Lord Brandon's Cottage. Proclaiming the charge to be "'not more than twopence'",
she nonetheless professed to have only threepence in change when offered
sixpence.[31] A similar anecdote appeared in the pages of the *Irish Times* in
1895, when a Dublin correspondent who had holidayed in Killarney, cycling
with two friends through the Gap of Dunloe, described how they arrived at
the demesne at the head of the Upper Lake, where a 1s. impost was levied.
Offering a half-sovereign to the gate-keeper, the party was informed she
could not make change.[32] Fortunately one member of the party found the
requisite change, as they were informed that they would otherwise have to
turn back, and retrace their steps—a distance of some ten miles.

While the wily locals' toll exactions mimicked—and even lampooned—
the tolls and, by extension, the authority of the landlord, more direct criticism of the formal toll regime came from those who condemned obstructions
to the tourist's free circulation. Indeed, these imposts were described by
one writer in the *Evening Telegraph* as "a system" of "the most aggressive
kind"; the writer added that "a poor man and his family anxious to have
a day's glimpse at the Lakes finds that tolls add ten or twelve shillings to
his day's expenses".[33] An outraged Patrick Spillane of Limerick, in an 1896
letter to the *Cork Examiner*, castigated the district's landlords for the exactions. He and his family (a party of four) had visited Killarney by train from
Limerick. They paid only 2s. 6d. per head by rail and then 6s. 6d. for a car
to convey them to various sites. But Spillane was incensed by tolls levied at
the entrance to Lord Kenmare's demesne at "Kelly's Gate" (6d. each). They
then paid the same sum to ascend Ross Castle. An additional 6d. per head
was levied "for the privilege of driving around Ross Island", and a further
6d. per head at the entrance gate to Deer Park. The party at last enjoyed
a site *gratis* at Aghadoe, before facing a 6d. impost per head again as they

drove through the "West Demesne", bringing their total disbursements, by Spillane's calculation, to 12*s*. at six toll-gates within a radius of five miles (he accounted for five tolls, amounting to 10*s*., in his letter).[34]

Newspapers provided a forum for dispute over aspects of these practices and to reveal contested notions of landscape and codes of travel that centred on them. In 1902 a pedestrian traveller writing to the *Irish Times* under the pseudonym "Londoner" criticised the private demesnes for cutting off scenic views to tourists on the public roads around the Lakes, lamented the absence of steamers on the Lower Lake, and commented on comparatively high costs of touring in Killarney, which the writer asserted to be twice the costs of a holiday in the English Lakes.[35] "Londoner" voiced frustration with the inconvenient situation of the town of Killarney and the absence of hotels near the Upper and Middle Lakes, which "force you to make the conventional tour by car and boat. These tours, which are numbered 1, 2, and 3, take you everywhere, and for those who do not object to being rushed round they are as satisfying as they are expensive."[36] Remarking that the English Lake district "is not nearly so much the subject of private property as Killarney", "Londoner" asserted that in the Lake District walkers found an unencumbered landscape amenable for touring without "covering the same ground twice", with villages to provide for them and no estates to block the lake-views. In contrast, the restrictions on hours of access to some sites such as Muckross Abbey frustrated the tourist's appreciation of Killarney by moonlight, just as the absence of smaller villages compelled tourists to join large parties of excursionists, frustrating acts of solitary touring.

John Benner, writing in reply, asserted that tourists could drive or walk to Ross Quay by way of a public road, and then hire a boat; the charm of the local characters and their conveyances were far greater than a conventional steamer. He disputed "Londoner's" assertion that a toll was levied to access Innisfallen, and pointed out that toll regimes prevailed at such famous British sites as Melrose and Furness Abbeys. Moreover, Benner insisted that the restrictions on access to demesnes were reasonable, as they could not be open "day and night".[37] "Surely," Benner asked, "he would not expect private property to be maintained for the public free of cost?"[38] In subsequent correspondence on the subject, Henry Hobbs of Limerick calculated that Lord Brandon's Gate, with a minimum of 500 excursionists passing through it daily four months of the year, netted the landlord an astonishing £3,000 annually.[39] Below Hobbs's letter, "Londoner" challenged Benner's assertion that no comparable tour could be had for the modest sum levied at the Gap by asserting that in the Tyrol pedestrians had at their disposal all the amenities every two or three miles to allow them to conduct themselves without being part of "grand tours".[40]

The debate raged on. Another rebuttal to "Londoner", pseudonymously penned by "Traveller", asserted that "[s]urely they cannot expect places to be kept up for visitors from all parts of the world without some charge to pay keepers, &c."[41] Indeed, "Traveller" argued that the charges at Muckross Abbey and demesne, and at Ross Castle paled beside the levies at Stonehenge. This letter was accompanied by another from John Benner:

> I do not share "Londoner's" acquaintance with the charges in the Tyrol, though I know something about Swiss rates. But, he will find, if he selects Killarney district for his next tramp, after each day's march through beautiful scenery, comfortable hotels and inns ready to receive him at moderate prices. English is spoken in all—a boon for travellers who have not the "gift of tongues."[42]

The debate in which "Traveller" and Benner defended Killarney's toll regime against "Londoner" and Henry Hobbs, enlisting British and continental comparators, ended with the newspaper's declaration on 11 September 1902 that correspondence on the matter was over. The war of letters centred on compulsory charges, the levels of such imposts, and the relative freedoms afforded travellers elsewhere. It evoked a recent dispute at one of Ireland's pre-eminent tourist sites, the Giant's Causeway, where a private syndicate had sought to demarcate the boundaries between private and public land, and had laid claim to the place—long seen, alongside Killarney, as one of Ireland's premier tourist attractions. The Giant's Causeway Company proposed to build railings and establish toll-gates for admission to the renowned geological formation on the Co. Antrim coast.[43] This initiative, the *Freeman's Journal* declared, was tantamount to vandalism: "The Giant's Causeway—one of the most remarkable natural curiosities in the world—is a national asset, and cannot be bartered away in this underhand manner."[44] A newspaper with an editorial stance on the opposite side of the Irish Home Rule debate, the *Belfast News-Letter*, weighed in, too, insisting that "[a] more ill-timed or a more audacious attempt to interfere with the People's Rights" was unequalled "within recent times in the history of the kingdom".[45] In October 1896 the *Belfast News-Letter* reported that an official had been deputised by the syndicate to take visitors' names, and had also stopped people on the grounds that they were trespassing on private land, requiring them first to sign their names in a book.[46] This practice, and rumours of differential fees for locals and those visiting from across the channel, provoked concern over the "obstruction" of access there. If a railing removed the risk of encountering the notoriously persistent local hawkers and guides, critics nonetheless charged that it excluded the public from customary access to the site. Despite professing a desire to flee from the local hordes, they balked at the prospect of paying charges to a syndicate. A Giant's Causeway Defence Fund, spearheaded in part by F.W. Crossley (no opponent of syndicates *per se*), formed in opposition to the initiative, and launched an ultimately unsuccessful effort to prevent the closing off of the site in 1898. In Co. Antrim, as in Killarney, diverse defenders of the "public's" right to access enlisted support from across the Irish Sea in an effort to defeat a syndicate's efforts to erect railings and impose charges for accessing the site.

The regime of tolls at Killarney was depicted as an obstacle to movement in a markedly different way than those associated with Kate's customary exactions and the mountain dew girls' imposts. As they were debated in the press, the toll-gate became a symbol of a wider system of land proprietorship in Ireland that retarded social and commercial progress. The American Presbyterian minister and prominent travel writer Dr Henry M. Field, for instance, who recounted his long journey "from Killarney to the Golden Horn" in a popular travelogue, found in the Irish district evidence of poor principles of land ownership, decried the physical enclosure of the Kenmare and Herbert demesnes by walls, which he saw as a metaphor for "the great rule of English exclusiveness",[47] and lamented the condition of the tenantry, which he contrasted with the sturdy independence of New England farmers. He ended his account of Irish travels by expressing the hope that a future visitor to Killarney

> shall not have his delight in the works of God spoiled by sight of the wretchedness of man; when instead of troops of urchins in rags, with bare feet, running for miles to catch the pennies thrown from jaunting cars, we shall see happy, rosy-cheeked children issuing from schoolhouses, and see the white spires of pretty churches gleaming in the valleys and on the hills.[48]

His short description of the Killarney leg of his wider globe-spanning journey suggested that the improvement of the peasantry's condition and the demise of the "great rule of English exclusiveness" might be resolved in tandem.

As we have seen, the contentious issue of tolls was linked to these wider discussions over the national condition, rural proprietorship, the freedom to roam, and the uplifting effects of both scenery and tourism. The charges levied by guides and hawkers, and the tributes demanded by Kate's "granddaughter" and the mountain dew girls, were inflected with complex cultural performances within an informal tourist economy; they offered contrasts to naked exactions at the landlord's toll-gate for tourists to merely move over land and lake. This was an era in which the system and structure of local landholding was changing dramatically, with the failing fortunes of both the Kenmare and Herbert estates. Tolls were stark reminders that Killarney, dubbed "Nature's Home", was in private hands. In fact, the weakness of the estates raised hopes that as land changed hands in Killarney,[49] reform of the system of tolls might open up sights to the tourist *gratis*. These contests over access came to a head in 1899. In October that year, opportunities, and risks, attached to changes in proprietorship were heralded by the announcement that the Herberts would be selling their remaining lands in the district.

The area in question was the 14,000 acres freehold with mansion and demesne that had belonged to the Herbert family for many decades. It comprised such celebrated sites as O'Sullivan's Cascade, Lord Brandon's Cottage, the Torc and Tomies Mountains, the ruins of Muckross Abbey, the islands of Dinish and Brickeen, as well as the Middle Lake, half of the Devil's Punch Bowl, half of Mangtertown Mountain, and two-thirds of the Purple Mountain.[50] The Herbert estate had passed into the hands of the Standard Life Company as mortgagees; the estate's agricultural holdings had been disposed of, and the mortgages were now preparing to sell the mansion and demesne. In consequence, one of the two most important landed families in the district was preparing to relinquish its last ownership amongst the vast holdings. This vestige, the *Freeman's Journal* noted, included that portion of land across which tourists passed as they left the Gap of Dunloe to access the Lakes, and for which they paid 1s. a head—a high sum "for some hard working artisan from Cork or Limerick, who has scraped up the money to give himself and his wife and children a day's holiday at Killarney".[51]

The impending sale excited concern that existing rights-of-way enjoyed by tourists might be even more strictly circumscribed, as at the Giant's Causeway. Could such a calumny be visited upon Ireland's other great scenic wonder? A correspondent in the *Evening Telegraph*, noting that the classic Killarney tour involved passing through the Gap and then paying a toll on Herbert property, declared that:

> If Muckross is ever sold to a curmudgeon or a crank he could shut up all access from the Gap; could prevent all visits to the Abbey; could shut out from the world the beautiful Torc Waterfall and O'Sullivan's Cascade; could, we fear, cut off all access by land or water to the Middle or Upper Lakes; could, in fact, shut up the Lakes of Killarney.[52]

The *Freeman's Journal* endorsed the purchase of the estate by the government, lest it "pass into the hands of some speculator who will weigh down the tourist with extravagant tolls, or of some oddity like the late Duke of Portland, who might close them altogether".[53] The unionist *Cork Constitution*, in contrast, mocked such "loosely-worded statements" as exaggerations, asserting that even if a "vulgar churl" excluded the public from the land, the new proprietor would never be able to extinguish views that could be enjoyed from other vantages.[54] But even "an American syndicate, and still less a speculative showman, would care to take over and settle down on a property under such conditions".[55] Fears that the extension of capricious aristocratic proprietorship would privatise Killarney reflected the diminished social authority of the local landed class, and encoded a persistent theme which was especially prominent in, but not limited to, nationalist organs of the press. Indeed, this debate occurred on the eve of the 1903 Wyndham Land Act, which was to further the transformation

of tenurial systems in Ireland and accelerate the arrival of peasant proprietorship. It nourished hopes amongst tourists and tourism-sector promoters alike that Killarney's tolls could be eradicated altogether.[56] At the
same time, the framing of the Killarney landscape as a productive tourist
resource by advocates of a new form of proprietorship revealed simmering
tensions over the extent to which the extortions of the rapacious estate,
rather than the comparatively modest exactions of the wily locals (which
had by this time been naturalised as inevitable features of a Killarney tour)
constituted an egregious defilement of the district's charms.

"THE DESPOILING HAND OF THE VANDAL": NATIONAL LANDSCAPES IN KILLARNEY

If Killarney was often narrated as a majestic landscape marred by grubby
commercialisation and the heavy imprint of the cockney's foot, rumours
which swirled around the sale of the estate raised fears of a monstrous,
irreversible pollution of its scenic charms and the rights of the public to
traverse the landscape. Concern about public access to, and stewardship
of, the landscape burst into the open in 1899, just as the successful visit of
a parliamentary delegation to the district had drawn to a close, and as the
political discourse in both Ireland and the United Kingdom more widely
was dominated by the Boer War. Many Irish nationalists at home and in
America were forthright in embracing the Boer cause.[57] In this context,
F.W. Crossley, the quixotic tourism champion who had appealed in the
early 1890s for tourism to cement the union, now appealed to "practical
patriotism of Irishmen", fearing that the property "may fall into private
hands, perhaps of some American or African millionaire, and thus the
opportunity would be lost to the country of possessing this exquisite estate,
as a national, or rather international, tourist resort".[58] Tellingly, this "patriotic" appeal appraised the physical landscape—not indigenous culture—as
a national economic resource. Alluding to almost 25 years of experience in
connection with the tourist trade and his role in the "tourist movement",
Crossley compared the assets of Killarney to the goldfields of South Africa
and coalfields of England, and called for a fund to be established to which
"every lover of Ireland" might subscribe from upwards of one shilling (giving "an opportunity for all to contribute—the poor man or woman their
shillings, and those who desire the prosperity of Ireland, and can afford
to back their wishes, a more substantial amount"). He announced that he
had already forwarded a 1,000*s.* contribution to the Lord Mayor of Dublin, acting as trustee.[59] But if the value of the district's land was linked to
its resource in tourism, Crossley was uneasy about entrusting its stewardship to transatlantic actors. The *Irish Tourist*, edited by Crossley, inveighed
against the prospect of Killarney being purchased by an American millionaire or a group of charitably minded Irish-Americans: "[W]e like neither

the idea of purchase by an American millionaire, nor the acquisition of so charming a spot by a sort of outcrop of Tammany".[60] The partial conflation of Irish America with Tammany Hall, for which Crossley feared that Killarney might supply a beachhead, allowed him to rhetorically cast nationalist Irish America as a sectionalist interest that was ill-suited to steward the country's premier touring district.

If the principle of landscape "conservation" united nationalist and unionist, there were several strategies for Killarney's acquisition. The *Freeman's Journal* pressed for outright state ownership, rather than an elaborate scheme to purchase the property by subscription, and noted in April 1899 that "[i]n America the State has with characteristic magnificence bought up vast territories containing thousands of square miles and dedicated them for ever to the public," while in Europe "interesting buildings or places of beauty have been purchased as national property", and even closer in London "thousands have been lavished on the Parks".[61] This proposal referenced a growing trend towards the acquisition of land and conferral of symbolic value on it as states produced "public" land and landscapes—many of them identified also as places of indigenous cultural value.[62] In America and on the continent, the creation of national parks was inextricably linked to projects that representatively invested selected topographies as "national landscapes". In Sweden, a proposed law on nature conservation in 1909 explicitly stated that national parks would be "'visual material for teaching patriotism'".[63] They had created vast stages for the performance of citizenship through bodily engagement with iconic national landscapes through sightseeing, hiking, walking, canoeing, and other activities. Linking the apparent inaction of the British state to the wider question of Ireland's inequitable treatment under the Union, the *Freeman's Journal* pointedly asked: "Does any one imagine that an Irish Parliament would treat the fair places of Ireland as the British Parliament has treated them? Happy in the possession of a free Parliament, the English people have been most successful in securing respect for the picturesque and the beautiful."[64] Kerry County Council passed a resolution in May 1899 supporting the government's purchase of the estate, after a meeting in which it was asserted that the property could be commercially profitable. The prospect of Muckross House becoming a royal residence was discussed but not included in the unanimous resolution, following the objection of a nationalist MP in attendance that it would give the proposition a "political tinge".[65] The *Irish Times*, for its part, favoured investing the estate in the County Council, in trust for the people of the county, by special statute.[66] The corollary to these efforts at conservation was the dismantling of the regime of levies, starkly and visibly signalled by the toll-gate, which signified the system of private ownership itself, and suggested not only conservation but reconstruction of the district's tenurial, social, and economic foundations. In contrast, the parallel system of customary tolls levied by local figures in elaborate tourist performances became matters for individuals to navigate and negotiate as abiding features of the Killarney tour, the tributes and charges disparaged by writers, but often in the service of a lively narrative.

As this debate raged on, it suggested the unease that attended the commodification of the Irish landscape at Killarney, but this time in the form of a commercial tourist complex on a near-industrial scale. If Glendalough had its religious overtones, and the Giant's Causeway a narrative that supplied both a creation myth for the site and a politically salient linkage between Ulster and Scotland in north-east Ulster, there were myriad narratives of space in Killarney, from the wretched to the Romantic. Echoing R.A.S. Macalister's remarks of a few years earlier about the sanctity of Irish sites and the potential for their desecration, the *Freeman's Journal* suggested that the defilement of the ancient site of the crowning of Irish kings, the Mound of Tara, now judged to be irreparable, foreshadowed Killarney's fate. But now the vulgar and rapacious rich American, not the cockney excursionist, was rhetorically enlisted to caricature the polluting designs of the foreigner. A "Millionaire Peck" of New York apparently harboured designs to

> cut up the estate into building lots, to convert the wild glories of the Lakes into glaring villas and hideous gardens, the homes of rich soap-boilers from New York and wealthy oilmen from Philadelphia. In the meantime, Ireland must stand by. She has not the power to raise a finger to protect either Tara or Killarney. Ill fares the land that has the foreigner for a master.[67]

Other reports alleged that a syndicate had been formed to purchase the estate, with a view to profiting by cutting down the woods on Torc Mountain, employing hydroelectric power from Torc Waterfall to supply electricity to a new factory at Muckross House, and turning Innisfallen Island into a "Tea Garden, probably with negro minstrels, merry-go-rounds, and other amusements, such as prevail in similar places on the English coasts"; it harboured similar plans for Dinish Island, steam launches throughout the Lower Lake, and a large increase in tolls.[68] Exclusive rights would allegedly be granted by the syndicate to its own flotilla on Muckross Lake. A small tramway would be constructed to ferry tourists throughout Muckross Demense, and a funicular railway would be erected to Torc Mountain, providing excursionists with a view of frequent fireworks displays at Muckross Abbey.[69] Herbert Honohan, in *Donahoe's Magazine*, alleged that Muckross House, which had been "so much spoken of as a probable Royal residence" the year before, would become a factory to extract carbide of calcium from limestone.[70] The prospect of such wanton desecration, combining theme-park commerce with resource extraction on an industrial scale, aroused indignation amongst tourist-development champions who now pledged themselves to preserve Killarney for its principal consumers—travellers of all political stripes—so that they may appreciate the country's premier tourist landscape without the attendant despoilments of funiculars and factories.

Facing the prospect of desecrations which rendered the "granddaughter's" customary imposts comparatively trifling, one solution was to place Killarney in public hands and enshrine it as a place, as Herbert Honohan wrote unironically (given the ink that had been spilled for decades over the bedlam that attended tourism there), "unspoiled by man's desecrating hand".[71] Recounting a story in which an American tourist had sped through the Holy Land in one night in order that he could reach Killarney and enjoy three days there, Honohan declared that "[i]t is not easy for Irishmen to rest under the thought that steam whistles and music-hall ditties may soon profane the sacred quiet of Killarney where nought is worldly." He ended by exhorting "more well-to-do kith and kin" to acquire it as a "National property. We would save it from the despoiling hand of the vandal, and all countries that love their beauty spots will applaud our desire."[72] While, as we have seen, few travellers claimed to have found the "sacred quiet" of Killarney which Honohan extolled, a district long-dismissed as teeming with mendicants was now recast as a landscape boasting innumerable beauty sites in narratives that elided—even repudiated—the ludic narrative of Killarney travel. This Romantic landscape was enlisted to castigate both the landlords' prospective privatisation of the land, and Americans' crass plans to commercialise it.

The programme to conserve Killarney spanned the Irish Sea and united disparate interests. Under a headline "Can Killarney Be Saved?", the *Kerry Sentinel* voiced fears of a "Saxon manufacturing Joint Stock Company's" designs on Killarney, and recounted that a Judge Adams, speaking before English visitors at a dinner given by the Lord Mayor of Dublin, had urged upon them the need to preserve "'the beautiful places of Ireland'", and noted that "'Ireland was threatened with a tremendous calamity'."[73] On 3 June 1899 a letter from "Q.C." to the same newspaper lamented that in Ireland, "[o]utside the Guinness family" there was a marked paucity of "public-spirited millionaires" who might contemplate presenting the estate as a gift to the nation.[74] "Q.C." expressed concern that a new proprietor might, by closing access to the various sites, "wipe out the Killarney lakes as one of the world's great playgrounds", and called for the state to purchase the property (the rumoured price being £30,000). In language that revealed the prospective recreational value for this district, "Q.C" proclaimed that such a measure would secure "the Lakes of Killarney as an inheritance for Ireland and a pleasure-ground for the world".

The scheme's proponents enlisted the support of the National Trust for Places of Historic Interest or Natural Beauty at a meeting in Grosvenor House, London, at the home of the duke of Westminster in June 1899. It brought together luminaries, including the earls of Cork and Mayo, and the Lord Mayor of Dublin, and heard correspondence from the earls of Meath and Carlisle, as well as the American ambassador. The meeting approved a motion made by the marquess of Dufferin and Ava adopting a report that proposed securing Killarney as a "great national park"; Dufferin asserted that it could be secured along the same lines that the USA and the Dominion of Canada had secured Niagara Falls.[75] The resolution was adopted. A committee comprising luminaries of diverse political creeds—the earl of Cork, Lord Dunraven, Lord Iveagh, F.W. Crossley, John Redmond, and Horace Plunkett—was formed to explore the matter. The government made clear that it had little interest in the proposal.[76] Nonetheless, the *Irish Tourist*, under Crossley's editorship, praised this initiative, declaring that "[t]he Giant's Causeway and Killarney are Ireland's principal scenic attractions"—comparable to Yellowstone Park in the USA. It noted that the Causeway had been appropriated by a company running it on commercial lines, "thereby taking all of the poetry out of it".[77] By contrast, Killarney "might yet be saved", if the public's sympathy could be enlisted in promoting the Trust's plans. The *Belfast News-Letter* reported that the mortgagees of the estate, the Standard Life Insurance Company, might be willing to dispose of the property "for a sum not far in excess of £30,000", which cheered those who hoped that it might be possible to preserve the property for the public "in the manner of the Yellowstone Park".[78] As a result of the meeting, a "Joint English and Irish Committee" was charged with exploring whether the committee might be given the option of purchasing the estate at an agreed sum "for some period to be agreed upon".[79] Such ambitions were circumscribed by the practical constraints placed on raising such a large sum, and by the Committee's concern that such a bid would, perversely, raise the price of the property.

These lofty ambitions to conserve Killarney from the private designs of landlords and from large-scale exploitation were underpinned by the belief that Killarney held some special place in the imagined landscape of the Irish nation, too—a privileged position as "Beauty's Home" and *Ireland's* signature tourist landscape—terrain which was not claimed by any one political faction, or constructed as a place of cultural purity. If other places lay "off the beaten track", in the words of Eleanor Foster, Killarney (like the Giant's Causeway and the Blarney Stone) provided the "'show' places" to British travellers through which they gained an essential apprehension of Ireland.[80] While Foster hoped instead that the tourist's reach would extend beyond these well-known sites, the joint committee established to place Killarney in public hands wished to steward this national landscape and enhance its fame. By November 1899 Hugh Blakiston, its secretary, in a letter to *The Times*, outlined the committee's hope to secure guardianship of Dinish Island, Torc Falls, and rights-of-way by land and water which corresponded to those currently enjoyed by the public.[81] With some satisfaction for having warned readers against the mounting hyperbole, the *Cork Constitution* reported that the National Trust had proposed £40,000 for the property, which had gone to auction with few bidders, none offering more than £50,000.[82] Amid tepid state support for nationalisation, and continued uncertainty over the fate of the estate, the *Kerry Sentinel* expressed considerable relief when the property was purchased shortly thereafter by Lord Ardilaun (of the wealthy Guinness family, whose wife's grandmother was a Herbert[83]), for £60,000 (£10,00 more than was bid at the recent auction, from which it had been withdrawn). Noting his record of philanthropy in earlier gifting St Stephen's Green to Dublin, and also the famous generosity of his brother, Lord Iveagh, the newspaper declared that "it is a pleasure to know that the property has not passed into the hands of money-grabbers and iconoclasts."[84] The Irish people, the *Kerry Sentinel* asserted, surveying press opinion on the matter, considered this result to be "THE NEXT BEST THING TO THE ACQUISITION OF KILLARNEY AS A GIFT TO THE NATION".[85] The transaction was an Irish matter, not involving disposal on London markets amidst "Saxon peers and capitalists". In Ardilaun's hands, the nationalist organ asserted, Killarney would avoid the fate of "the sordid or unpatriotic purpose of revoking or modifying by a title the prespective right of the Irish people to glorify in Killarney as a magnificent scenic asset of the nation available to all comers". The *Kerry Sentinel* also asserted that the new proprietor "is a man who will rise superior to such petty considerations as tolls, and it can be depended upon that the present tolls levied on visitors, which are not unreasonable, will not be increased, if, indeed, they are not altogether abolished".[86]

In fact, Ardilaun disappointed not only the *Kerry Sentinel* but also many prominent tourist-development advocates. In April 1907 the newspaper compared him unfavourably with Lord Kenmare, regretting "to observe some hostility on the part of a non-resident proprietor, Lord Ardilaun, to representations made by the Association for small concessions which would be an advantage to the tourist development".[87] By underscoring his *non-resident* status, the nationalist organ clearly attempted to rhetorically embed its critique of his unpatriotic "neglect" of the interests of the estate and the wider locality within discourses excoriating the figure of the absentee landlord. At the first annual meeting of the Killarney, Cork, Glengarriff, and South of Ireland Tourist Association in April 1907, it was noted that the new owner of the estate, unlike Lord Kenmare, had also declined to support the extension of telephone call stations on his property, in consequence of which the proposal "fell through".[88] Furthermore, he had not replied to the association's request that he erect a luncheon room for tourists at the head of the Upper Lake. The association noted at its annual meeting in 1907 that its attention had been drawn to the "unreasonable toll" levied at the end of the Gap: "It is confidently hoped that some measures will be adopted to put an end to what is undoubtedly a great grievance to tourists and visitors to Killarney."[89]

Whereas Ardilaun's acquisition of Muckross had raised hopes that he would reproduce the munificence of his gift of St Stephen's Green to Dublin, the *Killarney Sentinel* opined that it might have been preferable for the property to have passed into the hands of the much-feared "American syndicate". It ominously warned that although negotiations between the landlord and the association were pending, there remained risks that "tourist privileges" could yet be hampered "by narrow-minded exercise of proprietorial rights".[90] The leader concluded by expressing hope "that Lord Ardilaun, with a higher if not more profitable interest in the country than the sale of Guinness's stout, will meet the views of the Association and do his part like Lord Kenmare in advancing the welfare of the famous lake district". Ardilaun's management of the newly acquired lands led many local tourism advocates to invoke the long and sad history of negligent landlordism.[91] Killarney's transition to the much-hoped-for national park was to be a protracted and conflict-ridden path. The district would not boast a national park until after partition, and the famous "indigenous" tolls levied by pretenders to Kate Kearney's mantle, though generating innumerable (often comedic) accounts of bewilderment and bother, attracted no comparable fiery invective. Indeed they survived beyond the estates and into independence as indispensible features of the Killarney travel narrative.

CONCLUSION

If the performance of exchanges deep in the Gap beyond Kate's poetic toll-bar affirmed her symbolic authority over distinctive social regimes, buttressed by custom and drawing on lore, the formal toll regime expressed the formal authority of the estate over the landscape and the contested politics of land in late-nineteenth-century and early-twentieth-century Ireland. The toll-gates' prospective dismantling was linked with wider national debates over patriotism, national landscapes, tourism, and exclusivist narratives of space and travel. The toll-gate rhetorically signified private interests and designs: it was depicted as a severe impediment to performances of travel by Irish, British, and foreign travellers alike. Comic descriptions of locals' extortions were elided in these serious-minded protests against a far more perfidious regime of tolls. Indeed, without its rich literary instrumentality, the cavalcade faded altogether in many accounts of Killarney travel. In a counterpoint to the narrative of bedlam, Romantic aesthetics supplied discourses for programmatic efforts to frame the district as a national landscape, requiring protection from the rapacious designs of the American millionaire and naked extortions at the landlord's toll-gate—and signalled the openness of the district to wider tourism. These debates emerged as the twentieth century was to usher in partition, but also as the Tourist Organisation Society of Ireland, established in 1915, sought to rekindle support for a sector buffeted by war, and facing a decade of war and strife. As Irish tourism entered this uncertain era, the rhetorical foil for the "conservation" of Killarney was not the despoiling hand of the wily Gap denizen, but that of the capricious English landlord and the avaricious American millionaire—both bent on subverting narratives of place that had defined the Killarney tour for decades.

Conclusion

When Burton E. Stevenson turned his attention to a district in Ireland that he compared to both Scotland's Trossachs and to Niagara Falls—insisting that in Killarney Thomas Cook's pervasive influence left tourists who wished to "see Killarney 'in the least fatiguing manner'" resigned to placing themselves under the firm's control—he remarked on a peculiar fascination with a place that had been stripped of intrinsically Irish features:[1]

> Killarney is the one place in Ireland which every tourist wants to see, not because it is characteristically Irish, but because it has been very carefully exploited. In my own opinion, a trip to Holy Cross and Cashel, or to Mellifont and Monasterboice and the tombs of the kings, or to the congested districts of Connaught, is far better worth while. But the great bulk of tourist traffic follows the beaten path, and in Ireland the beaten path leads straight to Killarney.[2]

Later, when Stevenson lifted a glass of mountain dew to his lips at Kate Kearney's well-appointed cottage, he wrote that he drank the famous libation "in the interests of this narrative".[3] So doing, he abandoned the persona of the astonished traveller and the pretence of having his designs undermined by artful locals. Many accounts of the Gap tour expressed an ironic sensibility—one that is often attributed to the late-twentieth- and twenty-first-century tourist.[4] Within the expanding network of Irish tourist sites and routes, the Killarney tour gained fame as a place where past, present, fact, and legend were blended as generously as Kerry mountain dew and goat's-milk. An encounter with larger-than-life characters at the Gap of Dunloe furnished writers with material with which to expound on Irish Otherness, narrate their own erudition, lament the condition of the peasantry, and, more often than not, spin a readable, saleable yarn. And, in a growing stream of travel writing, the misadventures of Killarney tour cascaded down to audiences across the globe.

Echoing a widespread, playful refrain of open scepticism and conscious of both the well-established, underlying script and his role in the performance, Burton Stevenson wrote that the neighbourhood of Kate Kearney's

Cottage, where he enjoyed his beverage, was "a long way from the 'banks of Killarney'" where Owenson's song placed her protagonist.[5] Moreover, he contended that the whiskey he imbibed "is supposed to be surreptitious, but of course it has paid the tax like any other".[6] In enshrining the Gap tour in popular imagination, guide-books, travelogues, photographs, postcards, and other texts mapped out interwoven features of landscape and performance that became as firmly rooted in the locality as the arbutus trees that dotted the landscape. However instrumental these tropes became, many writers still expressed underlying anxiety over the extent of the excursionist's control over the tourist encounter. They offered generous advice on how the tour might be navigated, and its various frustrations either partly circumvented or endured. *Murray's Handbook* advised readers that an exchange of money for goat's-milk and mountain dew was inevitable in the land of Kate Kearney. It also suggested that tourists pay a "small consideration" to the ubiquitous mountain dew girls, and hinted obliquely, and wistfully, at the eclipse of Romantic precepts by commenting that it would be preferable "to enjoy the scenery without being pestered by these itinerant vendors; but it is just as well to take it all with good humour".[7] Legions of travel writers enumerated figures whom tourists would encounter, from the skilful bugler to the Killarney boatman, to the fearsome landlady of Kate Kearney's Cottage, to coquettish mountain dew girls who plied their trade beyond it. These writers adopted diverse perspectives on this medley of characters, calibrated to a variety of reading audiences and reflecting a range of stances, from that of the serious social commentator, to the frustrated traveller, to figures such as Burton E. Stevenson, who professed simply to be playing along. To some, Killarney offered the potential for social and cultural hierarchies to be challenged and inverted, as girls proffered their hospitality to men in the form of fleeting mock-courtships, as guides recounted fantastical lore which the learned tourist disputed, as tourists expressed exasperation at the exorbitant cost of local services which they nonetheless procured, and as the "granddaughter" schooled excursionists in customs of the country, emphasising the generous gratuity which compensated her hospitality. To others, a visit to Killarney was occasion for commentary on venality that modern tourism visited upon rural realms. A much greater general anxiety gripped late-Victorian tourism advocates, whose discourses of pollution centred as much on the toll-gate and the ferris wheel as on Killarney's colourful characters. In evoking the pleasures of the place, they elided the carnival atmosphere altogether, extolled the district's bucolic charms, and laid responsibility for impeding the Killarney tour squarely at the feet not of greedy locals, whose antics were now firmly implanted in narratives of place, but rather rapacious landlords. Narratives of place and culture that unfolded in their writing must be understood against the background of contentious ideologies of tourist development, nationhood, and patriotism, as well as contested landscape aesthetics and political programmes, and in terms of performances inflected by class and gender. They accelerated and intensified on the eve of conflicts that would engulf Europe and the world, and visit rebellion, revolution, and civil war on Ireland.

This study has argued in favour of critically engaging the leisure tourist narrative—a largely under-studied part of the Irish travel-writing canon in this time—alongside other texts to understand these diverse travel performances. The grammar of these performances merits close attention. No matter how much surprise and disdain excursionists affected at the trappings of mass tourism, and no matter how loud their voices were raised in protest against alleged extortions or encumbrances along the path, few travellers in Killarney, however fleet of foot or determined to find solitude and not saturnalia, evaded Killarney's colourful entourage. And very few refrained from describing those encounters in equally colourful detail. Their accounts, many laced with irony, were often intended to entertain; but they also sought to establish narrative distance from both the toured and the touring. Complex and dynamic performances in the narrow defile of the Gap of Dunloe made it a site of extraordinary sensuous engagement, distinctive forms of movement, and regimes of intense and peculiar sociality. But just as features of the ludic master-narrative of Killarney travel had antecedents in the pre-Famine era (when William H.A. Williams locates the origins of Irish tourism *per se*), a narrative anchored in codes of Romantic landscape appreciation persisted through the era of large-scale commercial tourism and supplied a discourse mobilised by railway-travel promoters and cinematographers, and was also deployed against local estates at the turn of the twentieth century.

Tensions between immersion in carnival and splendours of solitude were evident in the vacillating responses of excursionists to conventions of touring Killarney—and their own less-than-firm grip over it. Many expressed frustration in their inability to evade locals, toll-gates, and the vulgar trappings of commercial tourism, and expressed a desire to experience "unmediated" encounters with the landscape. Some endeavoured to "escape" the expensive web of customary exchanges and even more pernicious estate levies, and evaluate the landscape on their own terms. Others lamented conditions which led the mountain dew girl to join this cavalcade of hucksters and imposters. Most recreational tourists approached the colourful cavalry at the Gap with a mixture of resignation, trepidation, and profound curiosity. Appraisals of its people, sounds, sights, and tastes resounded like Killarney's famous echoes in many travelogues and guidebooks, and inscribed strangeness, allure, and romance—and sometimes a mixture of all three—in the Killarney tour. Fuelled by myriad motivations and narrational strategies—entertainment, social critique, political polemic—they produced diverse narratives of travel, landscape, and identity that were set against a magnificent background of mountain rivulets, deep recesses, and rocky outcrops. They were also cast amidst fluid social, cultural, commercial, and political conditions in which performances of excursioning, flights from the tourist hordes, serious-minded social investigation, and proclamations of resistance to, and engulfment by, a world of myth, subterfuge, entertainment, and extortion revealed complex, interwoven enactments of travel.

Notes

NOTES TO THE INTODUCTION

1. Thomas W. Silloway and Lee L. Powers, *The Cathedral Towns and Inter-vening Places of England, Ireland, and Scotland: A Description of Cities, Cathedrals, Lakes, Mountains, Ruins, and Watering-Places* (Boston: A. Williams and Company, 1883), p. v.
2. Silloway and Powers, *The Cathedral Towns*, p. 27.
3. Silloway and Powers, *The Cathedral Towns*, p. 27.
4. Silloway and Powers, *The Cathedral Towns*, p. 27.
5. Silloway and Powers, *The Cathedral Towns*, pp. 27–28.
6. On tourism history, see John K. Walton, "Prospects in Tourism History: Evolution, State of Play and Future Developments", *Tourism Management*, 30, no. 6 (2009): 783–93. See also Walton's earlier review essay "Taking the History of Tourism Seriously", *European Quarterly Review*, 27, no. 4 (1997): 563–71, as well as John K. Walton, ed., *Histories of Tourism: Representation, Identity and Conflict* (Clevedon: Channel View Publications, 2005). Other valuable collections include Rudy Koshar, ed., *Histories of Leisure* (Oxford: Berg, 2002) and Hartmut Berghoff, Barbara Korte, Ralf Schneider, and Christopher Harvie, eds., *The Making of Modern Tourism: The Cultural History of the British Experience, 1600–2000* (Basingstoke: Palgrave Macmillan, 2002).
7. For geographically and chronologically expansive surveys of tourism, see John Towner, *An Historical Geography of Recreation and Tourism in the Western World, 1510–1940* (Chichester: John Wiley & Sons, 1996) and also Orvar Löfgren, *On Holiday: A History of Vacationing* (Berkeley: University of California Press, 1999). For a valuable theoretical treatment of Thomas Cook, see Trent Newmeyer, "'Under the Wing of Mr. Cook': Transformations in Tourism Governance", *Mobilities*, 3, no. 2 (July 2008): 243–67, while a more general tourism history survey is offered by Jack Simmons, "Railways, Hotels, and Tourism in Great Britain, 1839–1914", *Journal of Contemporary History*, 19, no. 2 (1984): 201–22. The Grand Tour has long featured as one of the key themes in the study of travel history: amongst the seminal studies are Jeremy Black, *The British and the Grand Tour* (Beckenham: Croom Helm, 1985) and James Buzard, "The Grand Tour and After (1660–1840)", in Peter Hulme and Tim Youngs, eds., *The Cambridge Companion to Travel Writing* (Cambridge: Cambridge University Press, 2002), pp. 37–52. More recent work includes Rosemary Sweet, "British Perceptions of Florence in the Long Eighteenth Century", *The Historical Journal*, 50, no. 4 (2007): 837–59 and Iain Gordon Brown, "Water,

Windows, and Women: The Significance of Venice for Scots in the Age of the Grand Tour", *Eighteenth-Century Life*, 30, no. 3 (2006): 1–50. James Buzard's pioneering study is also worthy of note here: *The Beaten Track: European Tourism, Literature, and the Ways to 'Culture', 1800–1918* (Oxford: Clarendon Press, 1993). See also Michael Heafford, "Between Grand Tour and Tourism: British Travellers to Switzerland in a Period of Transition, 1814–1860", *Journal of Transport History*, 27, no. 1 (2006): 25–47. The study of tourism in Scotland offers examples of two approaches to the subject, one primarily drawing on literary sources, the other on both archival and printed material: for the former, see Katherine Haldane Grenier, *Tourism and Identity in Scotland, 1770–1914: Creating Caledonia* (Aldershot: Ashgate, 2005), and for the latter Alastair J. Durie, *Scotland for the Holidays: Tourism in Scotland, c. 1780–1939* (East Linton: Tuckwell Press, 2003), as well as his study with James Bradley and Marguerite Dupree, *Water is Best: The Hydros and Health Tourism in Scotland, 1840–1940* (Edinburgh: John Donald Publishers Ltd., 2006). New work in the field of British travel emphasises the character of intercultural contact, often through the prism of Empire: see, for instance, Catherine Hall, *Civilising Subjects: Colony and Metropole in the English Imagination, 1830–1867* (Chicago: The University of Chicago Press, 2002); Linda Colley, *The Ordeal of Elizabeth Marsh: A Woman in World History* (London: HarperCollins, 2007); F. Robert Hunter, "Tourism and Empire: The Thomas Cook & Son Enterprise on the Nile, 1868–1914", *Middle Eastern Studies*, 40, no. 5 (2004): 28–54; and the reverse gaze employed in Julie F. Codell, "Reversing the Grand Tour: Guest Discourse in Indian Travel Narratives", *The Huntington Library Quarterly*, 70, no. 1 (2007): 173–89.
8. Buzard, *The Beaten Track*.
9. Helen Gilbert and Anna Johnston, "Introduction", in Helen Gilbert and Anna Johnston, eds., *In Transit: Travel, Text, Empire* (New York: Peter Lang, 2002), pp. 5–6.
10. See Shelley Baranowski's excellent review essay "An Alternative to Everyday Life? The Politics of Leisure and Tourism", *Contemporary European History*, 12, no. 4 (2003): 561–72. John K. Walton, *The Blackpool Landlady: A Social History* (Manchester: Manchester University Press, 1978); *The English Seaside Resort: A Social History, 1750–1914* (Leicester: Leicester University Press, 1983); *Blackpool* (Edinburgh: Edinburgh University Press/Carnegie Publishing, 1998); *The British Seaside: Holidays and Resorts in the Twentieth Century* (Manchester: Manchester University Press, 2000); "Beaches, Bathing and Beauty: Health and Bodily Exposure at the British Seaside from the 18th to the 20th Century", *Revue Française de Civilisation Britannique*, 14, no. 3 (2007): 117–34. See also T. Bennett, "A Thousand and One Troubles: Blackpool Pleasure Beach", in [no editor identified], *Formations of Pleasure* (London: Routledge and Kegan Paul, 1983), pp. 138–55; Rob Shields, "Ritual Pleasures of a Seaside Resort: Liminality, Carnivalesque, and Dirty Weekends", chap. 2 in *Places on the Margin: Alternative Geographies of Modernity* (London: Routledge, 1991), pp. 73–116; and Darren Webb's critique, "Bakhtin at the Seaside: Utopia, Modernity and the Carnivalesque", *Theory, Culture & Society*, 22, no. 3 (2005): 121–38. See also A.J. Durie and M.J. Huggins, "Sport, Social Tone and the Seaside Resorts of Great Britain, c. 1850–1914", *International Journal of the History of Sport*, 15, no. 1 (1998): 173–87; John F. Travis, *The Rise of the Devon Seaside Resorts, 1750–1900* (Exeter: Exeter University Press, 1993); and for Wales, Peter Borsay, "Welsh Seaside Resorts: Historiography, Sources and Themes", *Welsh History Review*, 24, no. 2 (2008): 92–119.

11. Robert Preston-Whyte, "The Beach as a Liminal Space", in Alan A. Lew, C. Michael Hall, and Allan M. Williams, eds., *A Companion to Tourism* (Oxford: Blackwell Publishing Ltd., 2004), pp. 349–59; Shields, "Ritual Pleasures".
12. Theano S. Terkenli, "Tourism and Landscape", in Lew, Hall, and Williams, eds., *A Companion to Tourism*, pp. 339–48.
13. Adrian Franklin, *Tourism: An Introduction* (London: SAGE Publications, 2003), pp. 24–26; scholars have further argued that the state remains a primary sponsor of tourism, and that notions of "cultural tourism" are framed by the system of nation-states, wherein specific cultures are inscribed and demarcated by political borders. See, for instance, Mike Robinson and Melanie Smith, "Politics, Power and Play: The Shifting Contexts of Cultural Tourism", in Melanie K. Smith and Mike Robinson, eds., *Cultural Tourism in a Changing World: Politics, Participation, and (Re)presentation* (Clevedon: Channel View Publications, 2006), pp. 1–17.
14. Séamas Ó Saothraí, "Russell, Thomas O'Neill (1828–1908)", *Oxford Dictionary of National Biography* (Oxford University Press, 2004) <http://www.oxforddnb.com.subzero.lib.uoguelph.ca/view/article/35885> (11 February 2010).
15. T.O. Russell, *Beauties and Antiquities of Ireland, Being a Tourist's Guide to Its Most Beautiful Scenery & an Archaeologist's Manual for Its Most Interesting Ruins* (London: Kegan Paul, Trench Trübner & Co. Ltd, 1897), p. 1.
16. Russell, *Beauties and Antiquities of Ireland*, pp. 3–4.
17. Russell, *Beauties and Antiquities of Ireland*, p. 4.
18. *Picturesque Scenery in Ireland, drawn by Thomas Creswick, R.A., Engraved on Steel, with Descriptive Jottings by a Tourist* (New York: R. Worthington, 1881), p. 71.
19. See, for instance, the excursions outlined in John Cooke, ed., *Handbook for Travellers in Ireland*, 5th ed. (London: John Murray, 1896), pp. 423–29.
20. Glenn Hooper, *Travel Writing and Ireland, 1760–1860: Culture, History, Politics* (Basingstoke: Palgrave Macmillan, 2005); Glenn Hooper, ed., *The Tourist's Gaze: Travellers to Ireland, 1800–2000* (Cork: Cork University Press, 2001); Martin Ryle, *Journeys in Ireland: Literary Travellers, Rural Landscapes, Cultural Relations* (Aldershot: Ashgate, 1999); Christopher Morash, *Writing the Irish Famine* (Oxford: Clarendon Press, 1995); Margaret Kelleher, *The Feminization of Famine: Expressions of the Inexpressible?* (Durham: Duke University Press, 1997); Melissa Fegan, *Literature and the Irish Famine, 1845–1919* (Oxford: Clarendon Press, 2002); Elizabeth Meloy, "Touring Connemara: Learning to Read a Landscape of Ruins, 1850–1860", *New Hibernia Review/ Iris Éireannach Nua*, 13, no. 3 (2009): 21–46.
21. Hooper, *Travel Writing and Ireland*.
22. Éadaoin Agnew, "Travel Writing", in James H. Murphy, ed., Robert Welch and Brian Walker, general eds., *The Oxford History of the Irish Book*, vol. 4, *The Irish Book in English, 1800–1890* (Oxford: Oxford University Press, 2011), pp. 389–98.
23. Susan Kroeg, "Cockney Tourists, Irish Guides, and the Invention of the Emerald Isle", *Éire-Ireland* 44, nos 3–4 (2009): 200–28.
24. For histories of Irish tourism, see Eric G.E. Zuelow, "'Ingredients for Cooperation': Irish Tourism in North-South Relations, 1924–1998", *New Hibernia Review*, 10, no. 1 (2006): 17–39; Angela Mehegan, "The Cultural Analysis of Leisure: Tourism and Travels in Co. Donegal", *CIRCA*, 107 (spring 2004): 58–62. For Killarney tourism, see Donal Horgan, "The Development of Tourism in Killarney, 1720–2000", in Jim Larner, ed., *Killarney: History & Heritage* (Wilton, Cork: The Collins Press, 2005), pp. 122–38.

25. See, for instance, James Deegan and Donal A. Dineen, *Tourism Policy and Performance: The Irish Experience* (London: International Thomson Business Press, 1997); C. Michael Hall and Stephen J. Page, *The Geography of Tourism and Recreation: Environment, Place and Space* (London: Routledge, 1999), pp. 198–212; Moya Kneafsey, "Tourism Images and the Construction of Celticity in Ireland and Brittany", in David C. Harvey, Rhys Jones, Neil McInroy, and Christine Milligan, eds., *Celtic Geographies: Old Culture, New Times* (London: Routledge, 2002), pp. 123–38; and several important edited collections, including Ullrich Kockel, ed., *Culture, Tourism and Development: The Case of Ireland* (Liverpool: Liverpool University Press, 1994); Barbara O'Connor and Michael Cronin, eds., *Tourism in Ireland: A Critical Analysis* (Cork: Cork University Press, 1993); Michael Cronin and Barbara O'Connor, eds., *Irish Tourism: Image, Culture and Identity* (Clevedon: Channel View Publications, 2003). Recent contributions to the field are Michael Clancy, *Brand New Ireland? Tourism, Development and National Identity in the Irish Republic* (Farnham: Ashgate, 2009) and Kelli Ann Costa, *Coach Fellas: Heritage and Tourism in Ireland* (Walnut Creek, CA: Left Coast Press, Inc., 2009).
26. Eric G.E. Zuelow, *Making Ireland Irish: Tourism and National Identity since the Irish Civil War* (Syracuse: Syracuse University Press, 2009); Eric G.E. Zuelow, "'Ingredients for Cooperation'".
27. Irene Furlong, *Irish Tourism, 1880–1980* (Dublin: Irish Academic Press, 2009).
28. William H.A. Williams, *Creating Irish Tourism: The First Century, 1750–1850* (London: Anthem Press, 2010); *Tourism, Landscape, and the Irish Character: British Travel Writers in Pre-Famine Ireland* (Madison: The University of Wisconsin Press, 2008).
29. Jonathan Culler, "Semiotics of Tourism", *American Journal of Semiotics*, 1, nos 1–2 (1981): 127–40.
30. L.P. Curtis, Jr., *Anglo-Saxons and Celts: A Study of Anti-Irish Prejudice in Victorian England* (Bridgeport, CT: Conference on British Studies at the University of Bridgeport, 1968), expanded and revised as L. Perry Curtis, Jr., *Apes and Angels: The Irishman in Victorian Caricature* (Washington, D.C.: Smithsonian Institution Press, 1971); Michael de Nie, *The Eternal Paddy: Irish Identity and the British Press, 1798–1882* (Madison: The University of Wisconsin Press, 2004). For a critique of Curtis, now itself somewhat dated, see Sheridan Gilley, "English Attitudes to the Irish in England, 1789–1900", in Colin Homes, ed., *Immigrants and Minorities in British Society* (London: George Allen & Unwin), 1978, pp. 81–110, and also R.F. Foster, *Paddy and Mr Punch: Connections in Irish and English History* (London: The Penguin Press, 1993).
31. Tim Edensor, *National Identity, Popular Culture and Everyday Life* (Oxford: Berg, 2002); Tim Edensor, "Staging Tourism: Tourists as Performers", *Annals of Tourism Research*, 27, no. 2 (2000): 322–44; Tim Edensor, "Performing Rurality", in Paul Cloke, Terry Marsden, and Patrick Mooney, eds., *The Handbook of Rural Studies* (London: SAGE Publications, 2006), pp. 484–95; Tim Edensor, *Tourists at the Taj: Performance and Meaning at a Symbolic Site* (London: Routledge, 1998). For an early contribution to this literature, see Judith Adler, "Travel as Performed Art", *The American Journal of Sociology*, 94, no. 6 (1989): 1366–91, which informs the work of Jill Steward, "The Adventures of Miss Brown, Miss Jones and Miss Robinson: Tourist Writing and Tourist Performance from 1860 to 1914", *Journeys*, 1, nos 1–2 (2000): 36–58. See also Simon Coleman and Mike Crang, eds., *Tourism: Between Place and Performance* (Oxford: Berghahn Books, 2002)

and Jane C. Desmond, *Staging Tourism: Bodies on Display from Waikiki to Sea World* (Chicago: The University of Chicago Press, 1999); Jørgen Ole Bærenholdt, Michael Haldrup, Jonas Larsen, and John Urry, *Performing Tourist Places* (Aldershot: Ashgate, 2004).

32. See Gunnar Thór Jóhannesson, "Tourism Translations: Actor-Network Theory and Tourism Research", *Tourist Studies*, 5, no. 2 (2005): 133–50.

33. D. Soyini Madison and Judith Hamera, "Introduction: Performance Studies at the Intersections", in D. Soyini Madison and Judith Hamera, eds., *The SAGE Handbook of Performance Studies* (Thousand Oaks: SAGE Publications, 2006), pp. xi–xxv.

34. Judith Butler, "Performative Acts and Gender Constitution: An Essay in Phenomenology and Feminist Theory", *Theatre Journal*, 40, no. 4 (1988): 519–31.

35. See Bronislaw Szerszynski, Wallace Heim, and Claire Waterton, "Introduction", in Bronislaw Szerszynski, Wallace Heim, and Claire Waterton, eds., *Nature Performed: Environment, Culture and Performance* (Oxford: Blackwell Publishing/*The Sociological Review*, 2003), pp. 1–14.

36. See David Crouch, "Performances and Constitutions of Natures: A Consideration of the Performance of Lay Geographies", in Szerszynski, Heim, and Waterton, eds., *Nature Performed*, pp. 17–30. Crouch, in his theorising of performance and practice, borrows from Elizabeth Grosz, "Thinking the New: Of Futures Yet Unthought", in Elizabeth Grosz, ed., *Becomings: Explorations in Time, Memory, and Futures* (Ithaca: Cornell University Press, 1999), pp. 15–28.

37. See John Tribe, "New Tourism Research", *Tourism Recreation Research*, 30, no. 2 (2005): 5–8. Kevin Hannam details the directions which studies of tourism, and the related scholarly infrastructure, have taken in "*Tourism Geographies, Tourist Studies* and the Turn towards *Mobilities*", *Geography Compass*, 2, no. 1 (2008): 127–39.

38. Richard Ned Lebow, *White Britain and Black Ireland: The Influence of Stereotypes on Colonial Policy* (Philadelphia: Institute for the Study of Human Issues, 1976).

39. This approach stands in contrast to that of Louis Turner and John Ash, who in the 1970s adopted a highly critical view of tourist-guest interactions, which they regarded as expressing a form of economic and cultural imperialism, given what they regarded as the starkly different material resources at the disposal of each group, and the reduction of "foreign cultures" to tourist commodities through tourist transactions. See Louis Turner and John Ash, "The Barbarian and the Tourist", chap. 8 in *The Golden Hordes: International Tourism and the Pleasure Periphery* (London: Constable, 1975), pp. 129–48. This putatively intrinsic asymmetrical power relationship was elaborated in Valene L. Smith's collection *Hosts and Guests*, which exercised profound influence over the analysis of tourism for a decade and reinforced a binary within the study of tourism actors. See Valene L. Smith, ed., *Hosts and Guests: The Anthropology of Tourism* (Philadelphia: University of Pennsylvania Press, 1977); the collection was revised and reissued in 2001: Valene L. Smith and Maryann Brent, eds., *Hosts and Guests Revisited: Tourism Issues of the 21st Century* (Elmsford, NY: Cognizant Communication Corporation, 2001). Recent scholarship, however, challenges depictions of their immutable, negative cultural impacts, and attributes greater agency to locals, underscoring the heterogeneity of the host and guest populations, the protean character of their cultural performances, and the complex dialogues in which they engage. See, for instance, Rodrigo de Azeredo Grünewald, "Tourism and Cultural Revival", *Annals of Tourism Research*, 29, no. 4

(2002): 1004–21. For an interesting Australian case study which offers a problématique of the host-guest binary, see Kirsty Sherlock, "Revisiting the Concept of Hosts and Guests", *Tourist Studies*, 1, no. 3 (2001): 271–95.

40. Clement W. Scott, *Round about the Islands: or, Sunny Spots near Home* (London: Tinsley Brothers, 1874), pp. 11–15.
41. Scott, *Round about the Islands*, p. 75.
42. Madame de Bovet, *Three Months' Tour in Ireland*, trans. and condensed by Mrs Arthur Walter (London: Chapman and Hall, Ltd., 1891), pp. 93–94.
43. Burton E. Stevenson, *The Charm of Ireland* (New York: Dodd, Mead and Company, 1914), p. 481.
44. Stevenson, *The Charm of Ireland*, p. 482.
45. See, for instance, Liam O'Flaherty's excoriating observations on post-Independence Ireland in *A Tourist's Guide to Ireland* (London: Mandrake Press, n.d. [1929?]).
46. Hooper, *Travel Writing and Ireland*; Hooper, ed., *The Tourist's Gaze*; Ryle, *Journeys in Ireland*; Morash, *Writing the Irish Famine*; Kelleher, *The Feminization of Famine*; Fegan, *Literature and the Irish Famine*; Meloy, "Touring Connemara". Amongst the valuable bibliographic guides to travel writing are: John McVeagh, *Irish Travel Writing: A Bibliography* (Dublin: Wolfhound Press, 1996); C.J. Woods, "Review Article: Irish Travel Writings as Source Material", *Irish Historical Studies*, 28, no. 110 (1992): 171–83; and C.J. Woods, *Travellers' Accounts as Source-Material for Irish Historians* (Dublin: Four Courts Press, 2009).
47. David Nally, "'Eternity's Commissioner': Thomas Carlyle, the Great Irish Famine and the Geopolitics of Travel", *Journal of Historical Geography*, 32, no. 2 (2006): 313–35.
48. Erik Cohen, "Toward A Sociology of International Tourism", *Social Research*, 39, no. 1 (1972): 164–82; and Erik Cohen, "Who is a Tourist?: A Conceptual Clarification", *Sociological Review*, 22, no. 4 (1974): 527–55. These and other writings are compiled in Erik Cohen, *Contemporary Tourism: Diversity and Change* (Amsterdam: Elsevier, 2004).
49. Buzard, *The Beaten Track*.
50. See, for instance, "T.P.", "A Fortnight in Ireland", *The Eagle: A Magazine, Supported by Members of St. John's College* (Cambridge: W. Metcalfe, 1861), vol. 2, pp. 1–8.
51. This source-base includes a few translated narratives from such famous authors as Madame [Marie Anne] de Bovet and Julius Rodenberg, who penned evocative accounts of tourist encounters in which they constituted themselves as foreigners in ways that corresponded markedly to many British narratives.
52. "The Victim" [pseud.], "Killarney's Lakes and Dells", *The Idler Magazine. An Illustrated Monthly*, 6 (August 1894 to January 1895): 20–34.
53. *Irish Tourist* 8, no. 7 (October 1901): 6.
54. "A Member of the Evangelical Alliance, and of the Local Preachers' Mutual-Aid Association", "The Christian Tourist. A Fortnight's Recreation in Ireland in 1852", *The Local Preachers' Magazine and Christian Family Record, for the year 1853. The Authorised Organ of the Wesleyan Methodist Local Preachers' Mutual Aid Association*, 1, "new series" (October 1853): 408–11.
55. See Rudy Koshar, "'What Ought to Be Seen': Tourists' Guidebooks and National Identities in Modern Germany and Europe", *Journal of Contemporary History*, 33, no. 3 (1998): 323–40.
56. *Handbook for Travellers in Ireland. With Travelling Maps* (London: John Murray, 1864); the quotation is from the "Preface", n.p. The later (5th) edition

cited in this volume is Cooke, ed., *Handbook for Travellers in Ireland*, pp. 423–29. It is interesting to note that Murray was the publisher of the controversial travelogue by John Barrow, *A Tour Round Ireland, through the Sea-Coast Counties, in the Autumn of 1835* (London: John Murray, 1836).

57. John Bradbury, *Killarney and the South of Ireland. How to See them for Eight Guineas* (London: Simpkin, Marshall, & Co., n.d. [ca. 1871?]).
58. Esther Allen, "'Money and Little Red Books': Romanticism, Tourism, and the Rise of the Guidebook", *LIT*, 7, nos 2–3 (1996): 213–26.
59. Allen, "'Money and Little Red Books'", p. 216.
60. Allen, "'Money and Little Red Books'", p. 216.
61. Buzard, *The Beaten Track*, pp. 65–79.
62. Koshar, "'What Ought to Be Seen'".
63. Roland Barthes, "The *Blue Guide*", in Annette Lavers, comp. and ed., *Mythologies* (London: Jonathan Cape, 1972), pp. 74–77.
64. Aodh de Blacam, "Guide Books for the Gael", *The Irish Monthly*, 63, no. 745 (1935): 469.
65. de Blacam, "Guide Books for the Gael", p. 470.
66. Koshar, "'What Ought to Be Seen'".
67. See, for instance, *Specimens of Cook's Independent Tours in England, Scotland, and Ireland. Season 1901. A Selection of a Hundred Tours in the Most Interesting Parts of Great Britain and Ireland* (n.p. [London]: n.p. [Thomas Cook & Son], 1901).
68. See, for instance, *Tours in Ireland, 1905* (London: "Published by authority of the Irish Railways" by Walter Hill, 1905).
69. "How to See Killarney in One Day" (from the *Dublin University Magazine*), *Littell's Living Age*, 4, no. 42 (1 March 1845): 554–56.
70. Charles M. Taylor, Jr. *The British Isles through an Opera Glass* (Philadelphia: G.W. Jacobs & Co., 1899).
71. See, for instance, R.A. Scott-James, *An Englishman in Ireland. Impressions of a Journey in a Canoe by River, Lough and Canal* (London: J.M. Dent & Sons, Ltd., 1910); Alexander Corkey, *The Truth about Ireland, or Through the Emerald Isle with an Aeroplane* (Oskaloosa, IO: Shockley Bros. & Cook, 1910); Samuel G. Bayne, *On an Irish Jaunting-Car through Donegal and Connemara* (New York: Harper & Brothers, 1902).
72. A. Nicholson, *Ireland's Welcome to the Stranger: or, Excursions through Ireland, in 1844 & 1845, for the Purpose of Personally Investigating the Condition of the Poor* (London: Charles Gilpin, 1847).
73. Examples include *The Ladies' Treasury: A Household Magazine*, and *The Guardian. A Monthly Magazine, devoted to the Social, Literary, and Religious Interests of Young Men and Ladies*, and a periodical with an explicitly gendered and religious audience (with an implicit class dimension, too): *The Ladies' Repository: A Monthly Periodical, devoted to Literature and Religion.*
74. See Christopher Morash, *A History of the Media in Ireland* (Cambridge: Cambridge University Press, 2010), pp. 67–83.
75. See Francesca Benatti, "Land and Landscape in the *Dublin Penny Journal*, 1832–3", in Úna Ní Bhroiméil and Glenn Hooper, eds., *Land and Landscape in Nineteenth-Century Ireland* (Dublin: Four Courts Press, 2008), pp. 13–24.
76. Alastair J. Durie, "The Need for Legislation to Promote Tourism: A Cause that United all Irish Politicians", in Brenda Collins, Philip Ollerenshaw, and Trevor Parkhill, eds., *Industry, Trade and People in Ireland, 1650–1950: Essays in Honour of W.H. Crawford* (Belfast: Ulster Historical Foundation, 2005), pp. 192–204.
77. See Elihu Rich, esquire, F.R.H.S., "Thomas Mulock: An Historical Sketch", *Transactions of the Royal Historical Society*, 4 (1876): 424–38.

78. Pamela J. Kincheloe, "Two Visions of Fairyland: Ireland and the Monumental Discourse of the Nineteenth-Century American Tourist", *Irish Studies Review*, 7, no. 1 (1999): 41–51.

79. See Enda McKay, "A Century of Irish Trade Journals, 1860–1960", in Barbara Hayley and Enda McKay, eds., *Three Hundred Years of Irish Periodicals* (Dublin: Association of Irish Learned Journals, 1987), pp. 103–21.

80. See the *Irish Tourist*, 9, no. 1 (1902): 1.

81. D.J. Wilson, "The Tourist Movement in Ireland", *Journal of the Statistical and Social Inquiry Society of Ireland*, 11, no. 81 (1900–1): 56–63.

82. *Irish Tourist*, 1, no. 1 (June 1894): 1.

83. Erik Cohen, "Tourism as Play", *Religion*, 15, no. 3 (1985): 295.

84. Dean MacCannell, *The Tourist: A New Theory of the Leisure Class* (New York: Schocken Books, 1976).

85. Dean MacCannell, "Tourist Agency", *Tourist Studies*, 1, no. 1 (2001): 23–37 (at p. 30).

86. Edensor, *National Identity*, p. 37.

87. Richard Tresidder, "Tourism and Sacred Landscapes", in Crouch, ed., *Leisure/Tourism Geographies*, pp. 137–48. For a study employing this model, see John F. Sears, *Sacred Places: American Tourist Attractions in the Nineteenth Century* (Oxford: Oxford University Press, 1989).

NOTE TO CHAPTER 1

1. "Johnnie Gray" [Harry Speight], *A Tourist's View of Ireland* (London: Simpkin, Marshall & Co., 1885), p. 52. For bibliographic details, see John McVeagh, *Irish Travel Writing: A Bibliography* (Dublin: Wolfhound Press, 1996), p. 68.

2. Gray, *A Tourist's View*, p. 52.

3. Gray, *A Tourist's View*, p. 52.

4. Susan Egenolf, "Lady Morgan (Sydney Owenson) and the Politics of Romanticism", in Jim Kelly, ed., *Ireland and Romanticism: Publics, Nations and Scenes of Cultural Production* (Houndmills: Palgrave Macmillan, 2009), pp. 109–21.

5. *A Select Collection of Songs; or, an Appendage to the Piano-forte. Containing the Names of the Authors, Composers, Publishers, and Principal Singers* . . . (Newcastle upon Tyne: "Printed by and for S. Hodgson", 1806), p. 213. In this collection the author of the song is not identified.

6. See *Songs of Ireland: 100 Favorite Irish Songs*, comp. and arranged by J. Bodewalt Lampe (New York: Remick Music Corporation, 1916), p. 61.

7. Natasha Tessone, "Displaying Ireland: Sydney Owenson and the Politics of Spectacular Antiquarianism", *Éire-Ireland*, 37, nos 3–4 (2002): 169–86.

8. See, for instance, the excerpt in "Editor's Drawer", *Harper's New Monthly Magazine*, 58, no. 344 (January 1879): 318–19.

9. Thomas Carlyle, "Carlyle in Ireland: Reminiscences of my Irish Journey II", *The Century Illustrated Monthly Magazine*, 24, "new series" vol. 2, no. 2 (June 1882): 244–56. Carlyle's wider travels in Ireland are discussed in David Nally, "'Eternity's Commissioner': Thomas Carlyle, the Great Irish Famine and the Geopolitics of Travel", *Journal of Historical Geography*, 32, no. 2 (2006): 313–35. For a wider examination of Carlyle's views of the Irish, surveying many of his works, see Roger Swift, "Thomas Carlyle and Ireland", in D. George Boyce and Roger Swift, eds., *Problems and Perspectives in Irish History since 1800: Essays in Honour of Patrick Buckland* (Dublin: Four Courts Press, 2004), pp. 117–46.

10. Anne Plumptre, *Narrative of a Residence in Ireland during the Summer of 1814, and that of 1815* (London: "Printed for Henry Colburn", 1817), p. 273.
11. See William H.A. Williams, *Creating Irish Tourism: The First Century, 1750–1850* (London: Anthem Press, 2010), especially chap. 4, "The Sublime and the Picturesque in the Irish Landscape", pp. 69–88, and chap. 5, "Picturesque Tourist Sites in Ireland", pp. 89–106.
12. Claire Connolly, "Irish Romanticism, 1800–1830", in Margaret Kelleher and Philip O'Leary, eds., *The Cambridge History of Irish Literature*, vol. 1, to 1890 (Cambridge: Cambridge University Press, 2006), pp. 407–48. See also Tom Dunne, "Haunted by History: Irish Romantic Writing, 1800–50", in Roy Porter and Mikuláš Teich, eds., *Romanticism in National Context* (Cambridge: Cambridge University Press, 1988), pp. 68–91, in which Dunne presents three typologies of Irish Romantic writing, and explores them in cultural and political contexts specific to Ireland.
13. Ina Ferris, *The Romantic National Tale and the Question of Ireland* (Cambridge: Cambridge University Press, 2002), pp. 26–27; Melissa Fegan, "'Isn't It Your Own Country?': The Stranger in Nineteenth-Century Irish Literature", *The Yearbook of English Studies*, 34 (2004): 33; Melissa Fegan, "The Traveller's Experience of Famine Ireland", *Irish Studies Review*, 9, no. 3 (2001): 361–71 (see p. 361). I am grateful to Alex Clay, a former MA student in the Department of History at the University of Guelph, for his insights here.
14. Carl Thompson, "Travel Writing", in Nicholas Roe, ed., *Romanticism: An Oxford Guide* (Oxford: Oxford University Press, 2005), 555–73.
15. Philip Shaw, *The Sublime* (Abingdon: Routledge, 2006), pp. 2–3. See also Thomas Weiskel, *The Romantic Sublime: Studies in the Structure and Psychology of Transcendence* (Baltimore: The Johns Hopkins University Press, 1976).
16. Rt. Hon. Edmund Burke, *A Philosophical Enquiry into the Origin of Our Ideas of the Sublime and Beautiful. The Second Edition. With an Introductory Discourse Concerning Taste, and Several Other Additions* [1757], 2nd ed. (London: "Printed for R. and J. Dodsley", 1759), p. 58. The spelling in quotations has been modernised by the author.
17. Burke, *A Philosophical Enquiry*, p. 95.
18. Burke, *A Philosophical Enquiry*, p. 96.
19. Burke, *A Philosophical Enquiry*, p. 96.
20. Burke, *A Philosophical Enquiry*, p. 97.
21. Burke, *A Philosophical Enquiry*, pp. 127–29, 139–43.
22. Burke, *A Philosophical Enquiry*, p. 149.
23. Burke, *A Philosophical Enquiry*, pp. 150–51.
24. Burke, *A Philosophical Enquiry*, p. 156.
25. Michael Haldrup and Jonas Larsen, "Material Cultures of Tourism", *Leisure Studies*, 25, no. 3 (2006): 275–89. See also Malcolm Andrews, *The Search for the Picturesque: Landscape Aesthetics and Tourism in Britain, 1760–1800* (Stanford: Stanford University Press, 1989).
26. Sir Richard Colt Hoare, Bart., *Journal of a Tour in Ireland, A.D. 1806* (London: "Printed for W. Miller, Albemarle Street", 1807), pp. 80–81.
27. G.N. Smith, *Killarney, and the Surrounding Scenery: Being a Complete Itinerary of the Lakes . . .* (Dublin: "Printed for Johnston and Deas", 1822), pp. 163–64. In another guide to the district published in the same year, the Dublin-born Episcopalian minister Rev. George Newenham Wright gave explicit expression to the ideals of the sublime in his description of the Gap. See Rev. G.N. Wright, *A Guide to the Lakes of Killarney. Illustrated by Engravings,*

after the Designs of George Petrie, esq. (London: "Printed for Baldwin, Cradock, and Joy", 1822), pp. 81–83.

28. "Two Days at Killarney", *The Day, A Morning Journal of Literature, Art, Fine Arts, Fashion, & c.*, 101 (27 April 1832): 402–3 (at p. 402).

29. See also "Pike of the Gap of Dunloe, County of Kerry", *The Dublin Penny Journal*, 4, no. 159 (18 July 1835): 17–18.

30. John Carr, *The Stranger in Ireland: or, a Tour in the Southern and Western Parts of that Country, in the Year 1805* (Philadelphia: T. & G. Palmer, 1806), p. 240.

31. *Remains of William Reed, Late of Thornbury; including Rambles in Ireland . . .* (London: John Evans & Co., 1815), p. 18.

32. *Picturesque Scenery in Ireland, drawn by Thomas Creswick, R.A., with Descriptive Jottings by a Tourist* (New York: R. Worthington, 1881), p. 69.

33. Henry D. Inglis, *Ireland in 1834. A Journey throughout Ireland, during the Spring, Summer, and Autumn of 1834*, vol. 1, 3rd ed. (London: Whittaker & Co., 1835), pp. 223–24.

34. Carla Briggs, "The Landscape Painters", in Jim Larner, ed., *Killarney: History & Heritage* (Wilton, Cork: The Collins Press, 2005), pp. 145–55.

35. Briggs, "The Landscape Painters", pp. 153–54.

36. N.H. Carter, *Letters from Europe, Comprising the Journal of a Tour through Ireland, England, Scotland, France, Italy, and Switzerland, in the Years 1825, '26 and '27*, vol. 1 (New York: G. & C. Carvill, 1827), p. 29.

37. "J.K.", *Letters to the North, from a Traveller in the South* (Belfast: Hodgson, 1837), pp. 68–69. For evidence that the author may in fact be James Emerson Tennent, MP for Belfast and travel writer, see C.J. Woods, *Travellers' Accounts as Source-Material for Irish Historians* (Dublin: Four Courts Press, 2009), pp. 122–23.

38. See, for instructive comparison, the transformation of the tourist apprehension of Niagara, discussed in John Urry, *The Tourist Gaze*, 2nd ed. (London: SAGE Publications, 2002), pp. 55–56.

39. See Mike O' Sullivan, "Visiting Poets of the Romantic Period", in Larner, ed., *Killarney*, pp. 139–44; Carla Briggs, "The Landscape Painters", pp. 145–55.

40. Henry W. Longfellow, ed., *Poems of Places. Ireland* (Boston: James R. Osgood and Company, 1876), p. 125. Longfellow, however, credited the author as "anonymous".

41. "The Victim" [pseud.], "Killarney's Lakes and Dells", *The Idler Magazine. An Illustrated Monthly*, 6 (August 1894 to January 1895): 20–34 (at p. 32).

42. See Nicola J. Watson, "Ladies and Lakes", chap. 4 in *The Literary Tourist: Readers and Places in Romantic & Victorian Britain* (Basingstoke: Palgrave Macmillan, 2006), pp. 131–68. Amongst myriad guide-books that drew tourists' attention to the sites of the poem was James F. Hunnewell, *The Lands of Scott* (Edinburgh: Adam and Charles Black; Boston: James R. Osgood and Company, 1871), pp. 53–75.

43. Cecilia Morgan, *"A Happy Holiday": English Canadians and Transatlantic Tourism, 1870–1930* (Toronto: University of Toronto Press, 2008), p. 136.

44. C.P. Crane, *Kerry*, 2nd ed., revised (London: Methuen & Co. Ltd., 1914), p. 64.

45. *Irish Times*, 9 July 1898.

46. *Irish Times*, 9 July 1898.

47. Mary Gorges asserted that Moore had done inestimable service to the district by popularising it in England: see Mary Gorges, *Beautiful Ireland: Killarney* (London: Adam and Charles Black, 1912), pp. 16–17.

48. *Irish Times*, 20 April 1871.

49. John Clare, "Kate O'Killarney", in Eric Robinson and David Powell, eds., associate ed. Margaret Grainger, *The Later Poems of John Clare, 1837–1864*, vol. 2, (Oxford: Clarendon Press, 1984), p. 945.

50. *Twelve Original Hibernian Melodies, with English Words, Imitated and Translated, from the Works of the Ancient Irish Bards, with an Introductory Preface & Dedication by Miss S. Owenson* . . . (London: Preston [?], n.d.).

51. *Twelve Original Hibernian Melodies*, pp. 4–5.

52. Julie Donovan, *Sydney Owenson, Lady Morgan, and the Politics of Style* (Bethesda: Maunsel & Company, 2009), pp. 62–63.

53. See Watson, "Ladies and Lakes", pp. 131–68.

54. See Donald H. Reiman, "The Beauty of Buttermere as Fact and Romantic Symbol", *Criticism*, 26, no. 2 (1984): 139–70; Debbie Lee, "The Gentleman, the Witch, and the Beauty", chap. 3 in *Romantic Liars: Obscure Women who Became Imposters and Challenged an Empire* (London: Palgrave Macmillan, 2006), pp. 79–137. Melvyn Bragg's *The Maid of Buttermere* (London: Hodder & Stoughton, 1978) is a fictionalised account of her life, but it draws heavily from contemporary sources that recorded her experiences.

55. See, for instance, Gertrude Bacon, "Scenes of Famous Songs", *The Strand Magazine*, 32, no. 188 (August 1906): 213–22.

56. Christopher Morash, "The Remains of Ellen Hanley: Theatre, Commodification and Irish Identity in the Nineteenth Century", in Nicholas Allen and Eve Patten, eds., *That Island Never Found* (Dublin: Four Courts Press, 2007), pp. 19–32.

57. See *Southern Ireland: Its Lakes and Landscapes. The New Fishguard Route*, revised ed. (London: Great Western Railway, 1906), pp. 38–47.

58. "Grace Greenwood" [Sarah Jane Lippincott], *Europe. Its People, Places and Princes.—Its Pleasures and Palaces* (Philadelphia: Hubbard Brothers, 1888), p. 87. See Kevin J. Hayes, "Lippincott, Sara Jane Clarke", *American National Biography Online* (February 2000) <http://www.anb.org.proxy.lib.uwaterloo.ca/articles/16/16–01003.html> (11 February 2010).

59. In the *Irish Tourist*, 6, no. 2 (June 1899): 29.

60. *Southern Ireland*, p. 37.

61. *Illustrated Handbook to Cork, the Lakes of Killarney, and the South of Ireland* . . . (London: W. Smith & Sons; Dublin: McGlashan & Gill, 1859), p. 86.

62. *Illustrated Handbook to Cork*, p. 86.

63. See, for instance, *The Scotsman*, 6 October 1871.

64. See, for instance, the *Irish Tourist*, 6, no. 1 (May 1899): 17 and *Irish Tourist*, 16, no. 1 (1909): 9.

65. *Irish Tourist*, 8, no. 7 (October 1901): 6–7.

66. *Illustrated Handbook to Cork*, p. 89.

67. This story was recounted in a pamphlet entitled "Old Stories and Legends of Killarney and the Lakes", which was reviewed by the *Irish Times* in 1909. See the *Irish Times*, 14 May 1909.

68. "Kate Kearney of the Lake of Killarney [from *The Morning Chronicle*]", *The Spirit of the Public Journals for 1812*, 16 (1813): 9–12.

69. "Kate Kearney of the Lake of Killarney", p. 9.

70. "Kate Kearney of the Lake of Killarney", p. 11.

71. "Kate Kearney of the Lake of Killarney", p. 11.

72. "Extracts from the Secretary's Notes, Taken during the Late Visit to Ireland", *The Chronicle of the British & Irish Baptist Home Mission* (September 1872): 637–39 (at p. 638).

73. *Kerry Sentinel*, 31 January 1903.

74. *Kerry Sentinel*, 31 January 1903.

75. Clifton Bingham (lyrics) and Walter Slaughter (music), "The Gap of Dunloe" (London: J.B. Cramer & Co., Limited, 1898).
76. Leith Davis, *Music, Postcolonialism, and Gender: The Construction of Irish National Identity, 1724–1872* (Notre Dame: University of Notre Dame Press, 2006), p. 211. See also Figure 8.2 on p. 210, which depicts Kate Kearney as a shawled young mountain girl holding shamrocks in both hands.
77. John Clare, "Pretty Kate Kearney", in Eric Robinson, ed., *The Later Poems of John Clare, 1837–1864*, vol. 2, pp. 1039–40.
78. Glennis Byron, "Landon, Letitia Elizabeth (1802–1838)", *Oxford Dictionary of National Biography* (Oxford University Press, September 2004; online ed. October 2006) <http://www.oxforddnb.com.subzero.lib.uoguelph.ca/view/article/15978> (11 February 2010).
79. "L.E.L.", *The Zenana and Minor Poems of L.E.L., with a Memoir by Emma Roberts* (London: Fisher, Son, & Co., n.d. [ca. 1839?]), pp. 72–74.
80. See the synopsis appearing in *The Dramatic Magazine. Theatrical Journal* (1 May 1829): 68–70.
81. See Richard M. Dorson's seminal, and highly controversial, study *Folklore and Fakelore: Essays toward a Discipline of Folk Studies* (Cambridge, MA: Harvard University Press, 1976).
82. Thomas Campbell Foster, *Letters on the Condition of the People of Ireland* (London: Chapman and Hall, 1846), p. 388.
83. Foster, *Letters on the Condition*, pp. 371–98.
84. The report "Letters from Ireland" was reprinted in the *Kerry Sentinel*, 31 December 1886.
85. Paul Dillon, "James Connolly and the Kerry Famine of 1898", *Saothar*, 25 (2000): 29–42.
86. Kieran Foley, "Kerry during the Great Famine, 1845–52" (unpublished PhD dissertation, University College Dublin, Department of Modern History, 1997), p. 53. On occasion, even tourism could insulate tourist centres from crises: in 1898, inhabitants of the popular resort of Waterville experienced widespread destitution. See, for instance, a letter to the Lord Mayor of Dublin in the *Freeman's Journal*, 20 April 1898, from the Rector of Dromod and Prior of Waterville commenting on conditions there and calling for the development of the fishing industry.
87. *Irish Times*, 20 October 1886.
88. Aodh de Blacam, "Guide Books for the Gael", *The Irish Monthly*, 63, no. 745 (1935): 467–75 (at p. 470).
89. See, for instance, the excursions outlined in John Cooke, ed., *Handbook for Travellers in Ireland*, 5th ed. (London: John Murray, 1896), pp. 438–39.
90. *Liverpool Mercury*, 18 April 1885. The *Kerry Sentinel*, 1 June 1907, details the reception accorded Daniel O'Shea, a reinstated tenant of the Kenmare estate, who had been evicted 20 years earlier.
91. James S. Donnelly, Jr. has provided an illuminating analysis of how, from a position of lagging other districts of the south and west, Co. Kerry became a prominent centre of agrarian agitation in the 1880s, with the Kenmare estate an epicentre of the Land Campaign, underpinned by rapid structural transformations in demographic and agricultural regimes, and an increasingly focussed programme protesting rates of rent. See James S. Donnelly, Jr., "The Kenmare Estates during the Nineteenth Century", Part I, *Kerry Archaeological and Historical Society Journal*, 21 (1988): 5–41; Part II, *Kerry Archaeological and Historical Society Journal*, 22 (1989): 61–98; Part III, *Kerry Archaeological and Historical Society Journal*, 23 (1990): 5–45. The financially strapped earl of Kenmare and his agents, especially Samuel Hussey, became targets of local hostility (and, in the latter case, of several

failed assassination attempts). See the memoirs of a former estate agent, S.M. Hussey, *The Reminiscences of an Irish Land Agent, being those of S.M. Hussey, compiled by Home Gordon* (London: Duckworth and Company, 1904).
92. *The Times*, 2 February 1889.
93. Eric G.E. Zuelow, "'Kilts *versus* Breeches': The Royal Visit, Tourism and Scottish National Memory", *Journeys*, 7, no. 2 (2006): 33–53.
94. James H. Murphy, *Abject Loyalty: Nationalism and Monarchy in Ireland During the Reign of Queen Victoria* (Washington, D.C.: The Catholic University of America Press, 2001), pp. 109–35.
95. *Freeman's Journal*, 29 August 1861.
96. *Freeman's Journal*, 29 August 1861.
97. *Freeman's Journal*, 29 August 1861.

NOTES TO CHAPTER 2

1. *Freeman's Journal*, 3 April 1852.
2. *Freeman's Journal*, 3 April 1852.
3. *The Parliamentary Gazetteer of Ireland, Adapted to the New Poor-Law, Franchise, Municipal and Ecclesiastical Arrangements, and Compiled with a Special Reference to the Lines of Railroad and Canal Communication, as Existing in 1844–5 . . .* , vol. 2, "D-M" (Dublin: A. Fullerton & Co., 1846), p. 460.
4. K.M. Davies, "For Health and Pleasure in the British Fashion: Bray, Co. Wicklow, as a Tourist Resort, 1750–1914", in Barbara O'Connor and Michael Cronin, eds., *Tourism in Ireland: A Critical Analysis* (Cork: Cork University Press), pp. 29–48.
5. Tricia Cusack, "'Enlightened Protestants': The Improved Shorescape, Order and Liminality at Early Seaside Resorts in Victorian Ireland", *Journal of Tourism History*, 2, no. 3 (2010): 165–85; John Heuston, "Kilkee—The Origins and Development of a West Coast Resort", in O'Connor and Cronin, eds., *Tourism in Ireland*, pp.13–28. For Lucan, see *Irish Builder*, 1 September 1891.
6. See *Irish Builder*, 15 October 1863.
7. See *Irish Builder,* 15 November 1863 and 1 October 1865.
8. John Cooke, "Ireland as a Tourist Resort", in "W.T. M-F" [William T. Macartney-Filgate], *Irish Rural Life and Industry. With Suggestions for the Future* (Dublin: Hely's, Limited, n.d. [1907?]), p. 16. See also "Ireland for Health", *The British Medical Journal*, 1, no. 2052 (28 April 1900): 1036–38.
9. Brian Griffin, *Cycling in Victorian Ireland* (Dublin: Nonsuch Publishing, 2006).
10. A.J. Hayes, "A Holiday in the Far West. Achill Island", *The Leisure Hour*, 43, part 512 (August 1894): 636–40.
11. See Gordon Ledbetter, "A Painter on Achill", *Irish Arts Review*, 23, no. 4 (2006): 106–11; Paul Deane, "Paul Henry on Achill Island: Paintings and Drawings", *Éire-Ireland*, 24, no. 1 (1989): 59–65.
12. *Irish Independent*, 6 July 1912.
13. *Ireland from Sea to Sea: A Practical Hand-book to Galway, Connemara, Achill and the West of Ireland* (Dublin: Browne & Nolan, Limited for the Midland Great Western Railway Company, 1900), p. 105.
14. *Ireland from Sea to Sea*, pp. 105–6.
15. *Ireland from Sea to Sea*, p. 106.

16. See Trent Newmeyer, "'Under the Wing of Mr Cook': Transformations in Tourism Governance", *Mobilities*, 3, no. 2 (2008): 243–67.

17. D. Edgar Flinn, F.R.C.S., *Ireland: Its Health-Resorts and Watering Places* (London: Kegan Paul, Trench & Co., 1888), p. 89; see also *The Climates and Baths of Great Britain, Being the Report of a Committee of the Royal Medical and Chirurgical Society of London, C. Theodore Williams, M.D., Chairman, P. Horton-Smith, M.D., Hon. Secretary*, vol. 2, *The Climates of London and of the Central and Northern Parts of England, Together with Those of Wales and of Ireland* (London: Macmillan and Co., Ltd., 1902), pp. 492–94.

18. Flinn, *Ireland: Its Health-Resorts and Watering Places*, p. 13.

19. *Kerry Sentinel*, 20 April 1898.

20. *Irish Times*, 18 August 1894.

21. *Glasgow Daily Herald*, 29 September 1894.

22. See John K. Walton, "Thomas Cook: Reality", in Richard W. Butler and Roslyn A. Russell, eds., *Giants of Tourism* (Wallingford: CABI, 2010), pp. 81–92, and Susan Barton, *Working-Class Organisations and Popular Tourism, 1840–1970* (Manchester: Manchester University Press, 2005).

23. *Freeman's Journal*, 3 April 1852.

24. *Freeman's Journal*, 3 April 1852.

25. *Irish Times*, 6 June 1872.

26. *Killarney Echo*, 22 September 1900.

27. *Killarney Echo*, 22 September 1900.

28. *Irish Tourist*, 17, no. 6 (1910): 84–85.

29. *The Times*, 15 June 1849.

30. See K.J. James "A 'Vice among Tourists'? Trans-national Narratives of the Irish Landscape, 1886–1914", in Peter M. Burns, Cathy Palmer, and Jo-Anne Lester, eds., *Tourism and Visual Culture*, vol. 1, *Theories and Concepts* (Wallingford: CABI, 2010), pp. 52–63, and Kevin James, "'In No Degree Inferior': Scotland and 'Tourist Development' in Late-Victorian Ireland", in Frank Ferguson and James McConnel, eds., *Ireland and Scotland in the Nineteenth Century* (Dublin: Four Courts Press, 2009), pp. 11–22.

31. G.E. Mingay, "Caird, Sir James (1816–1892)", *Oxford Dictionary of National Biography* (Oxford University Press, 2004) <http://www.oxforddnb.com.subzero.lib.uoguelph.ca/view/article/4339> (11 February 2010).

32. James Caird, *The Plantation Scheme; or, the West of Ireland as a Field for Investment* (Edinburgh: William Blackwood and Sons, 1850), pp. 99–102. See also the review that appears in the *Freeman's Journal*, 1 February 1850.

33. *Daily News*, 10 September 1851.

34. *Irish Tourist*, 2, no. 1, "new series" (1895): 1.

35. See, for instance, the meeting discussed in the *Glasgow Herald*, 18 October 1890.

36. *Kerry Sentinel*, 18 November 1899.

37. *Kerry Sentinel*, 18 November 1899.

38. *Freeman's Journal*, 26 August 1885.

39. *Pall Mall Gazette*, 11 June 1896.

40. In *Belfast News-Letter*, 30 June 1896.

41. *Irish Tourist*, 16, no. 3 (1909): 41.

42. Redmond is quoted in the *Irish Tourist*, 16, no. 3 (1909), 43.

43. *Freeman's Journal*, 12 June 1874.

44. See Irene Furlong, *Irish Tourism, 1880–1980* (Dublin: Irish Academic Press, 2009), and Irene Furlong, "Frederick W. Crossley: Irish Turn-of-the-Century Tourism Pioneer", *Irish History—A Research Yearbook*, vol. 2 (Dublin: Four Courts Press, 2003), pp. 162–76.

45. This orthodox account is outlined comprehensively in Frederick H.A. Aalen, "Constructive Unionism and the Shaping of Rural Ireland, *c.* 1880–1921", *Rural History*, 4, no. 2 (1993): 137–64.

46. See Ciara Breathnach, *The Congested Districts Board of Ireland, 1891–1923: Poverty and Development in the West of Ireland* (Dublin: Four Courts Press, 2005).

47. For an excellent discussion of Plunkett and the Committee, see Carla King, "Defenders of the Union: Sir Horace Plunkett", in D. George Boyce and Alan O'Day, eds., *Defenders of the Union: A Survey of British and Irish Unionism since 1801* (London: Routledge, 2001), pp. 137–58.

48. See Alvin Jackson, *The Ulster Party: Irish Unionists in the House of Commons, 1884–1911* (Oxford: Clarendon Press, 1989), pp. 131–69, for a very thorough discussion of the land question, including internal cleavages within unionism occasioned by the 1896 Irish Land Bill.

49. See Andrew Gailey, "The Destructiveness of Constructive Unionism: Theories and Practice, 1890s–1960s", in D. George Boyce and Alan O'Day, eds., *Defenders of the Union*, pp. 227–50, and Gailey's excellent study *Ireland and the Death of Kindness: The Experience of Constructive Unionism, 1890–1905* (Cork: Cork University Press, 1987).

50. Arthur Balfour served while the prospect for the Liberal-Parnellite programme of Home Rule loomed large, and Gerald while a more confident unionism enjoyed a huge majority, did not depend even on such liberal unionist figures as T.W. Russell, and faced a weakened home rule movement following Gladstone's retirement. See Gailey, *Ireland and the Death of Kindness*, p. 27.

51. *Manchester Guardian*, 15 June 1910.

52. *Irish Times*, 15 August 1900.

53. *Irish Tourist*, 11, no. 5 (1904): 3–4.

54. *Irish Tourist*, 11, no. 5 (1904), 1.

55. *Irish Tourist*, 11, no. 5 (1904), 1.

56. *Irish Tourist*, 11, no. 5 (1904), 1.

57. Æ, "Nationality and Imperialism", in Lady Gregory, ed., *Ideals in Ireland* (London: "At the Unicorn", 1901), pp. 13–22.

58. R.A.S. Macalister, "The Debit Account of the Tourist Movement", *The New Ireland Review*, 8, no. 2 (October 1897): 87–92.

59. Macalister, "The Debit Account", p. 87.

60. Macalister, "The Debit Account", p. 87.

61. Macalister, "The Debit Account", p. 88.

62. Macalister, "The Debit Account", p. 89.

63. Macalister, "The Debit Account", p. 89.

64. Macalister, "The Debit Account", p. 90.

65. Macalister, "The Debit Account", p. 91.

66. Macalister, "The Debit Account", p. 92.

67. Macalister, "The Debit Account", p. 92.

68. Martin Ryle, *Journeys in Ireland: Literary Travellers, Rural Landscapes, Cultural Relations* (Aldershot: Ashgate, 1999), pp. 35–38.

69. Walter J. Farquharson, "The Coming of the British Tourist", *The New Ireland Review*, 5, no. 6 (August 1896): 339–43 (at p. 343).

70. K.J. James, "Imprinting the Crown on Irish Holiday-ground: Marking and Marketing the Duke of York Route, 1897", in Philip Long and Nicola J. Palmer, eds., *Royal Tourism: Excursions around Monarchy* (Clevedon: Channel View Publications. 2008), pp. 62–79.

71. *United Ireland*, 18 September 1897.

72. L.M. McCraith, "Does Ireland Want Tourists?", *The New Ireland Review*, 29, no. 6 (August 1908): 349–53 (at p. 351). For a short biography of Laura

M. McCraith, see Tina O'Toole, general ed., *Dictionary of Munster Women Writers* (Cork: Cork University Press, 2005), pp. 141–42. Though this writing appears consonant with Laura M. McCraith's work, a reply to this piece by F.W. Crossley referred to the author as "Mr. McCraith".

73. McCraith, "Does Ireland Want Tourists?", p. 351.
74. McCraith, "Does Ireland Want Tourists?", p. 352.
75. McCraith, "Does Ireland Want Tourists?", p. 352.
76. McCraith, "Does Ireland Want Tourists?", p. 352.
77. McCraith, "Does Ireland Want Tourists?", p. 352.
78. McCraith, "Does Ireland Want Tourists?", p. 353.
79. F.W. Crossley, "Does Ireland Want Tourists? A Reply to Mr. McCraith's Article in the *New Ireland Review*, 1908", *New Ireland Review*, 30, no. 3 (November 1908): 185–88 (at pp. 185–86).

NOTES TO CHAPTER 3

1. *Kerry Sentinel*, 20 December 1902.
2. *Kerry Sentinel*, 20 December 1902.
3. *Kerry Sentinel*, 20 December 1902.
4. *Killarney Echo*, 11 July 1903.
5. *Killarney Echo*, 11 July 1903.
6. *Irish Times*, 16 May 1907.
7. Spurgeon W. Thompson, "The Postcolonial Tourist: Irish Tourism and Decolonization since 1850" (unpublished PhD dissertation, University of Notre Dame, Department of English, 2000), p. 23.
8. See Susan Kroeg, "Cockney Tourists, Irish Guides, and the Invention of the Emerald Isle", *Éire-Ireland*, 44, nos 3–4 (2009): 200–28.
9. Edward G. Lengel, *The Irish through British Eyes: Perceptions of Ireland in the Famine Era* (Westport, CT: Praeger, 2002), pp. 141–42.
10. For an interesting modern comparator, see Hazel Tucker, "Welcome to Flinstones-Land: Contesting Place and Identity in Goreme, Central Turkey", in Simon Coleman and Mike Crang, eds., *Tourism: Between Place and Performance* (New York: Berghahn Books, 2002), pp. 143–59.
11. Glenn Hooper and Martin Ryle, in exploring the Famine's influence over narratives of travel and landscape, have diverged in their analysis of themes in post-Famine travel literature: Hooper detects an increasing emphasis on the idea of potential and "improvement". See Glenn Hooper, *Travel Writing and Ireland, 1760–1860: Culture, History, Politics* (Basingstoke: Palgrave Macmillan, 2005). Ryle contends that markedly critical cultural commentaries were formulated, and that discussions of scenery and the pleasures of travel in Ireland were considerably less prominent than in the pre-Famine writings by such figures as John Barrow, William Makepeace Thackeray, and Samuel Carter and Anna Maria Hall. Indeed, post-Famine narratives have seemed, to Ryle, to encode a rejection of the very prospects for improvement there. See Martin Ryle, *Journeys in Ireland: Literary Travellers, Rural Landscapes, Cultural Relations* (Aldershot: Ashgate, 1999), pp. 35–38.
12. In Kieran Foley, "Kerry during the Great Famine, 1845–52" (unpublished PhD dissertation, University College Dublin, Department of Modern History, 1997), p. 53.
13. Thomas Campbell Foster, *Letters on the Condition of the People of Ireland* (London: Chapman and Hall, 1846), p. 387.
14. William H.A. Williams, *Creating Irish Tourism: The First Century, 1750–1850* (London: Anthem Press, 2010), pp. 121–27.

15. Leitch Ritchie, *Ireland: Picturesque and Romantic, with Engravings from Drawings by D. Maclise, Esq., A.R.A., and T. Creswick, Esq.*, vol. 2 (London: Rees, Orme, Brown, Green, Longman, 1838), pp. 124–25.
16. Foster, *Letters on the Condition*, pp. 387–88.
17. John Cooke, ed., *Handbook for Travellers in Ireland*, 5th ed. (London: John Murray, 1896), p. 419.
18. C.S. Ward, *Ireland (Part II.) East, West, and South, including Dublin and Howth*, 3rd ed. (London: Dulau & Co., 1895), pp. 110–11.
19. Mrs Frederic West [Theresa Cornwallis], *A Summer Visit to Ireland in 1846*, 3rd ed. (London: Richard Bentley, 1846), p. 93.
20. John U. Higinbotham, *Three Weeks in the British Isles* (Chicago: The Reilly & Britton Co., 1911), p. 267.
21. Foley, "Kerry", pp. 22–30.
22. Foley, "Kerry", pp. 28–32.
23. Foley, "Kerry", pp. 65–69.
24. Foley, "Kerry", pp. 69–88.
25. Foley, "Kerry", pp. 198–208.
26. Foley, "Kerry", pp. 73–77, 125.
27. Foley, "Kerry", pp. 202–4.
28. Foley, "Kerry", pp. 239–41.
29. Foley, "Kerry", p. 218.
30. For an excellent discussion of these features, see James S. Donnelly, Jr., "The Kenmare Estates during the Nineteenth Century", Part I, *Kerry Archaeological and Historical Society Journal*, 21 (1988): 5–41.
31. Foster, *Letters on the Condition*, pp. 387–88.
32. Nassau William Senior, *Journals, Conversations and Essays Relating to Ireland*, vol. 1, 2nd ed. (London: Longmans, Green, and Co., 1868), p. 305.
33. T.O. Russell, *Beauties and Antiquities of Ireland, Being a Tourist's Guide to Its Most Beautiful Scenery & an Archaeologist's Manual for Its Most Interesting Ruins* (London: Kegan Paul, Trench Trübner & Co. Ltd, 1897), p. 5.
34. Indeed, the *Thorough Guide* writer C.S. Ward expressed surprise that a town so dependent on summer tourists manifested "so little care to render itself attractive". See Ward, *Ireland (Part II.)*, p. 110.
35. Ward, *Ireland (Part II.)*, p. 111.
36. James M. Hoyt, *Glances on the Wing at Foreign Lands* (Cleveland: Fairbanks, Benedict & Co, 1872), p. 35.
37. Clement W. Scott, *Round about the Islands: or, Sunny Spots near Home* (London: Tinsley Brothers, 1874), p. 68.
38. [Charles Lever], "Twaddling Tourists in Ireland. No. II. The Grant. With a Hint on Killarney", *The Dublin University Magazine: A Literary and Political Journal*, 24, no. 144 (December 1844): 740–48 (at pp. 745–46).
39. [Charles Lever], "Twaddling Tourists", p. 746.
40. [Charles Lever], "Twaddling Tourists", p. 747.
41. See So-Min Cheong and Marc L. Miller, "Power and Tourism: A Foucauldian Observation", *Annals of Tourism Research*, 27, no. 2 (2000): 371–90; Bernadette Quinn, "Performing Tourism: Venetian Residents in Focus", *Annals of Tourism Research*, 34, no. 2 (2007): 458–76; and Hazel Tucker, "The Ideal Village: Interactions through Tourism in Central Anatolia", in Simone Abram, Jacqueline Waldren, and Donald V.L. Macleod, eds., *Tourists and Tourism: Identifying with People and Places* (Oxford: Berg, 1997), pp. 107–28.
42. Rev. G.N. Wright, *A Guide to the Lakes of Killarney, Illustrated by Engravings, after the Designs of George Petrie, esq.* (London: "Printed for Baldwin, Cradock, and Joy", 1822), p. 9.

43. *The Scotsman*, 7 September 1850.
44. Margaret Tyner, "Irish Professionals", *The Ladies' Treasury: A Household Magazine* (1 April 1885): 191–93 (at p. 192).
45. "The Lake Scenery of Ireland", *The Ladies' Repository: A Monthly Periodical, devoted to Literature and Religion*, 12 (May 1852): 194–96 (at pp. 195–96).
46. *Kerry Sentinel*, 9 September 1899.
47. Alastair J. Durie, *Scotland for the Holidays: Tourism in Scotland, c. 1780–1939* (East Linton: Tuckwell Press, 2003), pp. 133–34.
48. *Kerry Sentinel*, 9 September 1899.
49. *Irish Times*, 7 June 1895.
50. "Irish Jottings", *The Suburban Magazine. A Local and General Periodical*, 1 (November 1866): 89–92 (at p. 90).
51. *The Scotsman*, 7 September 1850.
52. *The Scotsman*, 7 September 1850.
53. In addition to specific discussions of sights in their detailed delineation of tours, both guide-books included an introductory section which discussed Ireland's geology, transport infrastructure, etc. See, for instance, the introductory pages in John Cooke, *Handbook for Travellers in Ireland*, pp. 1–44, and *Black's Tourist's Guide to Ireland*, 19th ed. (Edinburgh: Adam and Charles Black, 1886), pp. 1–12.
54. Cooke, ed., *Handbook for Travellers*, p. 425.
55. M.D. Frazar, *Practical Guide to Great Britain and Ireland: Preparation, Cost, Routes, Sightseeing*, vol. 2, *Ireland and Scotland* (Boston: Small, Maynard & Company, 1909), p. 5.
56. Whereas the civil parish of Knockane had seen its population decline by 19 percent, and Co. Kerry by a similar number, the great, largely uninhabited swathe of land around of the Gap was ripe for narration as a site of peasant "persistence"; it was not until much later, in the decade between 1881 and 1891, that it experienced an appreciable decrease in population, which was lower than the parish and the county as a whole. See The Census of Ireland for the year 1851. Part I. Showing the area, population, and number of houses, by townlands and electoral divisions. County of Kerry [1543], HC 1852–53, vol; xci; The Census of Ireland for the year 1861. Part I. Showing the area, population, and number of houses, by townlands and electoral divisions, vol. I [3204], HC 1863, vol. liv; Census of Ireland, 1871. Part I. Area, houses, and population: also the ages, civil condition, occupations, birthplaces, religion, and education of the people. Vol. II. Province of Munster [C.873], HC 1873, vol. lxxii, pt ii; Census of Ireland, 1881 Part I. Area, houses, and population: also the ages, civil or conjugal condition, occupations, birthplaces, religion, and education of the people. Vol. II. Province of Munster [C.3148]. HC 1882, vol. lxxvii; Census of Ireland, 1891. Part I. Area, houses, and population; also the ages, civil or conjugal condition, occupations, birthplaces, religion, and education of the people. Vol. II. Province of Munster [C.6567], HC 1892, vol. xci; Census of Ireland, 1901. Part I. Area, houses, and population: also the ages, civil or conjugal condition, occupations, birthplaces, religion, and education of the people. Vol. II. Province of Munster [Cd.1058], HC 1902, vols. cxxiv, cxxv; Census of Ireland, 1911. Area, houses, and population: Also the ages, civil or conjugal condition, occupations, birthplaces, religion, and education of the people. Province of Munster [Cd. 6050], HC 1911–12, vol. cxv.
57. See Joep Leerssen, "Imagology: History and Method", in Manfred Beller and Joep Leerssen, eds., *Imagology: The Cultural Construction and Literary Representation of National Characters: A Critical Survey* (Amsterdam: Editions Rodopi B.S., 2007), pp. 17–32.

58. Georges Denis Zimmerman, *The Irish Storyteller* (Dublin: Four Courts Press, 2001).
59. *Irish Tourist*, 5, no. 1 (May 1898): 2.
60. *Irish Tourist*, 5, no. 1 (May 1898), 2.
61. Henry M. Field, *From the Lakes of Killarney to the Golden Horn*, 10ᵗʰ ed. (New York: Charles Scribner's Sons, 1876), pp. 20–21.
62. Field, *From the Lakes of Killarney*, p. 21.
63. D. Soyini Madison and Judith Hamera, "Introduction: Performance Studies at the Intersections", in D. Soyini Madison and Judith Hamera, eds., *The SAGE Handbook of Performance Studies* (Thousand Oaks, CA: SAGE Publications, 2006), pp. xiii–xiv.
64. John Bradbury, *Killarney and the South of Ireland. How to See Them for Eight Guineas* (London: Simpkin, Marshall, & Co., n.d. [ca. 1871?]), p. 54.
65. Joep Leerssen, "English Words in Irish Mouths in English Books", in Charles M. Taylor, Jr., *The British Isles through an Opera Glass* (Philadelphia: George W. Jacobs & Co., 1899), p. 112.
66. Luke Gibbons, "Romanticism, Realism and Irish Cinema", in Kevin Rockett, Luke Gibbons, and John Hill, eds., *Cinema and Ireland* (Syracuse: Syracuse University Press, 1988), pp. 194–258 (at p. 215).
67. Charles M. Taylor, Jr., *The British Isles through an Opera Glass* (Philadelphia: George W. Jacobs & Co., 1899), p. 111.
68. Taylor, *The British Isles*, p. 111.
69. Canniff Haight, *Here and There in the Home Land. England, Scotland and Ireland, as Seen by a Canadian* (Toronto: William Briggs, 1895), p. 554.
70. *Illustrated Handbook to Cork, the Lakes of Killarney and the South of Ireland* . . . (London: W. Smith & Sons; Dublin: McGlashan and Gill, 1859), p. 86.
71. *Illustrated Handbook to Cork*, pp. 86, 88.
72. "An Englishman" [W.W. Barry], *A Walking Tour round Ireland in 1865* (London: Richard Bentley, 1867), p. 225.
73. See Leitch Ritchie, *Ireland: Picturesque and Romantic, with Engravings from Drawings by D. Maclise, Esq., A.R.A., and T. Creswick, Esq.*, vol. 1. (London: Longman, Rees, Orme, Brown, Green, and Longman, 1837), p. 82. George Winder—Leitch Ritchie's guide—was another character who fused with Joe Irwin to form a composite character. See Zimmermann, *The Irish Storyteller*, pp. 153–54. I am grateful to Alex Clay, a former MA student in the Department of History at the University of Guelph, for drawing my attention to this figure.
74. Kroeg, "Cockney Tourists".
75. *Manchester Guardian*, 11 August 1852.
76. *Manchester Guardian*, 11 August 1852.
77. T. Crofton Croker, *Legends of the Lakes; or, Sayings and Doings at Killarney, Collected Chiefly from the Manuscripts of R. Adolphus Lynch, esq*, vols. 1–2 (London: John Ebers and Co., 1829).
78. Bradbury, *Killarney and the South of Ireland*, p. 54.
79. Zimmerman, *The Irish Storyteller*, p. 149.
80. *Illustrated Handbook to Cork*, p. 86.
81. *Pall Mall Gazette*, 30 October 1896.
82. *Pall Mall Gazette*, 30 October 1896.
83. *Killarney Echo*, 26 August 1899, 16 September 1899.
84. *Aberdeen Journal*, 27 October 1879.
85. *Aberdeen Journal*, 27 October 1879.
86. *Aberdeen Journal*, 27 October 1879.
87. Grimshaw was an Ulster-born convert to Catholicism and popular travel writer. See Clare McCotter, "Woman Traveller/Colonial Tourist", *Irish Studies Review*, 15, no. 4 (2007): 481–506.

88. Beatrice Grimshaw, "Killarney", *The Irish Monthly*, 30, no. 351 (September 1902): 532–35 (at pp. 532–33).
89. Grimshaw, "Killarney", p. 533.
90. "Irish Jottings", *The Suburban Magazine. A Local and General Periodical*, 1 (November 1866): 91.
91. William H.A. Williams, "Blow, Bugle, Blow: Romantic Tourism and the Echoes of Killarney", in Santiago Henríquez, ed., *Travel Essentials: Collected Essays on Travel Writing* (Las Palmas de Gran Canaria: Chandlon Inn Press, 1998), pp. 133–47.
92. *Manchester Guardian*, 11 August 1852.
93. Rob Shields, *Places on the Margin: Alternative Geographies of Modernity* (London: Routledge, 1991), pp. 89–100.
94. Burton E. Stevenson, *The Charm of Ireland* (New York: Dodd, Mead and Company, 1914), p. 183.
95. "Social Science and Sunny Scenes in Ireland", *Bentley's Miscellany*, 51 (1862): 162–72 (at p. 166).
96. John F. Sears, *Sacred Places: American Tourist Attractions in the Nineteenth Century* (New York: Oxford University Press, 1989), p. 27.
97. Stevenson, *The Charm of Ireland*, p. 177.
98. "Social Science", p. 167.
99. Mr and Mrs S.C. Hall, *A Week at Killarney, with Descriptions of the Routes thither . . .* (London: Virtue Brothers and Co., 1865), p. 110. See similar comments in an earlier edition by the same authors, *A Week at Killarney* (London: Jeremiah How, 1843), pp. 142–43.
100. Mr and Mrs S.C. Hall, *Ireland: Its Scenery, Character, & c.*, vol. 1 (London: How and Parsons, 1841), pp. 207–8.
101. Mr and Mrs S.C. Hall, *Ireland: Its Scenery*, p. 208.
102. See, for instance, R.M. Ballantyne, *The Lakes of Killarney* (London: T. Nelson and Sons, 1865), p. 65.
103. Julius Rodenberg, *The Island of the Saints. A Pilgrimage through Ireland*, trans. Lascelles Wraxall (London: Chapman and Hall, 1861), pp. 120–21.
104. Rodenberg, *The Island of the Saints*, pp. 121–22.
105. Mary Campbell, *Lady Morgan: The Life and Times of Sydney Owenson* (London: Pandora Press, 1988), pp. 98–102. See also Natasha Tessone, "Displaying Ireland: Sydney Owenson and the Politics of Spectacular Antiquarianism", *Éire-Ireland*, 37, nos 3–4 (2002): 169–86.
106. [Charles Mackay], *Illustrated London News*, 4 August 1849.
107. Cooke, ed., *Handbook for Travellers*, p. 425.
108. Ward, *Ireland (Part II.)*, p. 113.
109. Ward, *Ireland (Part II.)*, p. 113.
110. *Southern Ireland: Its Lakes and Landscapes. The New Fishguard Route*, revised ed. (London: Great Western Railway, 1906), p. 40.
111. E.K. Washington, *Echoes of Europe; or, World Pictures of Travel* (Philadelphia: James Challen & Son, 1860), p. 249.
112. "J.K.", *Letters to the North, from a Traveller in the South* (Belfast: Hodgson, 1837), p. 65.
113. Haight, *Here and There*, p. 553.
114. Haight, *Here and There*, p. 554.
115. Haight, *Here and There*, p. 554.
116. *The Scotsman*, 6 October 1871.
117. "An Oxonian" [T.S. Reynolds Hole], *A Little Tour in Ireland . . .* (London: Bradbury & Evans, 1859), p. 140. A translation is "O fairer daughter of a fair mother". By then the Dean of Rochester, Samuel Reynolds Hole was identified as the author of the original travelogue on the 1892 reprint of what

his biographer describes as a "well-informed and witty letterpress". See G. Le G. Norgate, "Hole, Samuel Reynolds (1819–1904)", rev. M.C. Curthoys, *Oxford Dictionary of National Biography* (Oxford University Press, 2004) <http://www.oxforddnb.com.subzero.lib.uoguelph.ca/view/article/33934> (11 February 2010).

118. Junius Henri Brown[e], "Pictures of Ireland", *Harper's New Monthly Magazine*, 42, no. 250 (March 1871): 496–514 (at p. 510).

119. See Simon Dentith, *Bakhtinian Thought: An Introductory Reader* (London: Routledge, 1995), pp. 66–67.

120. "Our Autumn Trip through Munster", *Eliza Cook's Journal*, 6, no. 137 (13 December 1851): 106–9 (at p. 107).

121. *Freeman's Journal*, 11 August 1879.

122. Noel Ruthven, "A Dash through the Green Isle", *Frank Leslie's Sunday Magazine*, 22, no. 5 (November 1887): 373–82 (at p. 382).

123. For a discussion of Glena, see Philip Dixon Hardy, *Hardy's Tourists' Guide through Ireland; in Four Tours* (Dublin: Hardy and Sons, 1860), pp. 227–28.

124. See Mike O' Sullivan, "Visiting Poets of the Romantic Period", in Jim Larner, ed., *Killarney: History & Heritage* (Wilton, Cork: The Collins Press, 2005), pp. 139–44; Carla Briggs, "The Landscape Painters", in Larner, ed., *Killarney*, pp. 145–55.

125. Brian P. Kennedy, "The Traditional Irish Thatched House: Image and Reality, 1793–1993", in Adele M. Dalsimer, ed., *Visualizing Ireland: National Identity and the Pictorial Tradition* (Boston: Faber and Faber, 1993), pp. 165–79.

126. Thomas Carlyle, "Carlyle in Ireland: Reminiscences of my Irish Journey II", *The Century Illustrated Monthly Magazine*, 24, "new series" vol. 2, no. 2 (June 1882): 251.

127. "Our Autumn Trip through Munster", p. 107.

128. *Illustrated Handbook to Cork*, p. 89.

129. Mr and Mrs S.C. Hall, *Ireland: Its Scenery*, p. 208.

130. Mr and Mrs S.C. Hall, *Ireland: Its Scenery*, p. 208.

131. The cottage came to serve as a kind of synecdoche for Irish rural culture: a signifier of the "improvement" which had been effected locally, and throughout Ireland (indeed in 1841 the barony of Dunkerron in which the Gap was located had the highest degree of poor-quality "4th class" inhabited houses in Kerry. Kerry in turn had the highest level in Munster). See Foley, "Kerry", pp. 40–42.

132. *Freeman's Journal*, 29 May 1893.

133. *Clare Journal*, 20 July 1893. I am indebted to Chris Quinn, a former MA student in the Department of History at the University of Guelph, for drawing my attention to this reference.

134. Neil Harris, "Selling National Culture: Ireland at the World's Columbian Exposition", in T.J. Edelstein, ed., *Imagining an Irish Past: The Celtic Revival, 1840–1940* (Chicago: The David and Alfred Smart Museum of Art, 1992), pp. 82–105.

135. See also Karen Sayer, *Country Cottages: A Cultural History* (Manchester: Manchester University Press, 2000). The extent to which Lady Aberdeen elevated this cottage into the exemplar of the Irish peasant abode in her production of rural "authenticity" also reflects the influences of the Celtic Revival over the Aberdeens and the vice-regal court during their tenure, during which the countess became an especially prominent patron of the Celtic arts and "peasant" handicraft generally. See Jeanne Sheehy, *The Rediscovery of Ireland's Past: The Celtic Revival, 1830–1930* (London: Thames and

Hudson Ltd., 1980), pp. 103–5. See also Janice Helland's excellent study *British and Irish Home Arts and Industries, 1880–1914: Marketing Craft, Making Fashion* (Dublin: Irish Academic Press, 2007).

136. Taylor, *The British Isles*, p. 111.
137. See Canniff Haight, *Country Life in Canada Fifty Years Ago: Personal Recollections and Reminiscences of a Sexagenarian* (Toronto: Hunter, Rose & Co., 1885).
138. Haight, *Here and There*, p. 553.
139. Haight, *Here and There*, p. 554.
140. *Three Weeks in Europe*, by John U. Higinbotham [review], *The Critic*, 46, no. 3 (March 1905): 286.
141. John U. Higinbotham, *Three Weeks*, p. 269.
142. Higinbotham, *Three Weeks*, p. 270.
143. In *The Scotsman*, 7 September 1850.
144. For an excellent discussion of this theme, see Simon Coleman and John Eade, "Introduction: Reframing Pilgrimage", in Simon Coleman and John Eade, eds., *Reframing Pilgrimage: Cultures in Motion* (London: Routledge, 2004), pp. 1–25. For a discussion of tourist "site-making", see Kevin Meethan, "Place, Image and Power: Brighton as a Resort", in Tom Selwyn, ed., *The Tourist Image: Myths and Myth Making in Tourism* (Chichester: John Wiley & Sons Ltd., 1996), pp. 179–96. See also Simon Coleman and Mike Crang, "Grounded Tourists, Travelling Theory", in Simon Coleman and Mike Crang, eds., *Tourism: Between Place and Performance* (New York: Berghahn Books, 2002), pp. 1–17.
145. See Nelson H.H. Graburn, "The Anthropology of Tourism", *Annals of Tourism Research*, 10, no. 1 (1983): 9–33; "Secular Ritual: A General Theory of Tourism", in Sharon Bohn Gmelch, ed., *Tourists and Tourism: A Reader* (Long Grove, Illinois: Waveland Press, Inc., 2004), pp. 23–34. See also John B. Allcock, "Tourism as a Sacred Journey", *Loisir et Société*, 11, no. 1 (1988): 33–48, for a novel argument in favour of the model of "implicit religion" in the study of tourism.
146. See, for instance, Bryan Pfaffenberger, "Serious Pilgrims and Frivolous Tourists: The Chimera of Tourism in the Pilgrimages of Sri Lanka", *Annals of Tourism Research*, 10, no. 1 (1983): 57–74; Richard Sharpley and Priya Sundaram, "Tourism: A Sacred Journey? The Case of Ashram Tourism, India", *International Journal of Tourism Research*, 7, no. 3 (2005): 161–71. See also N. Collins-Kreiner, "The Geography of Pilgrimage and Tourism: Transformations and Implications for Applied Geography", *Applied Geography*, 30, no. 1 (2010): 153–64.
147. Victor Turner and Edith L.B. Turner, *Image and Pilgrimage in Christian Culture: Anthropological Perspectives* (New York: Columbia University Press, 1978).
148. *Manchester Guardian*, 11 August 1852.
149. Bradbury, *Killarney and the South of Ireland*, p. 57.
150. Tim Edensor, "Walking in the British Countryside: Reflexivity, Embodied Practices and Ways to Escape", *Body & Society*, 6, nos 3–4 (2000): 81–106.
151. Tim Edensor, *Tourists at the Taj: Performance and Meaning at a Symbolic Site* (London: Routledge, 1998), pp. 114–15.
152. James N. Matthews, *My Holiday; How I Spent It: Being Some Rough Notes of a Trip to Europe and Back in the Summer of 1866* (Buffalo: Martin Taylor, 1867), p. 236.
153. See, for the Romantic period, Robin Jarvis, *Romantic Writing and Pedestrian Travel* (Basingstoke: Macmillan Press, Ltd., 1997).

154. See Dentith, "Bakhtin's Carnival", chap. 3 in *Bakhtinian Thought*, pp. 65–104. See Mikhail Bakhtin's famous work *Mikhail Bakhtin, Rabelais and his World,* trans. Helene Iswolsky (Cambridge, MA: The MIT Press, 1968). Rob Shields has adopted Bakhtin in his analysis of the beach at Blackpool, and argues that it became a zone where the initial inversion of the norms of "'high' culture" was expressed in "rowdy fun" and forms of "unlicensed, relativising, minor transgression along with the licensed, commodified, leisure 'attractions' that lined the beach". See Rob Shields, "Ritual Pleasures of a Seaside Resort: Liminality, Carnivalesque, and Dirty Weekends", chap. 2 in *Places on the Margin* (these quotations at pp. 92, 96–97).

155. Westoth Ide, "Reminiscences of Killarney", *London Society. A Monthly Magazine of Light and Amusing Literature for the Hours of Relaxation*, 70, no. 418 (July to December 1896): 432–37 (at pp. 434–35).

NOTES TO CHAPTER 4

1. *Western Mail*, 22 August 1899.
2. Sybil Sylvester, "Satan's Basin, no. II of 'Sketches Abroad'", *Godey's Lady Book*, 32, no. 17 (May 1846): 230.
3. For instructive comparison, see Margaret Byrne Swain, "Desiring Ashima: Sexing Landscape in China's Stone Forest", in Carolyn Cartier and Alan A. Lew, eds., *Seductions of Place: Geographical Perspectives on Globalization and Touristed Landscapes* (London: Routledge, 2005), pp. 246–59.
4. See, for instance, "The Author of 'Impressions at Home and Abroad'", "A Run through the West of Ireland; or, My Month in Connemara, Chapter VIII", *The Dublin Saturday Magazine*, 2, no. 32 (n.d., 1866 [?]): 119–20; N. Robinson, "A Dash through Connemara", *Frank Leslie's Popular Monthly*, 11, no. 3 (March 1881): 279–86.
5. *The Scotsman*, 22 July 1873.
6. *Illustrated Handbook to Cork, the Lakes of Killarney and the South of Ireland . . .* (London: W. Smith & Sons, 1859), p. 89.
7. *A Familiar and Accurate Hand-Book from London to the Lakes of Killarney, Glengarif, and Gougane Barra, by way of Bristol and Cork . . .* (London: E. Churton, 1846), p. 20.
8. "Three Days at Killarney", *Dublin University Magazine, A Literary and Political Journal*, 56, no. 332 (August 1860): 174–87 (at p. 180).
9. Helen L.S. Roberts, "Kate Kearney's Country", *Wings*, 12 (1 December 1899): 165.
10. "Extracts from the Secretary's Notes, Taken during the Late Visit to Ireland", *The Chronicle of the British & Irish Baptist Home Mission* (September 1872): 637–39 (at p. 638).
11. "Norah" [Margaret Dixon McDougall], *The Letters of "Norah" on her Tour through Ireland, Being a Series of Letters to the Montreal 'Witness' as Special Correspondent to Ireland* (Montreal: "Published by Public Subscription as a Token of Respect by the Irishmen of Canada", 1882), p. 265.
12. Cecilia Morgan, *"A Happy Holiday": English Canadians and Transatlantic Tourism, 1870–1930* (Toronto: University of Toronto Press, 2008), pp. 147–60.
13. *Glasgow Daily Herald*, 10 September 1858.
14. *Picturesque Scenery in Ireland, drawn by Thomas Creswick, R.A., with Descriptive Jottings by a Tourist* (New York: R. Worthington, 1881), p. 69.
15. "The author of 'John Halifax, Gentleman'" [Dinah Maria Mulock Craik], *About Money and Other Things. A Gift Book* (New York: Harper and Brothers, 1887), pp. 224–25.

16. The London, Canada resident Chester Glass recounted such claims in his account of the Irish leg of his world travels; he described his party's encounter with a barefooted, bare-headed crowd of women and girls: "One of the girls, aged sixteen, named Eily O'Connor, the Colleen Bawn, was a genuine beauty. I had a long talk with her on the road, and was impressed with her intelligence. She said that the girls usually got married when between eighteen and twenty years of age, but always had to supply the *fortune*, which means thirty-five shillings to pay for the priest's services." See Chester Glass, *The World: Round It and Over It* (Toronto: Rose-Belford Publishing Company, 1881), p. 74.

17. Margaret Tyner, "Irish Professionals", *The Ladies' Treasury: A Household Magazine* (1 April 1885): 191–93.

18. Tyner, "Irish Professionals", p. 191.

19. Tyner, "Irish Professionals", p. 192.

20. Tyner, "Irish Professionals", p. 191.

21. Tyner, "Irish Professionals", p. 192.

22. Tyner, "Irish Professionals", p. 193.

23. Susan Gavan Duffy, "How Irish!", *The Irish Monthly. A Magazine of General Literature*, 16, no. 183 (1888): 568.

24. See, for instance "C.W." [Charles Whymper], "An Artist's Notes. In an Irish Village", *The Leisure Hour*, 47, "new series" part 22 (August 1898): 637–41.

25. In the *Freeman's Journal*, 30 June 1874. See also the same remarks by Mary Elizabeth Braddon in "Ireland for Tourists. A Reminiscence of a Recent Excursion. Part I", *Belgravia: A London Magazine*, 4 -3rd series/24-1st series (July 1874): 88.

26. E.K. Washington, *Echoes of Europe; or, World Pictures of Travel* (Philadelphia: James Challen & Son, 1860), p. 251.

27. See Maria Luddy, *Prostitution and Irish Society, 1800–1940* (Cambridge: Cambridge University Press, 2007).

28. See Maria Luddy, "'Abandoned Women and Bad Characters': Prostitution in Nineteenth-Century Ireland", *Women's History Review*, 6, no. 4 (1997): 485–504, and Maria Luddy, *Women and Philanthropy in Nineteenth-Century Ireland* (Cambridge: Cambridge University Press, 1995).

29. *Aberdeen Journal*, 8 September 1882.

30. Andrew Shryock, "The New Jordanian Hospitality: House, Host, and Guest in the Culture of Public Display", *Comparative Studies in Society and History*, 46, no. 1 (2004): 35–62.

31. See Sinéad Sturgeon, "The Politics of Poitín: Maria Edgeworth, William Carleton, and the Battle for the Spirit of Ireland", *Irish Studies Review*, 14, no. 4 (2006): 431–45.

32. Clement W. Scott, *Round about the Islands: or, Sunny Spots near Home* (London: Tinsley Brothers, 1874), p. 69.

33. Erik Cohen and Nir Avieli, "Food in Tourism: Attraction and Impediment", *Annals of Tourism Research*, 31, no. 4 (2004): 755–58 (at p. 758).

34. Irena Ateljevic and Steven Doorne, "Cultural Circuits of Tourism: Commodities, Place, and Re-consumption", in Alan A. Lew, C. Michael Hall, and Allan M. Williams, eds., *A Companion to Tourism* (Oxford: Blackwell Publishing, Ltd., 2004), p. 294.

35. Charles D. Poston, *Europe in the Summer-Time* (Washington, D.C.: M'Gill & Witherow, 1868), p. 92.

36. David Bell and Gill Valentine, *Consuming Geographies: We Are Where We Eat* (London: Routledge, 1997); Cohen and Avieli, "Food in Tourism", p. 770.

37. "T.P.", "A Fortnight in Ireland", *The Eagle. A Magazine, Supported by Members of St. John's College*, 2 (1861): 1–8 (at p. 5).
38. John Bradbury, *Killarney and the South of Ireland. How to See Them for Eight Guineas* (London: Simpkin, Marshall, & Co., n.d. [ca. 1871?]), pp. 61, 67.
39. *Irish Tourist*, 4, no. 7 (October 1897): 134.
40. *Irish Tourist*, 4, no. 7 (October 1897), 135.
41. "Poteen-Hunting in the Wild West of Ireland", *Chambers's Journal*, sixth series, 2, no. 97 (28 October 1899), 761–63 (at p. 761).
42. "Poteen-Hunting", p. 763.
43. For instructive comparison with America, see Anthony Harkins, *Hillbilly: A Cultural History of an American Icon* (Oxford: Oxford University Press, 2004), pp. 33–45, and Wilbur E. Miller, *Revenuers & Moonshiners: Enforcing Federal Liquor Law in the Mountain South, 1865–1900* (Chapel Hill: The University of North Carolina Press, 1991); for comparisons with Scotland, see T.M. Devine, "The Rise and Fall of Illicit Whisky-Making in Northern Scotland, c. 1780–1840", *Scottish Historical Review*, 54, no. 158 (1975): 155–77. For Ireland, see Hewitt S. Thayer, "Distilling Spirits and Regulating Subjects: Whiskey and Beer in Romantic Britain", *Éire-Ireland*, 30, no. 3 (1995): 7–13.
44. E.B. McGuire, "Illicit Distillation", chap. 10 in *Irish Whiskey: A History of Distilling, the Spirit Trade and Excise Controls in Ireland* (Dublin: Gill and Macmillan Ltd., 1973), pp. 388–432.
45. See K.H. Connell, "Illicit Distillation: An Irish Peasant Industry", in *Historical Studies III: Papers Read before the Fourth Irish Conference of Historians* (London: Bowes & Bowes Publishers Ltd, 1961), pp. 58–91.
46. "A Member of the Evangelical Alliance, and of the Local Preachers' Mutual-Aid Association", "The Christian Tourist. A Fortnight's Recreation in Ireland in 1852", *The Local Preachers' Magazine and Christian Family Record, for the Year 1853. The Authorised Organ of the Wesleyan Methodist Local Preachers' Mutual Aid Association*, 1, "new series" (October 1853): 408–11 (at p. 410).
47. There has been a long-standing interest in the sexual division of labour within the tourist sector, and the "feminisation" of hospitality-linked occupations generally; this began as an interest within the applied area of tourism studies, but has since expanded to incorporate a broad range of methods and approaches. See, for instance, on sex-based tourism, Thomas G. Bauer and Bob McKercher, eds., *Sex and Tourism: Journeys of Romance, Love and Lust* (Binghamton: Haworth Hospitality Press, 2003); Steven Clift and Simon Carter, eds., *Tourism and Sex: Culture, Commerce and Coercion* (London: Pinter, 2000); Chris Ryan and C. Michael Hall, *Sex Tourism: Marginal People and Liminalities* (London: Routledge, 2001); Martin Oppermann, "Sex Tourism", *Annals of Tourism Research*, 26, no. 2 (1999): 251–66; Edward Herold, Rafael Garcia, and Tony DeMoya, "Female Tourists and Beach Boys: Romance or Sex Tourism?" *Annals of Tourism Research*, 28, no. 4 (2001): 978–97.
48. *Freeman's Journal*, 11 August 1879.
49. *The American Traveller's Guide. Harper's Hand-Book for Travellers in Europe and the East . . .* , vol. 1, *Great Britain, Ireland, France, Belgium, and Holland* (New York: Harper & Brothers, 1874), p. 50.
50. "R.W.C.T.", "To the Lakes of Killarney", *The St. James's Magazine*, 17 (August to November 1866): 494–504 (at p. 502).
51. Annette Pritchard and Nigel Morgan, "Encountering Scopophilia, Sensuality and Desire: Engendering Tahiti", in Annette Pritchard, Nigel Morgan,

Irena Ateljevic, and Candice Harris, eds., *Tourism and Gender: Embodiment, Sensuality and Experience* (Wallingsford: CABI, 2007), pp. 170–71.
52. Gareth Shaw and Allan M. Williams, *Tourism and Tourism Spaces* (London: SAGE Publications, 2004), pp. 151–53. The argument may be made that this is an extension of ways in which middle-class men interacted with "common" women outside the tourist theatre, too.
53. Canniff Haight, *Here and There in the Home Land. England, Scotland and Ireland, as Seen by a Canadian* (Toronto: William Briggs, 1895), p. 556.
54. Haight, *Here and There*, pp. 556–57.
55. "An Englishman" [William Whittaker Barry], *A Walking Tour round Ireland in 1865* (London: Richard Bentley, 1867), pp. 26–27.
56. "An Englishman" [W.W. Barry], *A Walking Tour*, pp. 232–33.
57. "An Englishman" [W.W. Barry], *A Walking Tour*, p. 236.
58. "An Englishman" [W.W. Barry], *A Walking Tour*, p. 238.
59. "An Englishman" [W.W. Barry], *A Walking Tour*, pp. 247–48.
60. "An Englishman" [W.W. Barry], *A Walking Tour*, pp. 248–49.
61. Seth Koven, *Slumming: Sexual and Social Politics in Victorian London* (Princeton: Princeton University Press, 2004).
62. "Cambrian Archaeological Association. The Forty-Sixth Annual Meeting held in Kerry, Ireland, during the Fortnight Commencing Aug. 11, 1891 . . . Report of the Proceedings at the Meetings and Excursions", *Archaeologia Cambrensis. The Journal of the Cambrian Archaeological Association*, vol. 9, fifth series, no. 33 (January 1892): 36–77 (at p. 55).
63. *Manchester Weekly Times—Supplement*, 13 August 1859.
64. Washington, *Echoes of Europe*, p. 251.
65. Taylor, *The British Isles*, p. 112.
66. Burton E. Stevenson, *The Charm of Ireland* (New York: Dodd, Mead and Company, 1914), p. 181.
67. One 1853 account of a tour, for instance, described how men partook of the mountain dew, while women were not even offered a sip of the libation. See "A Peep at Killarney", *Chambers's Edinburgh Journal*, 20, no. 506, "new series" (10 September 1853): 170–73 (at p. 171).
68. Madame de Bovet, *Three Months' Tour in Ireland*, trans. and condensed by Mrs Arthur Walter (London: Chapman and Hall, Limited, 1891), p. 148.
69. Grace Carew Sheldon, *As We Saw It in '90* (Buffalo: The Women's Exchange, 1890), p. 39.
70. Orvar Löfgren, "Know Your Country: A Comparative Perspective on Tourism and Nation Building in Sweden", in Shelley Baranowski and Ellen Furlough, eds., *Being Elsewhere: Tourism, Consumer Culture, and Identity in Modern Europe and North America* (Ann Arbor: The University of Michigan Press, 2001), pp. 137–54.
71. *Cook's Traveller's Gazette*, 11 March 1910.
72. Edward Chandler, *Photography in Ireland: The Nineteenth Century* (Dublin: Edmund Burke, 2001), pp. 57–62.
73. Patrick MacMonagle, "Pictorial Publicists", in Jim Larner, ed., *Killarney: History & Heritage* (Wilton, Cork: The Collins Press, 2005), pp. 222–23.
74. Michael Haldrup and Jonas Larsen, "Material Cultures of Tourism", *Leisure Studies*, 25, no. 3 (2006): 282–84; Jonas Larsen, "Families Seen Sightseeing: Performativity of Tourist Photography", *Space and Culture*, 8, no. 4 (2005): 416–34.
75. Lucy Langdon Williams and Emma V. McLoughlin, *A Too Short Vacation* (Philadelphia: J.B. Lippincott Company, 1892), p. 8.
76. Williams and McLoughlin, *A Too Short Vacation*, p. 35.
77. "The Victim" [pseud.], "Killarney's Lakes and Dells", *The Idler Magazine. An Illustrated Monthly*, 6 (August 1894 to January 1895): 25. The

capitalisation of the caption, and subsequent citations from captions in this book, are in the original version.

78. "The Victim" [pseud.], "Killarney's Lakes". p. 26.
79. "The Victim" [pseud.], "Killarney's Lakes", p. 27.
80. "An Englishman" [W.W. Barry], *A Walking Tour*, pp. 240–41.
81. See two examples of these images in Noel Kissane, comp. and ed., *Ex Camera 1860–1960: Photographs from the Collections of the National Library of Ireland* (Dublin: National Library of Ireland, 1990), p. 29.
82. See, for instance, Seth Koven, "Dr. Barnardo's 'Artistic Fictions': Photography, Sexuality, and the Ragged Child in Victorian London", *Radical History Review*, 69 (1997): 6–45.
83. J.J. Lee, "Introduction", in text by Carey Schofield, comp. by Sean Sexton, *Ireland in Old Photographs* (Boston: Bulfinch Press, 1994), pp. 10–11. See also Vivenne Pollock, "'All in a Day's Work': Robert John Welch and his World", in Ciara Breathnach, ed., *Framing the West: Images of Rural Ireland, 1891–1920* (Dublin: Irish Academic Press, 2007), pp. 1–28, and Marie Boran, "Tools of the Tourist Trade: The Photography of R.J. Welch in the Tourist Literature of Late-Nineteenth and Early-Twentieth Century Connemara and the West", in Breathnach, ed., *Framing the West*, pp. 48–60. For an analysis of other pictorial renderings of the Irish peasant, which elided such themes as privation, see Síghle Bhreathnach-Lynch, "Framing the Irish: Victorian Paintings of the Irish Peasant", chap. 4 in *Ireland's Art, Ireland's History: Representing Ireland, 1845 to the Present* (Omaha: Creighton University Press, 2007), pp. 52–71.
84. *Photographic News*, 26 January 1866.
85. *Photographic News*, 29 June 1866.
86. Margaret Harker, *The Linked Ring: The Secession Movement in Photography in Britain, 1892–1910* (London: Heinemann, 1979), p. 27.
87. See Margaret F. Harker, *Henry Peach Robinson: Master of Photographic Art, 1830–1901* (Oxford: Basil Blackwell Ltd., 1988), especially pp. 43–49 and chap. 6, "Picture Making by Photography", pp. 64–74. See also John Taylor, "Henry Peach Robinson and Victorian Theory", *History of Photography*, 3, no. 4 (1979): 295–303.
88. Harker, *The Linked Ring*, chap. 6, "The Secession Movement in Photography (The Aesthetic Movement)", pp. 64–81.
89. "Photography: Its History and Applications", *The British Quarterly Review*, 44, no. 88 (1 October 1866): 346–90 (at p. 378).
90. Jennifer Green Lewis, *Framing the Victorians: Photography and the Culture of Realism* (Ithaca: Cornell University Press, 1996), pp. 57–59.
91. Koven, "Dr. Barnardo's".
92. H.P. Robinson, *The Elements of a Pictorial Photograph* (Bradford: Percy Lund & Co, 1896), p. 94.
93. Robinson, *The Elements*, p. 94.
94. H.P. Robinson, *Picture-Making by Photography*, 5th ed. (London: Hazell, Watson, & Viney, Ltd., 1897), p. 54.
95. M.R. Solomon, "Preface", in M.R. Solomon, ed., *The Psychology of Fashion* (New York: Lexington, 1985), p. xi, quoted in Annette Pritchard and Nigel Morgan, "Encountering Scopophilia", p. 162.
96. The deliberate use of models in producing postcard photographs was not restricted to those who composed images of Kate Kearney or the mountain dew girls, though they were two of Killarney's most famous female "characters"; they were part of a wider rural motif in contemporary visual culture. See Harvey O'Brien, *The Real Ireland: The Evolution of Ireland in Documentary Film* (Manchester: Manchester University Press, 2004), p. 20.

97. Robinson, *Picture-Making*, p. 52.
98. Robinson, *Picture-Making*, p. 52.
99. Robinson, *Picture-Making*, p. 53.
100. Robinson, *The Elements*, p. 100.
101. Robinson, *The Elements*, p. 101.
102. Robinson, *The Elements*, p. 100.
103. Robinson, *The Elements*, p. 104; the image appears on p. 99.
104. See Martin A. Danahay, "Perversity at Work: Munby and Cullwick", chap. 5 in *Gender at Work in Victorian Culture: Literature, Art and Masculinity* (Aldershot: Ashgate, 2005), pp. 105–24. The ground-breaking study of Munby's diaries is Derek Hudson, *Munby, Man of Two Worlds: The Life and Diaries of Arthur J. Munby, 1828–1910* (London: John Murray, 1972).
105. Stevenson, *The Charm of Ireland*, p. 182.
106. See Harker, *Henry Peach Robinson*; see Plate 43, "Study of a Young Woman in Sun Bonnet with Water Jug, *c.* 1860", and Plate 64, "On the Way to Market, 1864–6", both n.p.

NOTES TO CHAPTER 5

1. *Kerry Sentinel*, 19 August 1891.
2. "Cambrian Archaeological Association. The 46th Annual Meeting held in Kerry, Ireland, during the Fortnight Commencing Aug. 11, 1891...Report of the Proceedings at the Meetings and Excursions", *Archaeologia Cambrensis, The Journal of the Cambrian Archaeological Association*, 9, "fifth series" (London: Pickering and Chatto, 1892): 36–77 (at p. 55).
3. Charles Greer, Shannon Donnelly, and Jillian M. Rickly, "Landscape Perspective for Tourism Studies", in Daniel C. Knudsen, Michelle M. Metro-Roland, Anne K. Soper, and Charles E. Greer, eds., *Landscape, Tourism, and Meaning* (Aldershot: Ashgate, 2008), p. 16.
4. See Ralph Kingston, "Review Essay. Mind over Matter? History and the Spatial Turn", *Cultural and Social History*, 7, no. 1 (2010): 111–21.
5. John Wylie, *Landscape* (Abingdon: Routledge, 2007), pp. 44–46.
6. See, for instance, Ian Ousby, *The Englishman's England: Taste, Travel and the Rise of Tourism* (Cambridge: Cambridge University Press, 1990); David Matless, *Landscape and Englishness* (London: Reaktion, 1998). For "readings" of Ireland, see William H.A. Williams, *Tourism, Landscape, and the Irish Character: British Travel Writers in Pre-Famine Ireland* (Madison: The University of Wisconsin Press, 2008); Joanna Brück, "Landscape Politics and Colonial Identities: Sir Richard Colt Hoare's Tour of Ireland, 1806", *Journal of Social Archaeology*, 7, no. 2 (2007): 224–49.
7. Martin Ryle, *Journeys in Ireland: Literary Travellers, Rural Landscapes, Cultural Relations* (Aldershot: Ashgate, 1999); see chap. 6, "Peddling the National Landscape", pp. 111–28.
8. William Bulfin, *Rambles in Eirinn*, 9th ed. (Dublin: M.H. Gill and Son, Ltd., 1957), pp. 222–25.
9. Ríona Nic Congáil, "'Life and the Dream': Utopian Impulses within the Irish Language Revival", *Utopian Studies*, 23, no. 2 (2012): 430–49. For examples, see the Central Branch of the Gaelic League's list of districts for Irish language holiday parties in Dublin's nationalist *Evening Telegraph*, 23 July 1902. I am grateful to Dara Folan for supplying me with information on the League's activities.
10. *The Parliamentary Gazetteer of Ireland, Adapted to the New Poor-Law, Franchise, Municipal and Ecclesiastical Arrangements, and Compiled with*

a *Special Reference to the Lines of Railroad and Canal Communication, as Existing in 1844–5*, vol. 2, "D-M" (London: A. Fullerton & Co., 1846), pp. 459–60.

11. *Illustrated Official Guide to Killarney, Glengariff, and the South-West of Ireland, including a Guide to Cork*, revised ed. (London: Ward, Lock and Co., Limited, n.d. [ca. 1898]), p. 6.

12. *Tours in the Emerald Isle. 1895* (Dublin: Thomas Cook & Son, 1895), p. 41.

13. *Tours in the Emerald Isle. 1895*, p. 41.

14. *Official Guide to the Lakes of Killarney and the Picturesque Parts of Southern Ireland. Issued by the Killarney, Cork, Glengarriff, & South of Ireland Tourist Association* (Dublin: Wilson, Hartnell & Co., n.d. [1908?]), p. 3.

15. Guide-books for Britain's Great Western Railway, for instance, while invoking the names of Kate Kearney and the Colleen Bawn to christen the district, did so in ways that heightened the area's romantic associations. See *Southern Ireland: Its Lakes and Landscapes. The New Fishguard Route*, revised ed. (London: Great Western Railway, 1906), pp. 38–47.

16. John O'Mahony, *The Sunny Side of Ireland. How to See It by the Great Southern and Western Railway . . .* , 2nd ed. (Dublin: Alex. Thom & Co. [Limited], n.d. [ca. 1902?]), p. 159.

17. See, for instance, *South of Ireland Illustrated and Described: Souvenir of Killarney* (Cork: Guy & Co. Ltd., n.d.) and, from the "Emerald Isle" album series, *Gems of the Killarney Lakes, Parknasilla, Kenmare, Glengarriff, and Bantry: Their Scenery and Antiquities* ("Printed in Ireland": n.p., n.d.). The 65 platinatone views are from photographs by William Lawrence; the identification of Muckross House as being in the possession of Lord Ardilaun suggests a date of publication after 1899, and before the transfer of the House to the Bourn Vincent family in the second decade of the twentieth century.

18. Luke Gibbons, "Romanticism, Realism and Irish Cinema", in Kevin Rockett, Luke Gibbons, and John Hill, eds., *Cinema and Ireland* (Syracuse: Syracuse University Press, 1988), pp. 194–258 (at p. 223). For a discussion of early film in Killarney, see Denis Condon, "Cinematographing Killarney", in Jim Larner, ed., *Killarney: History & Heritage* (Wilton, Cork: The Collins Press, 2005), pp. 215–20.

19. Luke McKernan, "The Familiarity of the New: The Emergence of a Motion Picture Industry in Late-Nineteenth-Century London", *Nineteenth Century Theatre and Film*, 33, no. 2 (2006): 30–44; Gibbons, "Romanticism", pp. 221–34; Denis Condon, *Early Irish Cinema, 1895–1921* (Dublin: Irish Academic Press, 2008), pp. 131–72.

20. Harvey O'Brien, *The Real Ireland: The Evolution of Ireland in Documentary Film* (Manchester: Manchester University Press, 2004), p. 29.

21. Condon, *Early Irish Cinema*, 155.

22. *Irish Tourist*, 14, no. 6 (1907): 9. This oft-printed quote in the pages of the journal also appeared in the *Irish Tourist*, 10, no. 1 (1903): 6.

23. "J.K.", *Letters to the North, from a Traveller in the South* (Belfast: Hodgson, 1837), p. 66. Lord Brandon's Gate was named for a former owner of the property who had made his eponymous cottage his principal home in later life and who had died in 1832. See Sylvanus Urban, "Lord Brandon. Obituary", *The Gentleman's Magazine, and Historical Chronicle*, 102, 25th "of a new series", "part the second" (July 1832): 78.

24. James S. Donnelly, Jr., "The Kenmare Estates during the Nineteenth Century", Part I, *Kerry Archaeological and Historical Society Journal*, 21 (1988): 5–41; Part II, *Kerry Archaeological and Historical Society Journal*, 22 (1989): 61–98; Part III, *Kerry Archaeological and Historical Society Journal*, 23 (1990): 5–45.

25. Kenmare established an annual carving school in the Town Hall, bringing a tutor from England who gave instruction in carving. By 1895 the school was also offering instruction in drawing and modelling, with terms from 7*s.* 6*d.* per season (*Kerry Sentinel*, 11 December 1895).
26. *Kerry Sentinel*, 11 December 1895.
27. *The Times*, 3 April 1902.
28. John U. Higinbotham, *Three Weeks in the British Isles* (Chicago: The Reilly & Britton Co., 1911), p. 272.
29. Clement W. Scott, *Round about the Islands: or, Sunny Spots near Home* (London: Tinsley Brothers, 1874), p. 72.
30. Victor Turner and Edith L.B. Turner, *Image and Pilgrimage in Christian Culture: Anthropological Perspectives* (New York: Columbia University Press, 1978).
31. *Glasgow Daily Herald*, 15 August 1864.
32. *Irish Times*, 7 June 1895.
33. In the *Kerry Sentinel*, 10 May 1899.
34. Patrick Spillane's letter to the *Cork Examiner*, 24 August 1895, was reprinted in the *Kerry Sentinel*, 21 March 1896.
35. *Irish Times*, 26 August 1902.
36. *Irish Times*, 26 August 1902.
37. *Irish Times*, 1 September 1902.
38. *Irish Times*, 1 September 1902.
39. *Irish Times*, 6 September 1902.
40. *Irish Times*, 6 September 1902.
41. *Irish Times*, 11 September 1902.
42. *Irish Times*, 11 September 1902.
43. Irene Furlong, "The Landscape for All—No Penny-in-the-Slot at the Giant's Causeway", in Úna Ní Bhroiméil and Glenn Hooper, eds., *Land and Landscape in Nineteenth-Century Ireland* (Dublin: Four Courts Press, 2008), pp. 63–77.
44. *Freeman's Journal*, 6 July 1896.
45. *Belfast News-Letter*, 6 July 1896.
46. *Belfast News-Letter*, 5 October 1896.
47. Henry M. Field, *From the Lakes of Killarney to the Golden Horn*, 10th ed. (New York: Charles Scribner's Sons, 1876), p. 22.
48. Field, *From the Lakes of Killarney*, p. 23.
49. On the protracted financial difficulties of both estates in the latter quarter of the nineteenth century, see Patricia O'Hare, "The Browne Family, Earls of Kenmare", in Larner, ed., *Killarney*, pp. 74–89; and Sinéad McCoole, "The Herberts of Muckross", in Larner, ed., *Killarney*, pp. 90–104.
50. *Kerry Sentinel*, 10 May 1899.
51. *Freeman's Journal*, 7 April 1899.
52. In the *Kerry Sentinel*, 10 May 1899.
53. *Freeman's Journal*, 6 May 1899.
54. *Cork Constitution*, 20 November 1899.
55. *Cork Constitution*, 20 November 1899.
56. If it could not be removed, the toll-gate could perhaps be circumvented: Michael Healy, the Town Clerk of Killarney, hoped that a proposal to open a road from the Gap of Dunloe to the Upper Lake would proceed, avoiding the toll paid by visitors to walk 200 yards. See *Killarney Echo*, 30 September 1899. Previous efforts by the defunct local tourist association to advance this proposal had not won the support of the estate. See *Kerry Sentinel*, 16 September 1899.
57. Donal P. McCracken, *Forgotten Protest: Ireland and the Anglo-Boer War*, revised ed. (Belfast: Ulster Historical Foundation, 2003); Keith Jeffery, "The

Irish Soldier in the Boer War", in John Gooch, ed., *The Boer War: Direction, Experience and Image* (London: Frank Cass Publishers, 2000), pp. 141–51.

58. F.W. Crossley in a letter published in the "Daily Press" and reprinted in the *Irish Tourist*, 6, no. 2 (June 1899): 23.
59. In the *Irish Tourist*, 6, no. 2 (June 1899), 23.
60. *Irish Tourist*, 6, no. 3 (July 1899): 43.
61. *Freeman's Journal*, 7 April 1899.
62. Margaret Werry, *The Tourist State: Performing Leisure, Liberalism, and Race in New Zealand* (Minneapolis and London: University of Minnesota Press, 2011); Courtney W. Mason, "The Construction of Banff as a 'Natural' Environment: Sporting Festivals, Tourism, and Representations of Aboriginal Peoples", *Journal of Sport History*, 35, no. 2 (2008): 221–39.
63. In Orvar Löfgren, "Know Your Country: A Comparative Perspective on Tourism and Nation Building in Sweden", in Shelley Baranowski and Ellen Furlough, eds., *Being Elsewhere: Tourism, Consumer Culture, and Identity in Modern Europe and North America* (Ann Arbor: The University of Michigan Press, 2001), pp. 137–54 (at p. 142).
64. *Freeman's Journal*, 7 April 1899.
65. *Freeman's Journal*, 30 May 1899.
66. *Irish Times*, 19 June 1899.
67. *Freeman's Journal*, 14 August 1899.
68. Report appearing originally in the *Evening Telegraph*, n.d., reprinted in the *Kerry Sentinel*, 17 May 1899.
69. Report appearing originally in the *Evening Telegraph*, n.d., reprinted in the *Kerry Sentinel*, 17 May 1899.
70. Herbert Honohan, "Heaven's Reflex—Killarney", *Donahoe's Magazine*, 42, no. 2 (August 1899): 165–66 (at p. 165).
71. Honohan, "Heaven's Reflex", p. 166.
72. Honohan, "Heaven's Reflex", p. 166.
73. In the *Kerry Sentinel*, 24 May 1899.
74. *Kerry Sentinel*, 3 June 1899.
75. *Kerry Sentinel*, 28 June 1899.
76. *Belfast News-Letter*, 26 June 1899.
77. *Irish Tourist*, 6, no. 3 (July 1899), 43.
78. *Belfast News-Letter*, 19 June 1899.
79. *Kerry Sentinel*, 8 July 1899.
80. Eleanor Foster, "Off the Beaten Track", *The Irish Monthly. A Magazine of General Literature*, 22 (1894): 432–35.
81. The letter from Hugh Blakiston, dated 1 November 1899, was reprinted in the *Kerry Sentinel*, 8 November 1899.
82. *Cork Constitution*, 28 November 1899.
83. *Kerry Sentinel*, 2 December 1899.
84. *Kerry Sentinel*, 29 November 1899.
85. *Kerry Sentinel*, 2 December 1899. The capitalisation in the original quotation is maintained here.
86. *Kerry Sentinel*, 2 December 1899.
87. *Kerry Sentinel*, 10 April 1907.
88. *Killarney Echo*, 13 April 1907.
89. *Kerry Sentinel*, 13 April 1907.
90. *Kerry Sentinel*, 10 April 1907.
91. In contrast, while such disappointment surrounded the management of the much larger neighbouring estate, the Mahony estate, comprising the Gap, became the first completed agreement for sale under the Wyndham Land Act of 1903—legislation that continued a process by which land in Ireland

was transferred to peasant proprietary, in this case to 82 tenants, almost all first-term, at prices between 10 and 19 years' purchase. See *Irish Times*, 6 April 1904. While the agreement between the estate and tenants had been reached under the terms of a preceding act, it was agreed by all parties that they would proceed under the Wyndham Act (*Irish Law Times and Solicitors' Journal*, 37, no. 1,912 [19 September 1903]: 397–98). John Mahony consented to have the prices to which he had agreed be left unaltered if the sales were completed after the passage of the act, which favoured him with a £2,000 bonus (Land Judges' Court [Ireland]), House of Commons Debate, 133 [13 April 1904], cc151-80). This agreement was preceded by a case before the Land Judges' Court in which John Mahony's sister, Marcella, the resident of Dunloe Castle, along with others, sought to deprive her brother of a desired postponement, so that she could enjoy the advantages of obtaining the entire purchase money for the lot on which she was a tenant (*Weekly Irish Times*, 18 July 1903). Others sales, including the lands of The McGillycuddy of the Reeks, produced friction between the tenants and estate.

NOTES TO THE CONCLUSION

1. Burton E. Stevenson, *The Charm of Ireland* (New York: Dodd, Mead and Company, 1914), p. 177.
2. Stevenson, *The Charm of Ireland*, p. 178.
3. Stevenson, *The Charm of Ireland*, p. 182.
4. Chris Rojek, *Ways of Escape: Modern Transformations in Leisure and Travel* (Lanham, MD: Rowman and Littlefield, 1994, "copyright 1993 by Chris Rojek").
5. Stevenson, *The Charm of Ireland*, p. 181.
6. Stevenson, *The Charm of Ireland*, p. 182.
7. John Cooke, ed., *Handbook for Travellers in Ireland*, 5th ed. (London: John Murray, 1896), pp. 419–20.

Bibliography

PRIMARY SOURCES

(a) Newspapers

Aberdeen Journal
Belfast News-Letter
Bristol Mercury and West Counties Advertiser
Clare Journal
Cook's Traveller's Gazette
Cork Constitution
Daily News
Evening Telegraph
Freeman's Journal
Glasgow Daily Herald/Glasgow Herald
Illustrated London News
Irish Builder
Irish Independent
Irish Law Times and Solicitors' Journal
Irish Times
Irish Tourist
Kerry Sentinel
Killarney Echo
Liverpool Mercury
Manchester Guardian
Manchester Weekly Times
Pall Mall Gazette
Photographic News
The Scotsman
The Times
United Ireland
Weekly Irish Times
Western Mail

(b) Books and Articles

Æ [George Russell]. "Nationality and Imperialism", in Lady Gregory, ed., *Ideals in Ireland* (London: "At the Unicorn", 1901), pp. 13–22.
The American Traveller's Guide. Harper's Hand-Book for Travellers in Europe and the East . . . vol. 1, Great Britain, Ireland, France, Belgium, and Holland (New York: Harper & Brothers, 1874).

"A Peep at Killarney", *Chambers's Edinburgh Journal*, 20, no. 506, "new series" (10 September 1853): 170–73.

"The Author of 'John Halifax, Gentleman'" [Dinah Maria Mulock Craik], *About Money and Other Things. A Gift Book* (New York: Harper and Brothers, 1887).

"The author of 'Impressions at Home and Abroad'", "A Run through the West of Ireland; or, My Month in Connemara, Chapter VIII", *The Dublin Saturday Magazine*, 2, no. 32 (n.d. [1866?]): 119–20.

Bacon, Gertrude, "Scenes of Famous Songs", *The Strand Magazine*, 32, no. 188 (August 1906): 213–22.

Ballantyne, R.M., *The Lakes of Killarney* (London: T. Nelson and Sons, 1865).

Barrow, John, *A Tour round Ireland, through the Sea-Coast Counties, in the Autumn of 1835* (London: John Murray, 1836).

Bayne, Samuel G., *On an Irish Jaunting-Car through Donegal and Connemara* (New York: Harper & Brothers, 1902).

Bingham, Clifton (lyrics), and Walter Slaughter (music), "The Gap of Dunloe" (London: J.B. Cramer & Co., Limited, 1898).

Blacam, Aodh de, "Guide Books for the Gael", *The Irish Monthly*, 63, no. 745 (1935): 467–75.

Black's Tourist's Guide to Ireland, 19th ed. (Edinburgh: Adam and Charles Black, 1886).

de Bovet, Madame, *Three Months' Tour in Ireland*, translated and condensed by Mrs Arthur Walter (London: Chapman and Hall, Limited, 1891).

Bradbury, John, *Killarney and the South of Ireland. How to See Them for Eight Guineas* (London: Simpkin, Marshall, & Co., n.d. [ca. 1871?]).

Braddon, M.E., "Ireland for Tourists. A Reminiscence of a Recent Excursion. Part I", *Belgravia: A London Magazine*, 4–3rd series / 24-1st series (July 1874): 76–88.

Brown[e], Junius Henri, "Pictures of Ireland", *Harper's New Monthly Magazine*, 42, no. 250 (March 1871): 496–514.

Bulfin, William, *Rambles in Eirinn* [1907], 9th ed. (Dublin: M.H. Gill and Son, Ltd, 1957).

Burke, Rt. Hon. Edmund, *A Philosophical Enquiry into the Origin of Our Ideas of the Sublime and Beautiful. The Second Edition. With an Introductory Discourse Concerning Taste, and Several Other Additions* [1757], 2nd ed. (London: "Printed for R. and J. Dodsley", 1759).

"C.W." [Charles Whymper], "An Artist's Notes. In an Irish Village", *The Leisure Hour*, 47, "new series" part 22 (August 1898): 637–41.

Caird, James, *The Plantation Scheme; or, the West of Ireland as a Field for Investment* (Edinburgh: William Blackwood and Sons, 1850).

"Cambrian Archaeological Association. The Forty-Sixth Annual Meeting Held in Kerry, Ireland, during the Fortnight Commencing Aug. 11, 1891 . . . Report of the Proceedings at the Meetings and Excursions", *Archaeologia Cambrensis, The Journal of the Cambrian Archaeological Association*, 9, fifth series, no. 33 (January 1892): 36–77.

Carlyle, Thomas, "Carlyle in Ireland: Reminiscences of My Irish Journey II", *The Century Illustrated Monthly Magazine I*, 24, new series vol. 2, no. 2 (June 1882): 244–56.

Carr, John, *The Stranger in Ireland: or, a Tour in the Southern and Western Parts of That Country, in the Year 1805* (Philadelphia: T. & G. Palmer, 1806).

Carter, N.H., *Letters from Europe, Comprising the Journal of a Tour through Ireland, England, Scotland, France, Italy, and Switzerland, in the Years 1825, '26 and '27*, vol. 1 (New York: G. & C. Carvill, 1827).

The Climates and Baths of Great Britain, Being the Report of a Committee of the Royal Medical and Chirurgical Society of London, C. Theodore Williams,

M.D., *Chairman, P. Horton-Smith, M.D., Hon. Secretary*, vol. 2, *The Climates of London and of the Central and Northern Parts of England, Together with Those of Wales and of Ireland* (London: Macmillan and Co., Ltd., 1902).

Cooke, John, ed., *Handbook for Travellers in Ireland*, 5th ed. (London: John Murray, 1896).

Cooke, John, "Ireland as a Tourist Resort", in "W.T. M-F" [William T. Macartney-Filgate], ed., *Irish Rural Life and Industry. With Suggestions for the Future* (Dublin: Hely's, Limited, n.d. [1907?]), pp. 13–22.

Corkey, Alexander, *The Truth about Ireland, or Through the Emerald Isle with an Aeroplane* (Oskaloosa, IO: Shockley Bros. & Cook, 1910).

Crane, C.P., *Kerry*, 2nd ed., revised (London: Methuen & Co. Ltd., 1914).

Croker, T. Crofton, *Legends of the Lakes; or, Sayings and Doings at Killarney. Collected Chiefly from the Manuscripts of R. Adolphus Lynch, esq.* vols. 1–2 (London: John Ebers and Co., 1829).

Crossley, F.W., "Does Ireland Want Tourists? A Reply to Mr McCraith's Article in the *New Ireland Review*, 1908", *New Ireland Review*, 30, no. 3 (November 1908): 185–88.

Description of the Lakes of Killarney, and the Surrounding Scenery (London: W.H. Smith & Son, 1849).

"Dottings in the South of Ireland", *The Northern Magazine*, 1, no. 8 (October 1852): 217–21.

The Dramatic Magazine. Theatrical Journal (1 May 1829): 68–70.

Duffy, Susan Gavan, "How Irish!", *The Irish Monthly. A Magazine of General Literature*, 16, no. 183 (1888): 568–69.

"Editor's Drawer", *Harper's New Monthly Magazine*, 58, no. 344 (January 1879): 318–19.

"An Englishman" [W.W. Barry]. *A Walking Tour round Ireland in 1865* (London: Richard Bentley, 1867).

"Extracts from the Secretary's Notes, taken during the Late Visit to Ireland", *The Chronicle of the British & Irish Baptist Home Mission* (September 1872): 637–39.

"Faed", "An Irish Outing, Awheel", *Outing*, 12, no. 6 (September 1888): 521–28.

A Familiar and Accurate Hand-Book from London to the Lakes Of Killarney, Glengarif, and Gougane Barra, by way of Bristol and Cork . . . (London: E. Churton, 1846).

Farquharson, Walter J., "The Coming of the British Tourist", *The New Ireland Review*, 5, no. 6 (August 1896): 339–43.

Field, Henry M., *From the Lakes of Killarney to the Golden Horn*, 10th ed. (New York: Charles Scribner's Sons, 1876).

Flinn, D. Edgar, F.R.C.S., *Ireland: Its Health-Resorts and Watering Places* (London: Kegan Paul, Trench & Co., 1888).

Foster, Eleanor, "Off the Beaten Track", *The Irish Monthly. A Magazine of General Literature*, 22 (1894): 432–35.

Foster, Thomas Campbell, *Letters on the Condition of the People of Ireland* (London: Chapman and Hall, 1846).

Frazar, M.D., *Practical Guide to Great Britain and Ireland: Preparation, Cost, Routes, Sightseeing*, vol. 2, *Ireland and Scotland* (Boston: Small, Maynard & Company, 1909).

Gems of the Killarney Lakes, Parknasilla, Kenmare, Glengarriff, and Bantry: Their Scenery and Antiquities ("Printed in Ireland": n.p., n.d.).

Glass, Chester, *The World: Round It and Over It* (Toronto: Rose-Belford Publishing Company, 1881).

Gorges, Mary, *Beautiful Ireland: Killarney* (London: Adam and Charles Black, 1912).

"Grace Greenwood" [Sarah Jane Lippincott], *Europe. Its People, Places and Princes.—Its Pleasures and Palaces* (Philadelphia: Hubbard Brothers, 1888).

Graves, Alfred Perceval, *Songs of Killarney* (London: Bradbury, Agnew, & Co., 1873).

"Johnnie Gray" [Harry Speight], *A Tourist's View of Ireland* (London: Simpkin, Marshall & Co., 1885).

Grimshaw, Beatrice, "Killarney", *The Irish Monthly*, 30, no. 351 (September 1902): 532–35.

Haight, Canniff, *Country Life in Canada Fifty Years Ago: Personal Recollections and Reminiscences of a Sexagenarian* (Toronto: Hunter, Rose & Co., 1885).

———, *Here and There in the Home Land. England, Scotland and Ireland, as Seen by a Canadian* (Toronto: William Briggs, 1895).

Hall, Mr and Mrs S.C., *Ireland: Its Scenery, Character, & c.*, vol. 1 (London: How and Parsons, 1841).

———, *A Week at Killarney* (London: Jeremiah How, 1843).

———, *A Week at Killarney, with Descriptions of the Routes thither . . .* (London: Virtue Brothers and Co., 1865).

Handbook for Travellers in Ireland. With Travelling Maps (London: John Murray, 1864).

Hardy, Philip Dixon, *Hardy's Tourists' Guide through Ireland; in Four Tours* (Dublin: Hardy and Sons, 1860).

Hayes, A.J., "A Holiday in the Far West. Achill Island", *The Leisure Hour*, 43, part 512 (August 1894): 636–40.

Higinbotham, John U., *Three Weeks in the British Isles* (Chicago: The Reilly & Britton Co., 1911).

Hoare, Sir Richard Colt, Bart., *Journal of a Tour in Ireland, A.D. 1806* (London: "Printed for W. Miller, Albemarle Street", 1807).

Honohan, Herbert, "Heaven's Reflex—Killarney", *Donahoe's Magazine*, 42, no. 2 (August 1899): 165–66.

"How to See Killarney in One Day" (from *Dublin University Magazine*), in *Littell's Living Age* 4, no. 42 (1 March 1845): 554–56.

Hoyt, James M., *Glances on the Wing at Foreign Lands* (Cleveland: Fairbanks, Benedict & Co, 1872).

Hunnewell, James F., *The Lands of Scott* (Edinburgh: Adam and Charles Black; Boston: James R. Osgood and Company, 1871).

Hussey, S.M., *The Reminiscences of an Irish Land Agent, Being Those of S.M. Hussey, Compiled by Home Gordon* (London: Duckworth and Company, 1904).

Ide, Westoth, "Reminiscences of Killarney", *London Society. A Monthly Magazine of Light and Amusing Literature for the Hours of Relaxation*, 70, no. 418 (October 1896): 432–37.

Illustrated Handbook to Cork, the Lakes of Killarney, and the South of Ireland . . . (London: W. Smith & Sons; Dublin: McGlashan & Gill, 1859).

Illustrated Official Guide to Killarney, Glengariff, and the South-West of Ireland, Including a Guide to Cork, revised ed. (London: Ward, Lock and Co., Limited, n.d. [ca. 1898]).

Inglis, Henry D., *Ireland in 1834. A Journey throughout Ireland, during the Spring, Summer, and Autumn of 1834*, 3rd ed., vol. 1 (London: Whittaker & Co., 1835).

"Ireland for Health", *The British Medical Journal*, 1, no. 2052 (28 April 1900): 1036–38.

Ireland from Sea to Sea: A Practical Hand-Book to Galway, Connemara, Achill and the West of Ireland (Dublin: Browne & Nolan, Limited for the Midland Great Western Railway Company, 1900).

"Irish Jottings", *The Suburban Magazine. A Local and General Periodical*, 1 (November 1866): 89–92.

"J.K.", *Letters to the North, from a Traveller in the South* (Belfast: Hodgson, 1837).

"Kate Kearney of the Lake of Killarney [from *The Morning Chronicle*]", *The Spirit of the Public Journals for 1812*, 16 (1813): 9–12.

"L.E.L." [Letitia Elizabeth Landon], *The Zenana and Minor Poems of L.E.L., with a Memoir by Emma Roberts* (London: Fisher, Son & Co., n.d. [ca. 1839?]).

"The Lake Scenery of Ireland", *The Ladies' Repository: A Monthly Periodical, Devoted to Literature and Religion*, 12 (May 1852): 194–96.

Lampe, J. Bodewalt, comp. and arr., *Songs of Ireland: 100 Favorite Irish Songs* (New York: Remick Music Corporation, 1916).

[Lever, Charles], "Twaddling Tourists in Ireland. No. II. The Grant. With a Hint on Killarney", *The Dublin University Magazine: A Literary and Political Journal*, 24, no. 144 (December 1844): 740–48.

Longfellow, Henry W., ed., *Poems of Places. Ireland* (Boston: James R. Osgood and Company, 1876).

Macalister, R.A.S., "The Debit Account of the Tourist Movement", *The New Ireland Review*, 8, no. 2 (October 1897): 87–92.

Matthews, James N., *My Holiday; How I Spent It: Being Some Rough Notes of a Trip to Europe and Back in the Summer of 1866* (Buffalo: Martin Taylor, 1867).

McCraith, L.M., "Does Ireland Want Tourists?", *The New Ireland Review*, 29, no. 6 (August 1908): 349–53.

"A Member of the Evangelical Alliance, and of the Local Preachers' Mutual-Aid Association", "The Christian Tourist. A Fortnight's Recreation in Ireland in 1852", *The Local Preachers' Magazine and Christian Family Record, for the Year 1853. The Authorised Organ of the Wesleyan Methodist Local Preachers' Mutual Aid Association*, 1, "new series" (October 1853): 408–11.

Nicholson, A., *Ireland's Welcome to the Stranger: or, Excursions through Ireland, in 1844 & 1845, for the Purpose of Personally Investigating the Condition of the Poor* (London: Charles Gilpin, 1847).

"Norah" [Margaret Dixon McDougall], *The Letters of "Norah" on Her Tour through Ireland, Being a Series of Letters to the Montreal 'Witness' as Special Correspondent to Ireland* (Montreal: "Published by Public Subscription as a Token of Respect by the Irishmen of Canada", 1882).

O'Flaherty, Liam, *A Tourist's Guide to Ireland* (London: Mandrake Press, n.d. [1929?]).

O'Mahony, John, *The Sunny Side of Ireland. How to See It by the Great Southern and Western Railway . . .* , 2nd ed. (Dublin: Alex. Thom & Co. (Limited), n.d. [ca. 1902?]).

Official Guide to the Lakes of Killarney and the Picturesque Parts of Southern Ireland. Issued by the Killarney, Cork, Glengarriff, & South of Ireland Tourist Association (Dublin: Wilson, Hartnell & Co., n.d. [ca. 1908?]).

"Our Autumn Trip through Munster", *Eliza Cook's Journal*, 6, no. 137 (13 December 1851): 106–9.

"An Oxonian" [S. Reynolds Hole], *A Little Tour in Ireland . . .* (London: Bradbury & Evans, 1859).

The Parliamentary Gazetteer of Ireland, Adapted to the New Poor-Law, Franchise, Municipal and Ecclesiastical Arrangements, and Compiled with a Special Reference to the Lines of Railroad and Canal Communication, as Existing in 1844–5 . . . , vol. 2, "D-M" (Dublin: A. Fullerton & Co., 1846).

"Photography: Its History and Applications", *The British Quarterly Review*, 44, no. 88 (1 October 1866): 346–90.

Picturesque Scenery in Ireland, Drawn by Thomas Creswick, R.A., Engraved on Steel, with Descriptive Jottings by a Tourist (New York: R. Worthington, 1881).

"Pike of the Gap of Dunloe, County of Kerry", *The Dublin Penny Journal*, 4, no. 159 (18 July 1835): 17–18.

Plumptre, Anne, *Narrative of a Residence in Ireland during the Summer of 1814, and that of 1815* (London: "Printed for Henry Colburn", 1817).

Poston, Charles D., *Europe in the Summer-Time* (Washington, D.C.: M'Gill & Witherow, 1868).

"Poteen-Hunting in the Wild West of Ireland", *Chambers's Journal*, sixth series, 2, no. 97 (28 October 1899): 761–63.

"R.W.C.T.", "To the Lakes of Killarney", *The St. James's Magazine*, 17 (August to November 1866): 494–504.

Remains of William Reed, Late of Thornbury; Including Rambles in Ireland . . . (London: John Evans & Co., 1815).

Rich, Elihu, "Thomas Mulock: An Historical Sketch", *Transactions of the Royal Historical Society*, 4 (1876): 424–38.

Ritchie, Leitch, *Ireland: Picturesque and Romantic, with Engravings from Drawings by D. Maclise, Esq., A.R.A., and T. Creswick, Esq.*, vol. 1 (London: Longman, Rees, Orme, Brown, Green, and Longman, 1837).

———, *Ireland: Picturesque and Romantic, with Engravings from Drawings by D. Maclise, Esq., A.R.A., and T. Creswick, Esq.*, vol. 2 (London: Longman, Orme, Brown, Green, and Longmans, 1838).

Roberts, Helen L.S., "Kate Kearney's Country", *Wings*, 12 (1 December 1899): 165.

Robinson, H.P., *The Elements of a Pictorial Photograph* (Bradford & London: Percy Lund & Co, 1896).

———, *Picture-Making by Photography*, 5th ed. (London: Hazell, Watson, & Viney, Ltd., 1897).

Robinson, N., "A Dash through Connemara", *Frank Leslie's Popular Monthly*, 11, no. 3 (March 1881): 279–86.

Rodenberg, Julius, *The Island of the Saints. A Pilgrimage through Ireland*, translated by Lascelles Wraxall (London: Chapman and Hall, 1861).

Russell, T.O., *Beauties and Antiquities of Ireland, Being a Tourist's Guide to Its Most Beautiful Scenery & an Archaeologist's Manual for Its Most Interesting Ruins* (London: Kegan Paul, Trench Trübner & Co. Ltd, 1897).

Ruthven, Noel, "A Dash through the Green Isle", *Frank Leslie's Sunday Magazine*, 22, no. 5 (November 1887): 373–82.

Scott, Clement W., *Round about the Islands: or, Sunny Spots near Home* (London: Tinsley Brothers, 1874).

Scott-James, R.A., *An Englishman in Ireland. Impressions of a Journey in a Canoe by River, Lough and Canal* (London: J.M. Dent & Sons, Ltd., 1910).

A Select Collection of Songs; or, an Appendage to the Piano-Forte. Containing the Names of the Authors, Composers, Publishers, and Principal Singers . . . (Newcastle upon Tyne: S. Hodgson, 1806).

Senior, Nassau William, *Journals, Conversations and Essays Relating to Ireland*, 2nd ed., vol. 1 (Longmans, Green, and Co., 1868).

Sheldon, Grace Carew, *As We Saw It in '90* (Buffalo: The Women's Exchange, 1890).

Silloway, Thomas W., and Lee L. Powers, *The Cathedral Towns and Intervening Places of England, Ireland, and Scotland: A Description of Cities, Cathedrals, Lakes, Mountains, Ruins, and Watering-Places* (Boston: A. Williams and Company, 1883).

Smith, G.N., *Killarney, and the Surrounding Scenery: Being a Complete Itinerary of the Lakes . . .* (Dublin: "Printed for Johnston and Deas", 1822).

"Social Science and Sunny Scenes in Ireland", *Bentley's Miscellany*, 51 (1862): 162–72.

South of Ireland Illustrated and Described: Souvenir of Killarney (Cork: Guy & Co. Ltd., n.d.).

Southern Ireland: Its Lakes and Landscapes. The New Fishguard Route, revised ed. (London: Great Western Railway, 1906).

Specimens of Cook's Independent Tours in England, Scotland, and Ireland. Season 1901. A Selection of a Hundred Tours in the Most Interesting Parts of Great Britain and Ireland (n.p. [London]: n.p. [Thomas Cook & Son], 1901).

Stevenson, Burton E., *The Charm of Ireland* (New York: Dodd, Mead and Company, 1914).

Sylvester, Sybil, "Satan's Basin. No. II of 'Sketches Abroad'", *Godey's Lady's Book*, 32, no. 17 (May 1846): 226–31.

"T.P.", "A Fortnight in Ireland", *The Eagle. A Magazine, Supported by Members of St. John's College*, 2 (1861): 1–8.

Taylor, Charles M., Jr., *The British Isles through an Opera Glass* (Philadelphia: George W. Jacobs & Co., 1899).

"Three Days at Killarney", *Dublin University Magazine, A Literary and Political Journal*, 56, no. 332 (August 1860): 174–87.

Three Weeks in Europe, by John U. Higinbotham [review], *The Critic*, 46, no. 3 (March 1905): 286.

Tours in the Emerald Isle. 1895 (Dublin: Thomas Cook & Son, 1895).

Tours in Ireland, 1905 (London: "Published by Authority of the Irish Railways" by Walter Hill, 1905).

Twelve Original Hibernian Melodies, with English Words, Imitated and Translated, from the Works of the Ancient Irish Bards, with an Introductory Preface & Dedication by Miss S. Owenson . . . (London: Preston [?], n.d.).

"Two Days at Killarney", *The Day, a Morning Journal of Literature, Art, Fine Arts, Fashion, & c.*, 1, no. 101 (27 April, 1832): 402–3.

Tyner, Margaret, "Irish Professionals", *The Ladies' Treasury: A Household Magazine* (1 April 1885): 191–93.

Urban, Sylvanus, "Lord Brandon. Obituary", *The Gentleman's Magazine, and Historical Chronicle*, 102, 25th "of a new series", "part the second" (July 1832): 78.

"The Victim" [pseud.], "Killarney's Lakes and Dells", *The Idler Magazine. An Illustrated Monthly*, 6 (August 1894 to January 1895): 20–34.

Ward, C.S., *Ireland (Part II.) East, West, and South, including Dublin and Howth*, 3rd ed. (London: Dulau & Co., 1895).

Washington, E.K., *Echoes of Europe; or, World Pictures of Travel* (Philadelphia: James Challen & Son, 1860).

West, Mrs Frederic [Theresa Cornwallis], *A Summer Visit to Ireland in 1846* (London: Richard Bentley, 1847).

Williams, Lucy Langdon, and Emma V. McLoughlin, *A Too Short Vacation* (Philadelphia: J.B. Lippincott Company, 1892).

Wilson. D.J., "The Tourist Movement in Ireland", *Journal of the Statistical and Social Inquiry Society of Ireland*, 11, no. 81 (1900–1): 56–63.

Wright, Rev. G.N., *A Guide to the Lakes of Killarney. Illustrated by Engravings, after the Designs of George Petrie, Esq* (London: "Printed for Baldwin, Cradock, and Joy", 1822).

(c) Photographic and Visual Sources

"Gap of Dunloe, Killarney", Postcard, numbered 98, unidentified series, n.d., ca. 1900–10.

"Gap of Dunloe, Full-Length Portraits of Mary Hartnett, Bridge Sweeney, Mary Sullivan, Joanna Keefe, Mary O'Grady, Norah O'Connell, Mary Burke (Formerly Numbered as 1, 3, 5, 6, 8, 9, 10 in a Series Entitled Gap Girls), Killarney,

Kerry", n.d. ca. 1860–70, Stereo Collection, National Photographic Archive, National Library of Ireland, STP 2851, 2852, 2853, 2854, 2855, 2856, 2857.

(d) Census, Parliamentary and Archival Sources

The Census of Ireland for the year 1851. Part I. Showing the area, population, and number of houses, by townlands and electoral divisions. County of Kerry [1543], HC 1852–53, vol; xci.
The Census of Ireland for the year 1861. Part I. Showing the area, population, and number of houses, by townlands and electoral divisions, vol. I [3204], HC 1863, vol. liv.
Census of Ireland, 1871. Part I. Area, houses, and population: also the ages, civil condition, occupations, birthplaces, religion, and education of the people. Vol. II. Province of Munster [C.873], HC 1873, vol. lxxii, pt ii.
Census of Ireland, 1881 Part I. Area, houses, and population: also the ages, civil or conjugal condition, occupations, birthplaces, religion, and education of the people. Vol. II. Province of Munster.[C.3148]. HC 1882, vol. lxxvii.
Census of Ireland, 1891. Part I. Area, houses, and population; also the ages, civil or conjugal condition, occupations, birthplaces, religion, and education of the people. Vol. II. Province of Munster [C.6567], HC 1892, vol. xci.
Census of Ireland, 1901. Part I. Area, houses, and population: also the ages, civil or conjugal condition, occupations, birthplaces, religion, and education of the people. Vol. II. Province of Munster [Cd.1058], HC 1902, vols. cxxiv, cxxv.
Census of Ireland, 1911. Area, houses, and population: Also the ages, civil or conjugal condition, occupations, birthplaces, religion, and education of the people. Province of Munster [Cd. 6050], HC 1911–12, vol. cxv.
1901 Census of Ireland, Manuscript Census Returns, Kerry DED, Killarney Public Library.
Land Judges' Court (Ireland), House of Commons Debate, 133 (13 April 1904), cc151–80.

SECONDARY SOURCES

(a) Published Sources

Aalen, Frederick H.A., "Constructive Unionism and the Shaping of Rural Ireland, c. 1880–1921", *Rural History*, 4, no. 2 (1993): 137–64.
Adey, Peter, *Mobility* (Abingdon: Routledge, 2010).
Adler, Judith, "Travel as Performed Art", *The American Journal of Sociology*, 94, no. 6 (1989): 1366–91.
Agnew, Éadaoin, "Travel Writing", in Robert Welch and Brian Walker, general eds., *The Oxford History of the Irish Book*, vol. 4, James H. Murphy, ed., *The Irish Book in English, 1800–1890* (Oxford: Oxford University Press, 2011), pp. 389–98.
Allcock. John B., "Tourism as a Sacred Journey", *Loisir et Société*, 11, no. 1 (1988): 33–48.
Allen, Esther, "'Money and Little Red Books': Romanticism, Tourism, and the Rise of the Guidebook", *LIT*, 7, nos 2–3 (1996): 213–26.
Andrews, Malcolm, *The Search for the Picturesque: Landscape Aesthetics and Tourism in Britain, 1760–1800* (Stanford: Stanford University Press, 1989).
Ateljevic, Irena, and Stephen Doorne, "Cultural Circuits of Tourism: Commodities, Place, and Re-consumption", in Lew, Hall, and Williams, eds., *A Companion to Tourism*, pp. 291–302.

Bærenholdt, Jørgen Ole, Michael Haldrup, Jonas Larsen, and John Urry, *Performing Tourist Places* (Aldershot: Ashgate, 2004).

Bakhtin, Mikhail, *Rabelais and his World*, translated by Helene Iswolsky (Cambridge, MA: The MIT Press, 1968).

Baranowski, Shelley, "An Alternative to Everyday Life? The Politics of Leisure and Tourism", *Contemporary European History*, 12, no. 4 (2003): 561–72.

Barthes, Roland, "The *Blue Guide*", in Roland Barthes, *Mythologies*, comp. and ed. Annette Lavers (London: Jonathan Cape, 1972), pp. 74–77.

Barton, Susan, *Working-Class Organisations and Popular Tourism, 1840–1970* (Manchester: Manchester University Press, 2005).

Bauer, Thomas G., and Bob McKercher, eds., *Sex and Tourism: Journeys of Romance, Love and Lust* (Binghamton: Haworth Hospitality Press, 2003).

Bell, David, and Gill Valentine, *Consuming Geographies: We Are Where We Eat* (London: Routledge, 1997).

Benatti, Francesca: "Land and Landscape in the Dublin Penny Journal, 1832–3", in Ní Bhroiméil and Hooper, eds., *Land and Landscape*, pp. 13–24.

Bennett, T., "A Thousand and One Troubles: Blackpool Pleasure Beach", in [no editor], *Formations of Pleasure* (London: Routledge and Kegan Paul, 1983), pp. 138–55.

Berghoff, Hartmut, Barbara Korte, Ralf Schneider, and Christopher Harvie, eds., *The Making of Modern Tourism: The Cultural History of the British Experience, 1600–2000* (Basingstoke: Palgrave Macmillan, 2002).

Bhreathnach-Lynch, Síghle, *Ireland's Art, Ireland's History: Representing Ireland, 1845 to the Present* (Omaha: Creighton University Press, 2007).

Black, Jeremy, *The British and the Grand Tour* (Beckenham: Croom Helm Ltd., 1985).

Boran, Marie, "Tools of the Tourist Trade: The Photography of R.J. Welch in the Tourist Literature of Late-Nineteenth and Early-Twentieth Century Connemara and the West", in Breathnach, ed., *Framing the West*, pp. 48–60.

Borsay, Peter, "Welsh Seaside Resorts: Historiography, Sources and Themes", *Welsh History Review*, 24, no. 2 (2008): 92–119.

Boyce, D. George, and Alan O'Day, eds., *Defenders of the Union: A Survey of British and Irish Unionism since 1801* (London: Routledge, 2001).

Bragg, Melvyn, *The Maid of Buttermere* (London: Hodder & Stoughton, 1978).

Breathnach, Ciara, *The Congested Districts Board of Ireland, 1891–1923: Poverty and Development in the West of Ireland* (Dublin: Four Courts Press, 2005).

Breathnach, Ciara, ed., *Framing the West: Images of Rural Ireland, 1891–1920* (Dublin: Irish Academic Press, 2007)

Briggs, Carla, "The Landscape Painters", in Larner, ed., *Killarney*, pp. 145–55.

Brown, Iain Gordon, "Water, Windows, and Women: The Significance of Venice for Scots in the Age of the Grand Tour", *Eighteenth-Century Life*, 30, no. 3 (2006): 1–50.

Brück, Joanna, "Landscape Politics and Colonial Identities: Sir Richard Colt Hoare's Tour of Ireland, 1806", *Journal of Social Archaeology*, 7, no. 2 (2007): 224–49.

Butler, Judith, "Performative Acts and Gender Constitution: An Essay in Phenomenology and Feminist Theory", *Theatre Journal*, 40, no. 4 (1988): 519–31.

Buzard, James, *The Beaten Track: European Tourism, Literature, and the Ways to 'Culture', 1800–1918* (Oxford: Clarendon Press, 1993).

———, "The Grand Tour and After (1660–1840)", in Peter Hulme and Tim Youngs, eds., *The Cambridge Companion to Travel Writing* (Cambridge: Cambridge University Press, 2002), pp. 37–52.

Byron, Glennis, "Landon, Letitia Elizabeth (1802–1838)", *Oxford Dictionary of National Biography* (Oxford University Press, 2004; online ed. October 2006)

<http://www.oxforddnb.com.subzero.lib.uoguelph.ca/view/article/15978> (11 February 2010).
Campbell, Mary, *Morgan: The Life and Times of Sydney Owenson* (London: Pandora Press, 1988).
Chandler, Edward, *Photography in Ireland: The Nineteenth Century* (Dublin: Edmund Burke, 2001).
Cheong, So-Min, and Marc L. Miller, "Power and Tourism: A Foucauldian Observation", *Annals of Tourism Research*, 27, no. 2 (2000): 371–90.
Clancy, Michael, *Brand New Ireland? Tourism, Development and National Identity in the Irish Republic* (Farnham: Ashgate, 2009).
Clift, Steven, and Simon Carter, eds., *Tourism and Sex: Culture, Commerce and Coercion* (London: Pinter, 2000).
Codell, Julie F., "Reversing the Grand Tour: Guest Discourse in Indian Travel Narratives", *The Huntington Library Quarterly*, 70, no. 1 (2007): 173–89.
Cohen, Erik, *Contemporary Tourism: Diversity and Change* (Amsterdam: Elsevier, 2004).
———, "Tourism as Play", *Religion*, 15, no. 3 (1985): 291–304.
———, "Toward a Sociology of International Tourism", *Social Research*, 39, no. 1 (1972): 164–82.
———, "Who is a Tourist?: A Conceptual Clarification", *Sociological Review*, 22, no. 4 (1974): 527–55.
Cohen, Erik, and Nir Avieli, "Food in Tourism: Attraction and Impediment", *Annals of Tourism Research*, 31, no. 4 (2004): 755–58.
Coleman, Simon, and Mike Crang, eds., *Tourism: Between Place and Performance* (New York: Berghahn Books, 2002).
Coleman, Simon, and Mike Crang, "Grounded Tourists, Travelling Theory", in Coleman and Crang, *Tourism: Between Place and Performance*, pp. 1–17.
Coleman, Simon, and John Eade, "Introduction: Reframing Pilgrimage", in Simon Coleman and John Eade, eds., *Reframing Pilgrimage: Cultures in Motion* (London: Routledge, 2004), pp. 1–25.
Colley, Linda, *The Ordeal of Elizabeth Marsh: A Woman in World History* (London: HarperCollins, 2007).
Collins-Kreiner, N., "The Geography of Pilgrimage and Tourism: Transformations and Implications for Applied Geography", *Applied Geography*, 30, no. 1 (2010): 153–64.
Condon, Denis, "Cinematographing Killarney", in Larner, ed., *Killarney*, pp. 215–20.
———, *Early Irish Cinema, 1895–1921* (Dublin: Irish Academic Press, 2008).
Connell, K.H., "Illicit Distillation: An Irish Peasant Industry", in *Historical Studies III: Papers Read before the Fourth Irish Conference of Historians* (London: Bowes & Bowes Publishers Ltd, 1961), pp. 58–91.
Connolly, Claire, "Irish Romanticism, 1800–1830", in Margaret Kelleher and Philip O'Leary, eds., *The Cambridge History of Irish Literature*, vol. 1, to 1890 (Cambridge: Cambridge University Press, 2006), pp. 407–48.
Costa, Kelli Ann, *Coach Fellas: Heritage and Tourism in Ireland* (Walnut Creek, CA: Left Coast Press, Inc., 2009).
Cronin, Michael, and Barbara O'Connor, eds., *Irish Tourism: Image, Culture and Identity* (Clevedon: Channel View Publications, 2003).
Crouch, David, "Performances and Constitutions of Natures: A Consideration of the Performance of Lay Geographies", in Szerszynski, Heim, and Waterton, eds., *Nature Performed*, pp. 17–30.
Culler, Jonathan, "Semiotics of Tourism", *American Journal of Semiotics*, 1, nos 1–2 (1981): 127–40.

Curtis, L.P., Jr., *Anglo-Saxons and Celts: A Study of Anti-Irish Prejudice in Victorian England* (Bridgeport, CT: Conference on British Studies at the University of Bridgeport, 1968).

Curtis, L. Perry, Jr., *Apes and Angels: The Irishman in Victorian Caricature* (Washington, D.C.: Smithsonian Institution Press, 1971).

Cusack, Tricia, "'Enlightened Protestants': The Improved Shorescape, Order and Liminality at Early Seaside Resorts in Victorian Ireland", *Journal of Tourism History*, 2, no. 3 (2010): 165–85.

Danahay, Martin A., *Gender at Work in Victorian Culture: Literature, Art and Masculinity* (Aldershot: Ashgate, 2005).

Davies, K.M., "For Health and Pleasure in the British Fashion: Bray, Co. Wicklow, as a Tourist Resort, 1750–1914", in O'Connor and Cronin, eds., *Tourism in Ireland: A Critical Analysis*, pp. 29–48.

Davis, Leith, *Music, Postcolonialism, and Gender: The Construction of Irish National Identity, 1724–1874* (Notre Dame: University of Notre Dame Press, 2006).

Deane, Paul, "Paul Henry on Achill Island: Paintings and Drawings", *Éire-Ireland*, 24, no. 1 (1989): 59–65.

Deegan, James, and Donal A. Dineen, *Tourism Policy and Performance: The Irish Experience* (London: International Thomson Business Press, 1997).

de Nie, Michael, *The Eternal Paddy: Irish Identity and the British Press, 1798–1882* (Madison: The University of Wisconsin Press, 2004).

Dentith, Simon, *Bakhtinian Thought: An Introductory Reader* (London: Routledge, 1995).

Desmond, Jane C., *Staging Tourism: Bodies on Display from Waikiki to Sea World* (Chicago: The University of Chicago Press, 1999).

Devine, T.M., "The Rise and Fall of Illicit Whisky-Making in Northern Scotland, c. 1780–1840", *Scottish Historical Review*, 54, no. 158 (1975): 155–77

Dillon, Paul, "James Connolly and the Kerry Famine of 1898", *Saothar*, 25 (2000): 29–42.

Donnelly, James S., Jr., "The Kenmare Estates during the Nineteenth Century", Part I, *Kerry Archaeological and Historical Society Journal*, 21 (1988): 5–41.

———, Part II, *Kerry Archaeological and Historical Society Journal*, 22 (1989): 61–98.

———, Part III, *Kerry Archaeological and Historical Society Journal*, 23 (1990): 5–45.

Donovan, Julie, *Sydney Owenson, Lady Morgan and the Politics of Style* (Bethesda: Maunsel & Company, 2009).

Dorson, Richard M., *Folklore and Fakelore: Essays toward a Discipline of Folk Studies* (Cambridge, MA: Harvard University Press, 1976).

Dunne, Tom, "Haunted by History: Irish Romantic Writing, 1800–50", in Roy Porter and Mikuláš Teich, eds., *Romanticism in National Context* (Cambridge: Cambridge University Press, 1988), pp. 68–91.

Durie, Alastair J., "The Need for Legislation to Promote Tourism: A Cause that United All Irish Politicians", in Brenda Collins, Philip Ollerenshaw, and Trevor Parkhill, eds., *Industry, Trade and People in Ireland, 1650–1950: Essays in Honour of W.H. Crawford* (Belfast: Ulster Historical Foundation, 2005), pp. 192–204.

———, *Scotland for the Holidays: Tourism in Scotland, c. 1780–1939* (East Linton: Tuckwell Press, 2003).

Durie, Alastair J., James Bradley, and Marguerite Dupree, *Water is Best: The Hydros and Health Tourism in Scotland, 1840–1940* (Edinburgh: John Donald Publishers Ltd., 2006).

Durie, A.J., and M.J. Huggins, "Sport, Social Tone and the Seaside Resorts of Great Britain, *c.* 1850–1914", *International Journal of the History of Sport*, 15, no. 1 (1998): 173–87.

Edensor, Tim, *National Identity, Popular Culture and Everyday Life* (Oxford: Berg, 2002).

———, "Performing Rurality", in Paul Cloke, Terry Marsden, and Patrick Mooney, eds., *The Handbook of Rural Studies* (London: SAGE Publications, 2006), pp. 484–95.

———, "Staging Tourism: Tourists as Performers", *Annals of Tourism Research*, 27, no. 2 (2000): 322–44.

———, *Tourists at the Taj: Performance and Meaning at a Symbolic Site* (London: Routledge, 1998).

———, "Walking in the British Countryside: Reflexivity, Embodied Practices and Ways to Escape", *Body & Society*, 6, nos 3–4 (2000): 81–106.

Egenolf, Susan, "Lady Morgan (Sydney Owenson) and the Politics of Romanticism", in Jim Kelly, ed., *Ireland and Romanticism: Publics, Nations and Scenes of Cultural Production* (Houndmills: Palgrave Macmillan, 2009), pp. 109–21.

Fegan, Melissa, "'Isn't It Your Own Country?': The Stranger in Nineteenth-Century Irish Literature", *The Yearbook of English Studies*, 34 (2004): 31–45.

———, *Literature and the Irish Famine, 1845–1919* (Oxford: Clarendon Press, 2002).

———, "The Traveller's Experience of Famine Ireland", *Irish Studies Review*, 9, no. 3 (2001): 361–71.

Ferris, Ina, *The Romantic National Tale and the Question of Ireland* (Cambridge: Cambridge University Press, 2002).

Foster, R.F., *Paddy and Mr Punch: Connections in Irish and English History* (London: The Penguin Press, 1993).

Franklin, Adrian, *Tourism: An Introduction* (London: SAGE Publications, 2003).

Furlong, Irene, "Frederick W. Crossley: Irish Turn-of-the-Century Tourism Pioneer", in *Irish History—A Research Yearbook*, vol. 2 (Dublin: Four Courts Press, 2003), pp. 162–76.

———, *Irish Tourism, 1880–1980* (Dublin: Irish Academic Press, 2009).

———, "The Landscape for All—No Penny-in-the-Slot at the Giant's Causeway", in Ní Bhroiméil and Hooper, *Land and Landscape*, pp. 63–77.

Gailey, Andrew, "The Destructiveness of Constructive Unionism: Theories and Practice, 1890s–1960s", in Boyce and O'Day, eds., *Defenders of the Union*, pp. 227–50.

———, *Ireland and the Death of Kindness: The Experience of Constructive Unionism, 1890–1905* (Cork: Cork University Press, 1987).

Gibbons, Luke, "Romanticism, Realism and Irish Cinema", in Kevin Rockett, Luke Gibbons, and John Hill, eds., *Cinema and Ireland* (Syracuse: Syracuse University Press, 1988), pp. 194–258.

Gilbert, Helen, and Anna Johnston, "Introduction", in Helen Gilbert and Anna Johnston, eds., *In Transit: Travel, Text, Empire* (New York: Peter Lang, 2002), pp. 1–20.

Gilley, Sheridan, "English Attitudes to the Irish in England, 1780–1900", in Colin Homes, ed., *Immigrants and Minorities in British Society* (London: George Allen & Unwin, 1978), pp. 81–110.

Graburn, Nelson H.H., "The Anthropology of Tourism", *Annals of Tourism Research*, 10, no. 1 (1983): 9–33.

———, "Secular Ritual: A General Theory of Tourism", in Sharon Bohn Gmelch, ed., *Tourists and Tourism: A Reader* (Long Grove, IL: Waveland Press, Inc., 2004), pp. 23–34.

Green-Lewis, Jennifer, *Framing the Victorians: Photography and the Culture of Realism* (Ithaca: Cornell University Press, 1996).

Greer, Charles, Shannon Donnelly, and Jillian M. Rickly, "Landscape Perspective for Tourism Studies", in Daniel C. Knudsen, Michelle M. Metro-Roland, Anne K. Soper, and Charles E. Greer, eds., *Landscape, Tourism, and Meaning* (Aldershot: Ashgate, 2008), pp. 9–18.

Grenier, Katherine Haldane, *Tourism and Identity in Scotland, 1770–1914: Creating Caledonia* (Aldershot: Ashgate, 2005).

Griffin, Brian, *Cycling in Victorian Ireland* (Dublin: Nonsuch Publishing, 2006).

Grosz, Elizabeth, "Thinking the New: Of Futures Yet Unthought", in Elizabeth Grosz, ed., *Becomings: Explorations in Time, Memory, and Futures* (Ithaca: Cornell University Press, 1999), pp. 15–28.

Grünewald, Rodrigo de Azeredo, "Tourism and Cultural Revival", *Annals of Tourism Research*, 29, no. 4 (2002): 1004–21.

Haldrup, Michael, and Jonas Larsen, "Material Cultures of Tourism", *Leisure Studies*, 25, no. 3 (2006): 275–89.

Hall, Catherine, *Subjects: Colony and Metropole in the English Imagination, 1830–1867* (Chicago: The University of Chicago Press, 2002).

Hall, C. Michael, and Stephen J. Page, *The Geography of Tourism and Recreation: Environment, Place and Space* (London: Routledge, 1999).

Hannam, Kevin, "*Tourism Geographies, Tourist Studies* and the Turn towards Mobilities", *Geography Compass*, 2, no. 1 (2008): 127–39.

Harker, Margaret F., *Henry Peach Robinson: Master of Photographic Art, 1830–1901* (Oxford: Basil Blackwell Ltd., 1988).

———, *The Linked Ring: The Secession Movement in Photography in Britain, 1892–1910* (London: Heinemann, 1979).

Harkins, Anthony, *Hillbilly: A Cultural History of an American Icon* (Oxford: Oxford University Press, 2004).

Harris, Neil, "Selling National Culture: Ireland at the World's Columbian Exposition", in T.J. Edelstein, ed., *Imagining an Irish Past: The Celtic Revival, 1840–1940* (Chicago: The David and Alfred Smart Museum of Art, 1992), pp. 82–105.

Hayes, Kevin J., "Lippincott, Sara Jane Clarke", *American National Biography Online* (February 2000) <http://www.anb.org.proxy.lib.uwaterloo.ca/articles/16/16–01003.html> (11 February 2010).

Heafford, Michael, "Between Grand Tour and Tourism: British Travellers to Switzerland in a Period of Transition, 1814–1860", *Journal of Transport History*, 27, no. 1 (2006). 25–47.

Helland, Janice, *British and Irish Home Arts and Industries, 1880–1914: Marketing Craft, Making Fashion* (Dublin: Irish Academic Press, 2007).

Herold, Edward, Rafael Garcia, and Tony DeMoya, "Female Tourists and Beach Boys: Romance or Sex Tourism?", *Annals of Tourism Research*, 28, no. 4 (2001): 978–97.

Heuston, John, "Kilkee—The Origins and Development of a West Coast Resort", in O'Connor and Cronin, eds., *Tourism in Ireland*, pp. 13–28.

Hooper, Glenn, ed., *The Tourist's Gaze: Travellers to Ireland, 1800–2000* (Cork: Cork University Press, 2001).

———, *Travel Writing and Ireland, 1760–1860: Culture, History, Politics* (Basingstoke: Palgrave Macmillan, 2005).

Horgan, Donal, "The Development of Tourism in Killarney, 1720–2000", in Larner, ed., *Killarney*, pp. 122–38.

Hudson, Derek, *Munby, Man of Two Worlds: The Life and Diaries of Arthur J. Munby, 1828–1910* (London: John Murray (Publishers) Ltd., 1972).

Hunter, F. Robert, "Tourism and Empire: The Thomas Cook & Son Enterprise on the Nile, 1868–1914", *Middle Eastern Studies*, 40, no. 5 (2004): 28–54.

Jackson, Alvin, *The Ulster Party: Irish Unionists in the House of Commons, 1884–1911* (Oxford: Clarendon Press, 1989).

James. K.J., "A 'Vice among Tourists'? Trans-national Narratives of the Irish Landscape, 1886–1914", in Peter M. Burns, Cathy Palmer, and Jo-Anne Lester, eds., *Tourism and Visual Culture*, vol. 1, *Theories and Concepts* (Wallingford: CABI, 2010), pp. 52–63.

———, "Imprinting the Crown on Irish Holiday-Ground: Marking and Marketing the Duke of York Route, 1897", in Philip Long and Nicola J. Palmer, eds., *Royal Tourism: Excursions Around Monarchy* (Clevedon: Channel View Publications, 2008), pp. 62–79.

———, "'In No Degree Inferior': Scotland and 'Tourist Development' in Late-Victorian Ireland", in Frank Ferguson and James McConnel, eds., *Ireland and Scotland in the Nineteenth Century* (Dublin: Four Courts Press, 2009), pp. 11–22.

Jarvis, Robin, *Romantic Writing and Pedestrian Travel* (Basingstoke: Macmillan Press Ltd., 1997).

Jeffery, Keith, "The Irish Soldier in the Boer War", in John Gooch, ed., *The Boer War: Direction, Experience and Image* (London: Frank Cass Publishers, 2000), pp. 141–51.

Jóhannesson, Gunnar Thór, "Tourism Translations: Actor-Network Theory and Tourism Research", *Tourist Studies*, 5, no. 2 (2005): 133–50.

Kelleher, Margaret, *The Feminization of Famine: Expressions of the Inexpressible?* (Durham: Duke University Press, 1997).

Kennedy, Brian P., "The Traditional Irish Thatched House: Image and Reality, 1793–1993", in Adele M. Dalsimer, ed., *Visualizing Ireland: National Identity and the Pictorial Tradition* (Boston: Faber and Faber, 1993), pp. 165–79.

Kincheloe, Pamela J. "Two Visions of Fairyland: Ireland and the Monumental Discourse of the Nineteenth-Century American Tourist", *Irish Studies Review*, 7, no. 1 (1999): 41–51.

King, Carla, "Defenders of the Union: Sir Horace Plunkett", in Boyce and O'Day, *Defenders of the Union*, pp. 137–58.

Kingston, Ralph, "Review Essay. Mind over Matter? History and the Spatial Turn", *Cultural and Social History*, 7, no. 1 (2010): 111–21.

Kissane, Noel, comp. and ed., *Ex Camera 1860–1960: Photographs from the Collections of the National Library of Ireland* (Dublin: National Library of Ireland, 1990).

Kneafsey, Moya, "Tourism Images and the Construction of Celticity in Ireland and Brittany", in David C. Harvey, Rhys Jones, Neil McInroy, and Christine Milligan, eds., *Celtic Geographies: Old Culture, New Times* (London: Routledge, 2002), pp. 123–38.

Kockel, Ullrich, ed., *Culture, Tourism and Development: The Case of Ireland* (Liverpool: Liverpool University Press, 1994).

Koshar, Rudy, "'What Ought to Be Seen': Tourists' Guidebooks and National Identities in Modern Germany and Europe", *Journal of Contemporary History*, 33, no. 3 (1998): 323–40.

Koshar, Rudy, ed., *Histories of Leisure* (Oxford: Berg, 2002).

Koven, Seth, "Dr. Barnardo's 'Artistic Fictions': Photography, Sexuality, and the Ragged Child in Victorian London", *Radical History Review*, 69 (1997): 6–45.

———, *Slumming: Sexual and Social Politics in Victorian London* (Princeton: Princeton University Press, 2004).

Kroeg, Susan, "Cockney Tourists, Irish Guides, and the Invention of the Emerald Isle", *Éire-Ireland*, 44, nos 3–4 (2009): 200–28.

Larner, Jim, ed., *Killarney: History & Heritage* (Wilton, Cork: The Collins Press, 2005).

Larsen, Jonas, "Families Seen Sightseeing: Performativity of Tourist Photography", *Space and Culture*, 8, no. 4 (2005): 416–34.

Lebow, Richard Ned, *White Britain and Black Ireland: The Influence of Stereotypes on Colonial Policy* (Philadelphia: Institute for the Study of Human Issues, 1976).

Ledbetter, Gordon, "A Painter on Achill", *Irish Arts Review*, 23, no. 4 (2006): 106–11.

Lee, Debbie, *Romantic Liars: Obscure Women who Became Imposters and Challenged an Empire* (London: Palgrave Macmillan, 2006).

Lee, J.J., "Introduction", in text by Carey Schofield, comp. by Sean Sexton, *Ireland in Old Photographs* (Boston: Bulfinch Press, 1994), pp. 7–11.

Leerssen, Joep, "English Words in Irish Mouths in English Books", in Ton Hoenselaars and Marius Buning, eds., *English Literature and the Other Languages* (Amsterdam: Rodopi B.V., 1999), pp. 185–96.

———, "Imagology: History and Method", in Manfred Beller and Joep Leerssen, eds., *Imagology: The Cultural Construction and Literary Representation of National Characters: A Critical Survey* (Amsterdam: Editions Rodopi B.V., 2007), pp. 17–32.

Lengel, Edward G., *The Irish through British Eyes: Perceptions of Ireland in the Famine Era* (Westport, CT: Praeger, 2002).

Lew, Alan A., C. Michael Hall, and Allan M. Williams, eds., *A Companion to Tourism* (Oxford: Blackwell Publishing Ltd., 2004).

Löfgren, Orvar, "Know Your Country: A Comparative Perspective on Tourism and Nation Building in Sweden", in Shelley Baranowski and Ellen Furlough, eds., *Being Elsewhere: Tourism, Consumer Culture, and Identity in Modern Europe and North America* (Ann Arbor: The University of Michigan Press, 2001), pp. 137–54.

———, *On Holiday: A History of Vacationing* (Berkeley: University of California Press, 1999).

Luddy, Maria, "'Abandoned Women and Bad Characters': Prostitution in Nineteenth-Century Ireland", *Women's History Review*, 6, no. 4 (1997): 485–504.

———, *Prostitution and Irish Society, 1800–1940* (Cambridge: Cambridge University Press, 2007).

———, *Women and Philanthropy in Nineteenth-Century Ireland* (Cambridge: Cambridge University Press, 1995).

MacCannell, Dean, "Tourist Agency", *Tourist Studies*, 1, no. 1 (2001): 23–37.

———, *The Tourist: A New Theory of the Leisure Class* (New York: Schocken Books, 1976).

MacMonagle, Patrick, "Pictorial Publicists", in Larner, ed., *Killarney*, pp. 221–27.

Madison, D. Soyini, and Judith Hamera, "Introduction: Performance Studies at the Intersections", in D. Soyini Madison and Judith Hamera, eds., *The SAGE Handbook of Performance Studies* (Thousand Oaks, CA: SAGE Publications, 2006), pp. xi–xxv.

Mason, Courtney W., "The Construction of Banff as a 'Natural' Environment: Sporting Festivals, Tourism, and Representations of Aboriginal Peoples", *Journal of Sport History*, 35, no. 2 (2008): 221–39.

Matless, David, *Landscape and Englishness* (London: Reaktion, 1998).

McCoole, Sinéad, "The Herberts of Muckross", in Larner, ed., *Killarney*, pp. 90–104.

McCotter, Clare, "Woman Traveller/Colonial Tourist", *Irish Studies Review*, 15, no. 4 (2007): 481–506.

McCracken, Donal P., *Forgotten Protest: Ireland and the Anglo-Boer War*, revised ed. (Belfast: Ulster Historical Foundation, 2003).

McGuire, E.B., *Irish Whiskey: A History of Distilling, the Spirit Trade and Excise Controls in Ireland* (Dublin: Gill and Macmillan Ltd., 1973).

McKay, Enda, "A Century of Irish Trade Journals, 1860–1960", in Barbara Hayley and Enda McKay, eds., *Three Hundred Years of Irish Periodicals* (Dublin: Association of Irish Learned Journals, 1987), pp. 103–21.

McKernan, Luke, "The Familiarity of the New: The Emergence of a Motion Picture Industry in Late Nineteenth-Century London", *Nineteenth Century Theatre and Film*, 33, no. 2 (2006): 30–44.

McVeagh, John, *Irish Travel Writing: A Bibliography* (Dublin: Wolfhound Press, 1996).

Meethan, Kevin, "Place, Image and Power: Brighton as a Resort", in Tom Selwyn, ed., *The Tourist Image: Myths and Myth Making in Tourism* (Chichester: John Wiley & Sons Ltd., 1996), pp. 179–96.

Mehegan, Angela, "The Cultural Analysis of Leisure: Tourism and Travels in Co. Donegal", *CIRCA*, 107 (2004): 58–62.

Meloy, Elizabeth, "Touring Connemara: Learning to Read a Landscape of Ruins, 1850–1860", *New Hibernia Review/Iris Éireannach Nua*, 13, no. 3 (2009): 21–46.

Miller, Wilbur E., *Revenuers & Moonshiners: Enforcing Federal Liquor Law in the Mountain South, 1865–1900* (Chapel Hill: The University of North Carolina Press, 1991).

Mingay, G.E., "Caird, Sir James (1816–1892)", *Oxford Dictionary of National Biography*, (Oxford University Press, 2004) <http://www.oxforddnb.com.subzero.lib.uoguelph.ca/view/article/4339> (11 February 2010).

Morash, Christopher, *A History of the Media in Ireland* (Cambridge: Cambridge University Press, 2010).

———, "The Remains of Ellen Hanley: Theatre, Commodification and Irish Identity in the Nineteenth Century", in Nicholas Allen and Eve Patten, eds., *That Island Never Found* (Dublin: Four Courts Press, 2007), pp. 19–32.

———, *Writing the Irish Famine* (Oxford: Clarendon Press, 1995).

Morgan, Cecilia, *"A Happy Holiday": English Canadians and Transatlantic Tourism, 1870–1930* (Toronto: University of Toronto Press, 2008).

Murphy, James H., *Abject Loyalty: Nationalism and Monarchy in Ireland during the Reign of Queen Victoria* (Washington, D.C.: The Catholic University of America Press, 2001).

Nally, David, "'Eternity's Commissioner': Thomas Carlyle, the Great Irish Famine and the Geopolitics of Travel", *Journal of Historical Geography*, 32, no. 2 (2006): 313–35.

Nash, Dennison, *Anthropology of Tourism* (Kidlington: Pergamon, 1996).

Newmeyer, Trent, "'Under the Wing of Mr. Cook': Transformations in Tourism Governance", *Mobilities*, 3, no. 2 (2008): 243–67.

Ní Bhroiméil, Úna, and Glenn Hooper, eds., *Land and Landscape in Nineteenth-Century Ireland* (Dublin: Four Courts Press, 2008).

Nic Congáil, Ríona, "'Life and the Dream': Utopian Impulses within the Irish Language Revival", *Utopian Studies*, 23, no. 2 (2012): 430–49.

Norgate, G. Le G., "Hole, Samuel Reynolds (1819–1904)", rev. by M.C. Curthoys, *Oxford Dictionary of National Biography* (Oxford University Press, 2004) <http://www.oxforddnb.com.subzero.lib.uoguelph.ca/view/article/33934> (11 February 2010).

O'Brien, Harvey, *The Real Ireland: The Evolution of Ireland in Documentary Film* (Manchester: Manchester University Press, 2004).

O'Connor, Barbara, and Michael Cronin, eds., *Tourism in Ireland: A Critical Analysis* (Cork: Cork University Press, 1993).

O'Hare, Patricia, "The Browne Family, Earls of Kenmare", in Larner, ed., *Killarney*, pp. 74–89.

Ó Saothraí, Séamas, "Russell, Thomas O'Neill (1828–1908)", *Oxford Dictionary of National Biography* (Oxford University Press, 2004) <http://www.oxforddnb.com.subzero.lib.uoguelph.ca/view/article/35885> (11 February 2010).

O'Sullivan, Mike, "Visiting Poets of the Romantic Period", in Larner, ed., *Killarney*, pp. 139–44.

O'Toole, Tina, general ed., *Dictionary of Munster Women Writers* (Cork: Cork University Press, 2005).

Oppermann, Martin, "Sex Tourism", *Annals of Tourism Research*, 26, no. 2 (1999): 251–66.

Ousby, Ian, *The Englishman's England: Taste, Travel and the Rise of Tourism* (Cambridge: Cambridge University Press, 1990).

Pfaffenberger, Bryan, "Serious Pilgrims and Frivolous Tourists: The Chimera of Tourism in the Pilgrimages of Sri Lanka", *Annals of Tourism Research*, 10, no. 1 (1983): 57–74.

Pollock, Vivienne, "'All in a Day's Work': Robert John Welch and His World", in Breathnach, ed., *Framing the West*, pp. 1–28.

Preston-Whyte, Robert, "The Beach as a Liminal Space", in Lew, Hall, and Williams, eds., *A Companion to Tourism*, pp. 349–59.

Pritchard, Annette, and Nigel Morgan, "Encountering Scopophilia, Sensuality and Desire: Engendering Tahiti", in Annette Pritchard, Nigel Morgan, Irena Ateljevic, and Candice Harris, eds., *Tourism and Gender: Embodiment, Sensuality and Experience* (Wallingford: CABI, 2007), pp. 158–81.

Quinn, Bernadette, "Performing Tourism: Venetian Residents in Focus", *Annals of Tourism Research*, 34, no. 2 (2007): 458–76.

Reiman, Donald H., "The Beauty of Buttermere as Fact and Romantic Symbol", *Criticism*, 26, no. 2 (1984): 139–70.

Robinson, Eric, general ed., *The Later Poems of John Clare, 1837–1864*, vol. 2, Eric Robinson and David Powell, eds., Margaret Grainger, associate ed. (Oxford: Clarendon Press, 1984).

Robinson, Mike, and Melanie Smith, "Politics, Power and Play: The Shifting Contexts of Cultural Tourism", in Melanie K. Smith and Mike Robinson, eds., *Cultural Tourism in a Changing World: Politics, Participation, and (Re)presentation* (Clevedon: Channel View Publications, 2006), pp. 1–17.

Rojek, Chris, *Ways of Escape: Modern Transformations in Leisure and Travel* (Lanham, MD: Rowman and Littlefield, 1994, "copyright 1993 by Chris Rojek").

Ryan, Chris, and C. Michael Hall, *Sex Tourism: Marginal People and Liminalities* (London: Routledge, 2001).

Ryle, Martin, *Journeys in Ireland: Literary Travellers, Rural Landscapes, Cultural Relations* (Aldershot: Ashgate, 1999).

Sayer, Karen, *Country Cottages: A Cultural History* (Manchester: Manchester University Press, 2000).

Sears, John F., *Sacred Places: American Tourist Attractions in the Nineteenth Century* (Oxford: Oxford University Press, 1989).

Sharpley, Richard, and Priya Sundaram, "Tourism: A Sacred Journey? The Case of Ashram Tourism, India", *International Journal of Tourism Research*, 7, no. 3 (2005): 161–71.

Shaw, Gareth, and Allan M. Williams, *Tourism and Tourism Spaces* (London: SAGE Publications, 2004).

Shaw, Philip, *The Sublime* (Abingdon: Routledge, 2006).

Sheehy, Jeanne, *The Rediscovery of Ireland's Past: The Celtic Revival, 1830–1930* (London: Thames and Hudson Ltd., 1980).

Sherlock, Kirsty, "Revisiting the Concept of Hosts and Guests", *Tourist Studies*, 1, no. 3 (2001): 271–95.

Shields, Rob, *Places on the Margin: Alternative Geographies of Modernity* (London: Routledge, 1991).

Shryock, Andrew, "The New Jordanian Hospitality: House, Host, and Guest in the Culture of Public Display", *Comparative Studies in Society and History*, 46, no. 1 (2004): 35–62.

Simmons, Jack, "Railways, Hotels, and Tourism in Great Britain, 1839–1914", *Journal of Contemporary History*, 19, no. 2 (1984): 201–22.

Smith, Valene L., ed., *Hosts and Guests: The Anthropology of Tourism* (Philadelphia: University of Pennsylvania Press, 1977).

Smith, Valene L., and Maryann Brent, eds., *Hosts and Guests Revisited: Tourism Issues of the 21st Century* (Elmsford, NY: Cognizant Communication Corporation, 2001).

Steward, Jill, "The Adventures of Miss Brown, Miss Jones and Miss Robinson: Tourist Writing and Tourist Performance from 1860 to 1914", *Journeys*, 1, no. 1 (2000): 36–58.

Sturgeon, Sinéad, "The Politics of Poitín: Maria Edgeworth, William Carleton, and the Battle for the Spirit of Ireland", *Irish Studies Review*, 14, no. 4 (2006): 431–45.

Swain, Margaret Byrne, "Desiring Ashima: Sexing Landscape in China's Stone Forest", in Carolyn Cartier and Alan A. Lew, eds., *Seductions of Place: Geographical Perspectives on Globalization and Touristed Landscapes* (London: Routledge, 2005), pp. 245–59.

Sweet, Rosemary, "British Perceptions of Florence in the Long Eighteenth Century", *The Historical Journal*, 50, no. 4 (2007): 837–59.

Swift, Roger, "Thomas Carlyle and Ireland", in D. George Boyce and Roger Swift, eds., *Problems and Perspectives in Irish History since 1800: Essays in Honour of Patrick Buckland* (Dublin: Four Courts Press, 2004), pp. 117–46.

Szerszynski, Bronislaw, Wallace Heim, and Claire Waterton, eds., *Nature Performed: Environment, Culture and Performance* (Oxford: Blackwell Publishing/The Sociological Review, 2003).

Szerszynski, Bronislaw, Wallace Heim, and Claire Waterton, "Introduction", in Szerszynski, Heim, and Waterton, eds., *Nature Performed*, pp. 1–14.

Taylor, John, "Henry Peach Robinson and Victorian Theory", *History of Photography*, 3, no. 4 (1979): 295–303.

Terkenli, Theano S., "Tourism and Landscape", in Lew, Hall, and Williams, eds., *A Companion to Tourism*, pp. 339–48.

Tessone, Natasha, "'Displaying Ireland: Sydney Owenson and the Politics of Spectacular Antiquarianism", *Éire-Ireland*, 37, nos 3–4 (2002): 169–86.

Thayer, Hewitt S., "Distilling Spirits and Regulating Subjects: Whiskey and Beer in Romantic Britain", *Éire-Ireland*, 30, no. 3 (1995): 7–13.

Thompson, Carl, "Travel Writing", in Nicholas Roe, ed., *Romanticism: An Oxford Guide* (Oxford: Oxford University Press, 2005), pp. 555–73.

Towner, John, *An Historical Geography of Recreation and Tourism in the Western World, 1540–1940* (Chichester: John Wiley & Sons, 1996).

Travis, John F., *The Rise of the Devon Seaside Resorts, 1750–1900* (Exeter: Exeter University Press, 1993).

Tresidder, Richard, "Tourism and Sacred Landscapes", in David Crouch, ed., *Leisure/Tourism Geographies: Practices and Geographical Knowledge* (London: Routledge, 1999), pp. 137–48.

Tribe, John, "New Tourism Research", *Tourism Recreation Research*, 30, no. 2 (2005): 5–8.

Tucker, Hazel, "The Ideal Village: Interactions through Tourism in Central Anatolia", in Simone Abram, Jacqueline Waldren, and Donald V.L. Macleod, eds., *Tourists and Tourism: Identifying with People and Places* (Oxford: Berg, 1997), pp. 107–28.

———, "Welcome to Flinstones-Land: Contesting Place and Identity in Goreme, Central Turkey", in Coleman and Crang, *Tourism: Between Place and Performance*, pp. 143–59.

Turner, Louis, and John Ash, *The Golden Hordes: International Tourism and the Pleasure Periphery* (London: Constable, 1975).

Turner, Victor, and Edith L.B. Turner, *Image and Pilgrimage in Christian Culture: Anthropological Perspectives* (New York: Columbia University Press, 1978).

Urry, John, *The Tourist Gaze*, 2nd ed. (London: SAGE Publications, 2002).

Wallace, Anne D., *Walking, Literature, and English Culture: The Origins and Uses of Peripatetic in the Nineteenth Century* (Oxford: Clarendon Press, 1993).

Walton, John K., "Beaches, Bathing and Beauty: Health and Bodily Exposure at the British Seaside from the 18th to the 20th Century", *Revue Française de Civilisation Britannique*, 14, no. 2 (2007): 117–34.

———, *Blackpool* (Edinburgh: Edinburgh University/Carnegie Publishing, 1998).

———, *The Blackpool Landlady: A Social History* (Manchester: Manchester University Press, 1978).

———, *The British Seaside: Holidays and Resorts in the Twentieth Century* (Manchester: Manchester University Press, 2000).

———, *The English Seaside Resort: A Social History, 1750–1914* (Leicester: Leicester University Press, 1983).

———, ed., *Histories of Tourism: Representation, Identity and Conflict* (Clevedon: Channel View Publications, 2005).

———. "Prospects in Tourism History: Evolution, State of Play and Future Developments", *Tourism Management*, 30, no. 6 (2009): 783–93.

———, "Taking the History of Tourism Seriously", *European History Quarterly*, 27, no. 4 (1997): 563–7.

———, "Thomas Cook: Image and Reality", in Richard W. Butler and Roslyn A. Russell, eds., *Giants of Tourism* (Wallingford: CABI, 2010), pp. 81–92.

Watson, Nicola J., *The Literary Tourist: Readers and Places in Romantic & Victorian Britain* (Basingstoke: Palgrave Macmillan, 2006).

Webb, Darren, "Bakhtin at the Seaside: Utopia, Modernity and the Carnivalesque", *Theory, Culture & Society*, 22, no. 3 (2005): 121–38.

Weiskel, Thomas, *The Romantic Sublime: Studies in the Structure and Psychology of Transcendence* (Baltimore: The Johns Hopkins University Press, 1976).

Werry, Margaret, *The Tourist State: Performing Leisure, Liberalism, and Race in New Zealand* (Minneapolis and London: University of Minnesota Press, 2011).

Williams, William H.A., "Blow, Bugle, Blow: Romantic Tourism and the Echoes of Killarney", in Santiago Henríquez, ed., *Travel Essentials: Collected Essays on Travel Writing* (Las Palmas de Gran Canaria: Chandlon Inn Press, 1998), pp. 133–47.

———, *Creating Irish Tourism: The First Century, 1750–1850* (London: Anthem Press, 2010).

———, *Tourism, Landscape, and the Irish Character: British Travel Writers in Pre-Famine Ireland* (Madison: The University of Wisconsin Press, 2008).

Woods, C.J., "Review Article: Irish Travel Writings as Source Material", *Irish Historical Studies*, 28, no. 110 (1992): 171–83.

———, *Travellers' Accounts as Source-Material for Irish Historians* (Dublin: Four Courts Press, 2009).

Wylie, John, *Landscape* (Abingdon: Routledge, 2007).

Zimmermann, Georges Denis, *The Irish Storyteller* (Dublin: Four Courts Press, 2001).

Zuelow, Eric G.E., "'Ingredients for Cooperation': Irish Tourism in North-South Relations, 1924–1998", *New Hibernia Review*, 10, no. 1 (2006): 17–39.

———, "'Kilts *versus* Breeches': The Royal Visit, Tourism and Scottish National Memory", *Journeys*, 7, no. 2 (2006): 33–53.

———, *Making Ireland Irish: Tourism and National Identity since the Irish Civil War* (Syracuse: Syracuse University Press, 2009).

(b) Unpublished Dissertations

Foley, Kieran, "Kerry during the Great Famine, 1845–52" (unpublished PhD dissertation, University College Dublin, Department of Modern History, 1997).

Thompson, Spurgeon W., "The Postcolonial Tourist: Irish Tourism and Decolonization since 1850" (unpublished PhD dissertation, University of Notre Dame, Department of English, 2000).

Index

For Product Safety Concerns and Information please contact our EU
representative GPSR@taylorandfrancis.com
Taylor & Francis Verlag GmbH, Kaufingerstraße 24, 80331 München, Germany

www.ingramcontent.com/pod-product-compliance
Ingram Content Group UK Ltd.
Pitfield, Milton Keynes, MK11 3LW, UK
UKHW020941180425
457613UK00019B/497